A Country of Mem

By the same author
I BOUGHT A MOUNTAIN
I BOUGHT A STAR
BRIDE TO THE MOUNTAIN
LOG HUT

~~:~~

The dragon used on the cover is reproduced
by permission of
Mr. William O. Williams
Hafod yr Rhisgol
Nant Gwynant
Beddgelert

A Country of Memorable Honour

THOMAS FIRBANK

FLUELLEN.
I do believe your majesty takes no scorn to wear the leek upon Saint Tavy's day.

KING HENRY.
I wear it for a memorable honour;
For I am Welsh, you know, good countryman.

King Henry V, Act IV, Scene 7

JOHN JONES

A COUNTRY OF MEMORABLE HONOUR

This new paperback edition published May 1998.

First published in 1953 by George Harrap

ISBN 1 871083 21 4

Cover photographs of Snowdon and the Llangollen valley
by John Idris Jones

Cover designed and book printed by Cambrian Printers,
Aberystwyth

Published by John Jones Publishing Ltd, Clwydfro Business Centre, Ruthin, North Wales LL15 1NJ

INTRODUCTION

Dear Reader: This fresh publication of '*A Country of Memorable Honour*' is unchanged in text and sentiment. It carries the time-worn Preface that introduced the first edition printed in 1953, almost half a century ago. Lifestyles have changed since then. The whirlwinds of the electronic age blow our thoughts away into the distorting airwaves. Thoughts may be more conveniently anchored in print at home.

I had been a long while away from Wales before the original edition of this book was conceived and born. Years earlier I had been drawn to soldier through WWII by the body's versatile inner music box that sounds cataclysm with drumbeats, bugle calls, strident fifes and the rhythmic tramp of marching feet. There was fulfilment in meeting the call.

When war had struggled to an end, myriads of men and women returned from the armed services to peacetime Britain. I was among the swarms seeking a niche in a changed civilian lifestyle where estrangement between niche and seeker was often mutual. Many felt a lack of purpose. By chance I came upon a dream job for a restless man. A British engineering company hired me to open the Far East for its products.

A touch of Celtic clairvoyance hinted that the task might take time, the region being vast and most of the sovereign entities in tumult. Before departure I refreshed myself walking the length of my mother's country from mountainous Gwynedd in the north to the diversity of the south. The simple gleanings gathered from the farewell stroll were recorded in this nostalgic book before taking flight to the Far East.

In Wales today there is new political talk of self-determination, long sought; and the pattern of Europe is being re-drawn. May Wales secure its own good place. There is the blood in the veins to succeed: Tudor; the historic Llywellyns; Owain; Lloyd George, and plenty such as Mr Jones Flannel Mill.

ITO-SHI
SHIZUOKA-KEN
JAPAN

THOMAS FIRBANK
DOLWYDDELAN
APRIL 1998

PREFACE

WALES is a small country moated on three sides by sea, and walled on the fourth by mountains. Within its boundaries survive the Cymry, the Compatriots, the British Brotherhood. These British, named Welsh, or Foreigners, in the Anglo-Saxon tongue, are the most remarkable of the many monuments to history which remain in that small but storied land. They have preserved their race through two millennia against the destructive power of alien storms.

Much has been written by many able men of most aspects of Wales and the Welsh. I do not try to compete on the chosen grounds of the experts. I try only to capture the spirit of passionate nationality, which often eludes the material eye.

This, then, is not a guide-book, comprehensive in its lists of megaliths and castles and statistics. If it is in any sense a guide, it is towards an understanding of the Welsh people, whose generic name of 'British' has become the title of a world-wide Commonwealth. The seeds of Brotherhood sowed by Cunedda have fructified in a prolific and unpredicted way. By whatever transposition, and by whatever unrelated causation, it is the fact that the many nations of our modern British Brotherhood ought to make their pilgrimage of sentiment across the forecourt of moorland to the inner mountains of Wales.

To paint a word-picture of the Welsh nation requires a vast canvas, and I have but sketched a few living impressions. If these are judged inadequate or inaccurate, I will take comfort from the Roman Horace, who said:

"To have no errors is a privilege above the condition of humanity; under it happiest is he who has the fewest of them."

T. F.

SHALLOWS,
CHAGFORD, DEVON
November 1952

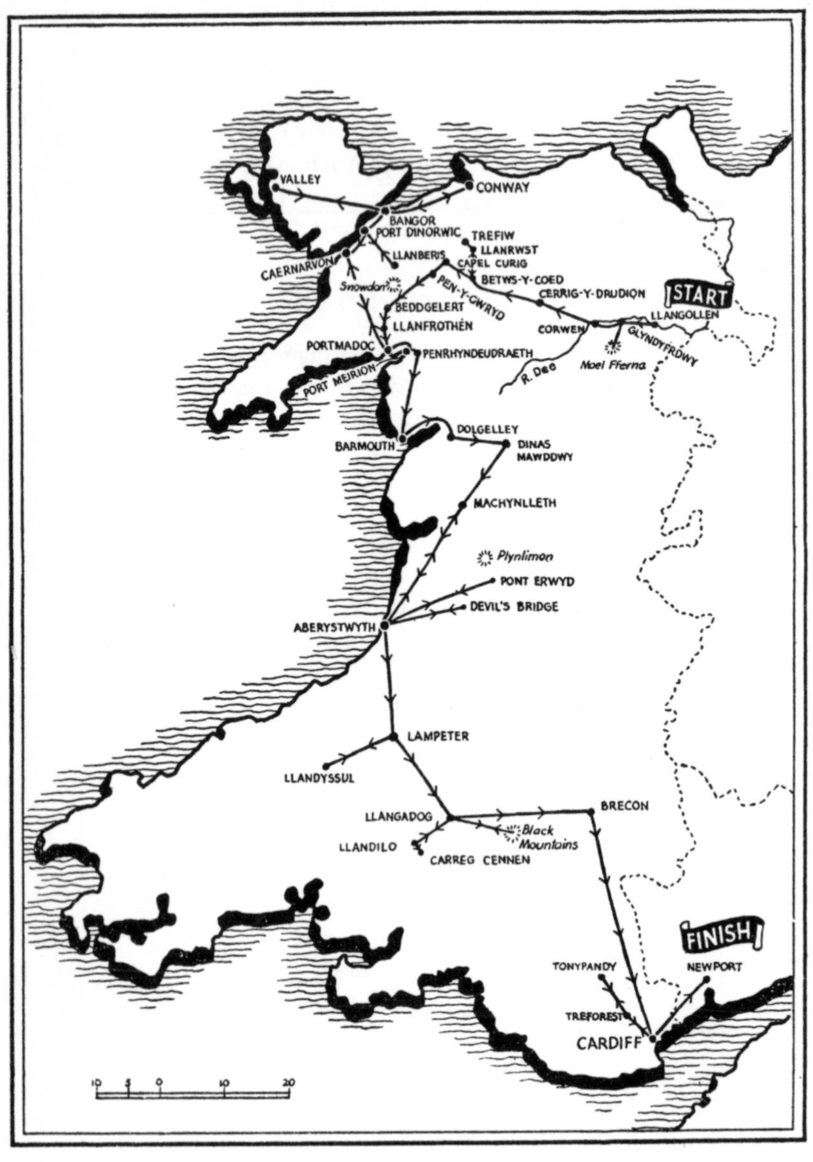

THE AUTHOR'S ROUTE

CONTENTS

CHAPTER ONE

Llangollen—My first Nationalist—Iberians and Celts—Roman occupation—English publican—International Eisteddfod—Ancient Greeks—Guns, trees, and sheep—A bed at Glyndyfrdwy

I CROSSED the border on foot. The little town which I reached on the mid-February morning lay in the cupped palm of the hills, through whose deep-cleft lifeline flowed a swift river. The sun was above the mountains and the pale winter rays struck cold light from the snow crystals which covered the bridge on which I paused. I stood in an embrasure above one of the abutments and looked up-river deeper into the strange country. The hills encircled the town with an unbroken rim, white on the skyline, but tree-clothed lower down, each branch of the topmost rows of larches fretted clear against the snow.

The river slid by quickly, blue-black when it lingered in the deeper pools, lathered with cold sweat when it leaped down the rapids. Just above the bridge the water divided to pass a flat rock which lay in its course like a stranded whale. Passers-by gave each other good morning and remarked on the weather in their melodious foreign tongue, for at this season there were no visitors or sightseers, and the place had lost the self-consciousness of the tourist centre.

I had determined to begin my walk through Wales here at Llangollen because the Dee valley opens a natural gateway into the hills. In mountain country history is written along the courses of the rivers. I had been a long time from Wales and, as I walked about the small town, felt something of a stranger until I saw a figure, vaguely familiar, dressed in very hairy tweeds and a deerstalker hat.

"Mr Jones Flannel Mill?" I asked.

He was, and we renewed slight acquaintance. Mr Jones was an oldish man, tall and broad, though now a little bowed. But if Nature had fettered the power of his physique, his eyes had inherited a fierce intolerance. He almost spat when I inquired how the woollen trade went.

"When I was young," he said, "a farmer would have his own sheep's wool woven into cloth and take it to a local tailor to make up into a suit that he could pass on to his son when he was gone. Changing fashions have ended that. Men change their fashions like silly women these days—wide trousers, narrow trousers, double-breasted jackets, single-breasted jackets."

I sympathized, and said that no doubt the multiple tailors catered for these fickle male fancies, and bought their cloth by the mile from the big Yorkshire mills.

"Petticoats were the days," insisted Mr Jones. "A woman would wear three or four, all good flannel. There *was* trade then."

He ruminated for a moment, then said that small concerns such as his must change their ideas, and that he was finding the Rural Industries Advisory Bureau at Machynlleth to be helpful with his designing. I wanted to ask more about this, but Mr Jones had harked back to petticoats and was banging the pavement with his stick.

"The biggest mistake a man can make is to get married," he stated. "Where's the sense in it? Some men can satisfy six women, and some women can't be satisfied by six men. How's a couple to get their arithmetic right?"

These were deep waters only to be navigated by Einstein in conjunction with Solomon, so I gave an intelligent grunt.

"Women," went on Mr Jones, as if wishful to finish with the subject once and for all, "women want children and men want satisfaction. What's love got to do with it? You don't have to love your grocer. But sleep with a woman once, and you're expected to keep her for the rest of your life."

I had to agree that, put in this way, society was making unfair demands. Mr Jones cut me short by demanding whether I would be travelling near my old farm at Capel Curig. He said that he had walked the Snowdon Horseshoe, and had promised himself a traverse of the Carneddau, but arthritis had forbidden him Anyway, he said, he was fond of the Berwyn Mountains, which cradled Llangollen. Had I seen the Ceiriog Falls? Did I not agree that they were grander than Pistyll Rhaiadr? Did I know why Chirk was so called? The Romans had named the place after the river Ceiriog. They were unable, he believed, to pronounce their 'R's,' and Ceiriog became Ceiog, thence Chirk. Anyway, he supposed Chirk was easy for the English to pronounce.

I said that I thought Llangollen had fully maintained its Welsh identity, in spite of the proximity of the English border.

"Aye!" agreed Mr Jones. "I suppose you'll have been to the International Eisteddfod in Llangollen? A great gathering it is for all the world, and a wonderful big achievement for a little Welsh town."

I knew of the Eisteddfod, and asked questions, but Mr Jones referred me to more competent persons.

"Go and ask Gwynn Williams," he said. "Musical organizer he is. Yes, Welsh the place keeps, except for the pubs. You're hard put to it to find a Welsh pub in the whole of Wales. I can remember when you could go in and be welcomed by your own folk, and nothing too much trouble, and proper beer from our own little breweries."

These little breweries, so praised by George Borrow a hundred years ago, were put out of business by the tied houses, which strangled their marketing facilities. Mr Jones confirmed this speculation.

"Too slow our breweries were to buy up pubs when the custom started. The big English companies bought our pubs and gave them English beer to sell. Yet I remember one time when the Government began to test beer after some poisoning cases, it was Llangollen brewery came out top and a famous English brewery second."

To pacify him I said that I hoped the Minister for Welsh Affairs might help put the country's case in such matters. I added that I hoped soon to see Wales have a full Secretary of State.

This aspiration did not satisfy Mr Jones.

"No, by damn!" he cried. "Home Rule!"

I was not at that time sure that I could with honesty go the whole way with him here, and argued that the economy of the two countries seemed to me to be inextricably entangled.

"Maybe," he said. "Maybe. But the English exploit us like they did the Indians."

I protested at this, saying that we left behind in India far more than we had ever taken away; that our dominion there had paid both sides; that no doubt English-Welsh relations were also to mutual advantage.

"I won't argue about industry," Mr Jones said, banging his stick again. "You ask them in South Wales. You ask why the English take our anthracite and soft coal so that they can export it and keep the money."

He began to walk away, obviously seething with emotion, and I took a step or two after him, anxious to go on with our talk.

"How would you set about Home Rule?" I asked.

"Look!" exclaimed Mr Jones, bringing his stick into play again. "If the bloody Irish managed it, so can we, man."

My old acquaintance had gone a little farther in his expression of opinion than some Welshmen were prepared to do, but the difference in feeling was only one of degree, for no other British nation has such a strong consciousness of its racial identity.

It is a pity that the English, who hold strong sway over the changing development of Wales, understand the people of the country so little. This ignorance is discourteous, for these islands owe much to the Welsh.

Many English give the Welsh a half-contemptuous consideration such as the Australians bestow upon their aborigines, and the North Americans upon the Red Indians. They imagine the Welsh people to be the survivors of the little dark men, smeared with woad, who fled to the Cambrian hills before the mighty Romans.

It is true that the Welsh of to-day are the only descendants of the British stock which the Romans found here, and their language the only living development of the old tongue, but the term 'Ancient Briton' has been lent a wrong colour by English history books.

The first numerous colonizers of the mountain country now known as Wales were the Hamitic Iberian migrants of prehistoric times who crept north and west from Africa, through Spain, and up the coastal fringe of France. Some took the direct sea-route which brought them to Cornwall, Wales, Strathclyde, and the eastern coast of Ireland. Later the Beaker folk from the lands about the Rhine delta intermingled with them. Later still, perhaps five hundred years before the birth of Jesus, came the Celts. The Celts were a conquering race who originated most likely from the upper

Danube basin. An old race-memory whispers to them that they fought at Troy.

It is not impossible that the Celts had a connexion with the shepherd tribe from the Danube basin who called themselves Hellenes, after Hellen, the son of Deucalion and Pyrrha, who were in Greek mythology the sole survivors of the Flood. The Hellenes drifted over to the Greek peninsula and, over a period of several centuries, settled there. They could not for a long while match their crude stone weapons with the metal ones of such Ægeans as survived in their hill fortifications. But in the end they learned the way of metal-working and many other trades, such as seafaring, and at last drove the remaining Ægeans to the off-shore islands.

Perhaps the dimly believed Græco-Celtic affinity has a foundation. Both had, in early days, a feeling for the stone, and the Achean clan of Hellenes in particular used to sing endlessly of their ancestors, as the Celts have always done.

In Britain the Celts imposed their rule and tongue upon the Iberian-Beaker stock. These Celts were of two strains. The Goidelic strain gave their language to Ireland, Scotland, and the Isle of Man, and to-day the language is all but dead. The Brythonic strain imposed its speech on Brittany, Cornwall, and Wales. The modern Welsh tongue is the direct lineal descendant, vigorous in Wales, but dead in Cornwall. In Britanny there are traces in dialect.

The Celts gained ascendancy not only by force of arms, but by force of character. Within a few hundred years they seem to have drawn the earlier peoples into themselves, and, acting as a catalyst, to have populated a great deal of Britain with a race, not a hotchpotch of breeds. They imposed their own Aryan language, but retained the idiom which they found here, and which, coming from the Middle East, is so Hebraic that a modern Welshman is quickly at home with Hebrew.

Wales and much of the rest of the island was now populated by a predominantly Brython race. Those in Wales were entrenched in a piece of land surrounded on three sides by sea, and cut off from England by a mountain rampart.

Now came the Romans. They Romanized the softer Brythons of the lowlands, but they made small impact upon the Brythons of the Welsh hills. Indeed, of the three legions which were permanently stationed in Britain, two were held up against the mountains of Wales, at Chester on the Dee, and Caerleon on the Usk. The third legion was at York to stem the incursions of the Celts and Picts from the northern part of the island. All the soft centre and south of Britain was lightly garrisoned under a Roman form of civil government rather than military occupation. The native people were of no danger to the invaders, but emulated their customs so far as they were able. The Romans were free to build their baths and villas and to settle down to a civilized life without fear of molestation. It was not so in Wales. The hill Brythons had developed the hardness of all peoples who are constantly exercised against the strokes of storm and the unrelenting enmity of soil and pasturage. Here the Romans penetrated, true enough, but they dared not relax their guard. Their camps remained on a war footing. They never grew to be garrison towns in whose amenities the natives participated. Nor were the Romans sufficiently secure to build villas in which to practise the arts of comfort. There were but a handful west of the Severn, and one solitary Roman town at Caerwent, just within the border of modern Wales. The Romans remained as military occupiers; the Welsh Britons as a nation were subdued but not conquered.

Throughout all the vicissitudes of their long history neither by Roman, Saxon, Norman, nor Englishman were the Welsh conquered. Physical occupation is not conquest so long as spirit remains unbroken.

It was a cold day to brood on history standing on Llangollen Bridge, and I had more miles to cover before dark. I remembered the advice of Mr Jones Flannel Mill to seek out Gwynn Williams and learn the story of the International Eisteddfod, and went into a hotel to discover where he lived. The landlord was English, a nominee of one of those Midlands breweries which had, as Mr Jones had pointed out, reached across with their tentacles to grasp the Welsh inns. It is unfortunate that it is mostly the Midland and Lancashire brewers who have exploited the Welsh inns. There is a brashness and braggadocio about some of the inhabitants of these parts of England which contrasts ill with the quiet dignity of the Welsh. I asked my English landlord how he liked his local customers.

"Clannish!" he said, looking at me with a superior air. "Fight one, fight all."

I suggested that history gave an honoured place to the Scots clans, and that the adjective need not necessarily be derogatory, and anyway why fight with them?

He said that he did not need to fight any more because he had taught his customers who was master. Knowing the Welsh, I could imagine a dozen ways in which they would amuse themselves romping in this fool's paradise, and he ignorant of their game.

I did not stay here long, but went searching refreshment and information in more congenial company, though I made several calls before I settled down in an inn served by an old Welsh lady who talked with me about the International Eisteddfod; the excellent moral effect of providing a class for youths' choirs which gave the participants a hobby to steady them through the turbulent years between school-leaving and discretion; how the stature of a man like Eden had eased the Egyptian difficulty; how money was short these days, and it was the worse that people had forgotten how to occupy themselves, but felt that they must pay to be entertained.

I left the old lady reluctantly, and, primed with English beer and Welsh directions, went to seek Gwynn Williams.

Mr Williams was a big man, built like an Italian tenor. He clearly had had practice in lecturing backward students, but it was soon apparent that, as is often the way with men who are masters of their subject, he could not plumb the depths of ignorance, and he began his musical explanations at a point above my greatest knowledge.

We talked in the study. It was a practical room devoted to music and books. There was a Rönisch upright piano with score sheets piled high on the lid; more piles of sheets on the floor; a bookcase filled mainly with works in Welsh on folklore, dance, verse, and song. On a ledge about the walls stood the houshold gods of the Welshman: lustre-ware jugs, pewter, willow-pattern china, and bright copper kettles.

The International Eisteddfod had begun in a most casual and haphazard way. During the Second German War there had been, Gwynn Williams reminded me, many foreign Governments in London who were spending a busy exile in wrangling and personal intrigue. Some of them had taken time off from these exercises to send representatives to the Welsh National Eisteddfod. They suggested that an international element might be introduced into the competition. But the committee was not able to find room for more events in the perennially crowded programme.

Gwynn Williams, the Eisteddfod's musical organizer, put the problem to his own town council at Llangollen, and so the scheme was born there in 1947 as a separate event altogether.

The town took on a tremendous task. Quite apart from the intricate organization of a complex programme which extended over six days, and which catered for instrumentalists and vocalists, soloists and large orchestras and choirs, dancers from the Far East and dancers from these islands, there was the problem of entertaining.

The competitors came as guests of Llangollen. The town helped those who had currency troubles, it transported them to prepared free lodgings in the district, it transported them free daily from the lodgings to the Eisteddfod, it treated them as a host of the old school would treat his house guests. Some of the choirs were sixty strong, and the total of competitors was in the thousands.

In Gwynn Williams's study I glanced at the last year's programme. At random I picked out names of competing countries: India, Belgium, Austria, France, Finland, Germany, Italy, Portugal, Yugoslavia, England, Norway, Chile, Switzerland, Holland, New Brunswick, Spain, Indonesia, and even, with astonishment, the Ukraine. I suppose that all these nations understood one another through the lingua franca of music.

Gwynn Williams pointed out to me the couplet by T. Gwynn Jones which encircled the harp and dragon medallion which graced the cover of the programme. It said:

Byd gwyn fydd byd a gano
Gwaraidd fydd ei gerddi fo.

These soft words from a warlike race mean:

Blessed is a world that sings,
Gentle are its songs.

It would take a Welshman to give practical expression to that sentiment. The Llangollen International Eisteddfod may be but a drop of soothing oil on the turbulent ocean of world passion, but blessed is the race which conceived so selfless a child of peace. I wondered aloud to Gwynn Williams whether a comparable English township could have done so. He did not immediately scout the idea, for fear of making an unfavourable comparison with his own people. He considered the question, but finally said that he did not think so; that he had had experience in England, and that he did not think the English had the necessary qualities.

"Of course," he added, true to the Welsh custom of making excuse for others not so fortunate, "of course, music is in our blood. We can do great things to serve music."

It was indeed in the Welsh blood. In the fourth century before Christ an unknown Greek author wrote: "The Celts practise the customs of the Greeks, being on the most friendly terms with Greece through the exchange of guest-friendship. They conduct their public assemblies to the accompaniment of music, zealously practising it for its softening effects."

In conversation the Welsh often confuse the foreign listener by their attitude to time. To a Welshman time is contemporaneous. He will tell you a tale as if he had himself witnessed the happenings, yet the event may have been a thousand years before. This bewildering habit becomes understandable when one remembers the long continuity of custom which has kept Welsh character within a mould. I realized that what now took place at Llangollen was in the pattern of which the Greek had written twenty-three hundred years before.

I asked Gwynn Williams how alive Welsh literature and music remained. He replied that it was live enough, but that he foresaw a danger to it from rising costs; that the liberal Welshman was too conservative to adapt himself to the rising prices of his books and song-sheets; that he insisted he had always paid just so much, and was damned if he would pay more. This attitude was particularly harmful in Wales, because the publishers had no other outlet. The English, for instance, had a vast English-speaking market throughout the world: not so the Welsh.

Gwynn Williams was a music publisher, and was not, he admitted, in such a predicament as the book publishers, whose costs had increased by a greater percentage owing to the ratio between total expenses and weight of paper.

However, of the Celtic peoples, it was among the Welsh that the language had remained preserved. The Cornish had lost the tongue: the Gaelic was very rare in Scotland, and modern Gaelic writings were negligible; and the compulsory revival of the language in Eire was but a self-conscious act of defiance by which the Irish were putting themselves to great inconvenience and confusion in order to spite an indifferent England. To say merely that the Welsh tongue has survived is to give a wrong emphasis. An Assyrian clay tablet may survive, but it survives only to be a museum piece. It would convey the fact better to say that the tongue has continued to flourish. It is no petrified tree dug from the bogs of time, but a flowering shrub.

I do not think that Gwynn Williams, as a world-famous adjudicator, was very satisfied with my performance so far. He looked at me suddenly with the calculating eye of a mentor who has determined to know the worst and is steeled against a shock.

"Cynghanedd has had much to do with keeping Welsh poetry and verse alive," he said. I replied that I was sure it had.

"Taliesin lived in the sixth century," he went on, not taking his eye off me. "His poems were written down unchanged in the twelfth century, and a Welsh village audience can understand them to-day."

Remembering fourteenth-century Chaucer, I thought that this particular example of Welsh conservatism must be thought admirable by the schoolboys of the country.

In the early days, I had heard, the bardic apprenticeship was of twenty years' duration. The aspirant learned his lessons by heart. His knowledge was stored not in books, but only in his mind. There was a system of prodigious memory training. Only much later in history were the products of these fertile versifiers snatched from the air, where they still echoed faithfully, and confined to paper.

But Gwynn Williams was not satisfied.

"Cynghanedd!" he remarked sharply.

He drew to him the Eisteddfod programme, and with a pencil ran lines about the couplet on the medallion:

It was clear now that there was in the couplet a harmony of consonants. It would have been difficult to have changed a letter without, to the expert, having obviously destroyed the balance. There are few chances to put a mistaken letter in a crossword puzzle without making a nonsense of another word. So the careful consonance of Welsh verse retains the words within a mould which remains for ever intact.

I thumbed quickly through a book written by Gwynn Williams, called *Welsh National Song and Dance*, and was struck at once by further examples of how changeless has been Welsh character and custom. They have fought for so long to retain their identity. It is clear that they have won their battle against all comers. In the book Giraldus Cambrensis, or Gerald de Barry, is quoted.

In the twelfth century he wrote of how a guest was treated in a Welsh house:

> Those who arrive in the morning are entertained till evening by the conversation of young women, and the music of the harp; . . . in each family the art of playing on the harp is held preferable to any other learning.

And again:

> These people being of a sharp and acute intellect, and gifted with a rich and powerful understanding, excel in whatever studies they pursue, and are more quick and cunning than the other inhabitants of a western climate. Their musical instruments charm and delight the ear with their sweetness.

I remembered that I had myself on occasions been entertained by music in out-of-the-way farms, and even in Welsh town villas. If one substitutes piano for harp, Giraldus might have written in this century, for the harp is no longer an everyday instrument in the home.

I noticed too that Giraldus had remarked the alien character of the Welsh among Western nations.

The Mediterranean strain in the Welsh ancestry brought unmistakable Eastern characteristics. Somewhere Giraldus says: "In war this nation is very severe in the first attack, terrible by their clamour and looks, filling the air with horrid shouts, and the deep toned clangour of very long trumpets."

Did those trumpets, in the hands of the sons of Ham, once blast down the walls of ancient Jericho?

I took leave of Gwynn Williams, who was a very busy man, and walked back through the small town. The shop windows were an example of Welsh lack of taste in matters outside their predominant artistic interests. The argot of the trade names trash 'Fancy Goods,' but trash it remains. Perhaps, though, I criticized too harshly. A shopkeeper must sell what is demanded of him, and I suppose tourists demand such tawdry trinkets as I saw.

Just the same, the display was sordid and out of place in a town which had burst spontaneously into a song whose beauty had drawn the nations of the world into the chorus.

Darkness was not so very far away over the hills as I headed along Thomas Telford's Holyhead Road, now rendered anonymous by the soubriquet A5. The outlines of the houses behind me were dimmed. Above them the castle of Dinas Bran stood on its conical hill, each rib of its skeleton outlined against a pale, cold sky. Seven hundred years and more ago Madoc, son of Gruffydd Maelor, Prince of Powys, roistered in that eyrie. His castle was now decayed. But the Dee still washed about the base of the hill. The Welsh tongue still drifted up to the stillness on the summit. But the ruin was the price of treachery, for the House of Maelor had turned coat more than once during the struggle which the northern Princedom of Gwynedd had so ceaselessly inspired against the English.

I meant to sleep that night at Glyndyfrdwy, which name means Valley of the Water of the Dee. A little short of the village I came upon a commotion in the road; a chattering of men; the movement of red warning lights. Two gun-and-tractor units, part of a convoy of Royal Artillery, had slid on the ice, blocking half the road.

A Welsh voice was saying: "Cheek it is to bring their old guns here, taking good land to shoot over."

This promoted a further anonymous expression of opinion: "Never mind the old guns. Them tree plantations is a lot worse, man. There won't be place for no sheep in the country after a few years."

I was glad that Mr Jones Flannel Mill was not present to fan the latent embers, for I was tired and wished to go to bed without further argument.

CHAPTER TWO

Moel Fferna slate quarry—Our homage to a dead King—The Throne and the Berwyn Hills—Welsh and stone-craft—I go inside a mountain—System of payment—Silicosis—Intellect of quarrymen

GLYNDYFRDWY is built on the north slope of the Berwyn Mountains. Like most North Welsh villages, it is a scattered community of small farm holdings and sheepwalks. The only other occupation of the able-bodied men is found below the surface of those hills on which their livestock grazes. For there is considerable mineral wealth secreted beneath the turf and heather of North Wales, and many villages win part of their living by burrowing for lead, copper, or slate. Above Glyndyfrdwy a great vein of slate bores through the very thickness of the mountain range from north-west to south-east.

The quarry lies at close on two thousand feet above sea-level, under the summit of Moel Fferna. A narrow, steep valley cleaves into the hills at right angles to the vale of the Dee, merging into the moor at the level of the quarry. Along one side of the valley runs a track which has been improved to take lorries, along the other is a tramway now disused.

When I went to visit the quarry I made my three-mile walk up the tramway with a certain nostalgia. In the days of my boyhood holidays in the village the tramway was in use to bring the slates down from the workings. They came in little open trucks whose descent down the easier gradients was controlled by a wind-on brake. On the steeper stretches the line was doubled, and the loaded trucks were hitched to a cable which, bent round a drum at the top, harnessed their momentum to pull up empties. To a boy the railway was fascinating in its course, which ran gently athwart the contours of spur and ravine, and I used to lie in wait until the last trip came bucketing down, the home-going quarrymen perched on top of the neat rows of slates. When all was quiet after their passing, and the hills had gathered to themselves again their wonted loneliness, I would search the occasional sidings for empty trucks, tip up the wooden blocks which were hinged across the rails as scotches, and gently ease a truck over the points.

Those runs were magnificent in their speed and daring, my heart doubly in my mouth lest the brakes should fail to take hold, or in case the ringing of the wheels on the iron rails, which echoed wildly in the valley, should attract attention. But now the tramway was dead; the rails ripped up; the sleepers rotted. No more would the Wells Fargo Express defy the shafts of Redskins, the tongues of prairie fires.

The snow grew crisp as I mounted higher, and near the quarry I had to kick steps in the steep final gradient, which had once merited a cable. It was very cold on the north-facing terrace above the pyramid of slate debris, and I went into the warm engine-shed. Jack Newnes greeted me. He was a burly man of medium height, and was known as the driver. In fact, the title was written on the lapels of a sort of uniform coat which he wore. It was, however, hardly necessary to label him, since there were less than forty men employed, and, though a comparative newcomer, Jack had been at work up there for only a decade less than the half-century. I told him that Willie Edwards, the assistant manager, had sponsored my visit.

It was a stationary engine which Jack drove. He led me to the pulsating power-unit and stood by it with a bedside manner compounded of confidence and admonition, like a doctor who is satisfied with the patient, but advises against taking liberties. It was a Ruston engine, a one-hundred-and-twenty horsepower triple-cylinder diesel, and drove a generator and air-compressor. I noticed that the generator, like the engine, was English, made by the Lancashire Dynamo and Crypto Company. I wanted to know what Crypto was, but thought that so silly a question might provoke a matching response. Instead I asked whether the machinery behaved itself. Jack said that on the whole it was not too bad. He added that it had been installed for twenty years and the original brushes were in the generator.

"I daresay they'll want renewing one of these days, though," he said, with Welsh disapproval of change.

I had the impression that Jack was not in love with his plant, though he gave it grudging respect. When he took me into the next shed I understood. Here was the original power-unit, only kept now as a stand-by. Jack eyed it with the affection of one contemporary for another in a world of uncertain future. The engine was a massive, horizontal single-cylinder affair. The bore was sixteen inches and the stroke as long as a man's arm. There was nothing paltry about it. It was as robust as the hills among which it had made its home. Jack stroked the massive cylinder barrel, and, like a man recalling an illness in the family, recounted a dreadful occurrence when the roof of the shed had collapsed under a weight of snow.

"The Ruston was out of action just then," he said, "and this one was doing all the work. It took us a day to dig her out. I greased her up, and she fired first time, man, and run so quiet you couldn't hear her."

Jack showed me the diamond-toothed saw which cut the slabs of slate into suitable pieces for the trimmers. It was the last mechanical process in the chain of production, for at the latter end a slate must be fashioned by the plain, skilled hand of man—and not any man, but one with inborn knowledge of stone. We went on to the trimming-shed, and, sure enough, I found there several old friends. We greeted each other, and Jack, who had been willing but puzzled during our tour, whispered a question or two and learned that I was not altogether just another bloody visitor.

The craft of slate-trimming is unlike any other. There are crafts in which the worker must have feeling for his material, such as carpentry. But no material is less tractable than the bones of the earth, and a slate-trimmer always seems to me to put a spell upon the slab on which he works. He turns it and twists it about, gravely learning its quality and the run of its grain. He taps it quite gently with hammer and cold chisel until irregularities drop away as easily as blown thistledown. He splits the rectangular remainder with the leisurely dexterity of a conjuror peeling cards off a pack.

Jack had lowered the barrier of formality now that he knew my antecedents, and presently took me back to his engine-house to give me cups of tea while he ate his lunch-time sandwiches. It was cold in the quarry. The trade was a hungry one. Yet the food the men were able to bring was not such as their bodies demanded. Up here was no equipped canteen with a hot meal of protein and vegetables; a meal extra to the rations of home. Instead there was a stone bench and a lump of bread and margarine and cheese. The factory-worker would not for long be able to stand the conditions under which these intelligent and dignified craftsmen plied their skill.

My friend Willie Edwards arrived by lorry up the mountain track. The time was nearly two o'clock. Several men questioned Willie about the observance of a silence in memory of their King. For that day the body of King George VI was being laid beside his ancestors at Windsor Castle. His body was even then under escort of picked detachments of the fighting Services which had owed him the supreme allegiance. The mourners in procession were sovereign rulers and the heads of States. Up here under the peak of Moel Fferna the small group of Welshmen paid their own tribute in gravity and silence and affection. For the dead man had been their King. The Royal lineage was nourished, true enough, by many roots which spread to other lands, but deep beneath the surface soil on which these fed the strong tap-root struck down into the history of Wales.

Through the complexities of breed and inheritance one constant strain had run linking the dead monarch, as by a golden thread, with the ancient Kings of the House of Cunedda, the Wledig, the leader of the Britons. The long history of our dead King had stirred to life in and about those hills in whose midst we stood quietly that snowy day.

Cunedda was a remarkable man. He and his Celtic forbears of Strathclyde had been entrusted by the Romans with the defence of the northern wall; a recognition of ability by Roman to provincial. It was when the legions left Britain, vainly to try to stem the tide of barbarism which was washing over their own country, that Cunedda and his eight sons swept down into Wales, and began to drive the Goidel settlers back to Ireland or to absorb such as were amenable. Cunedda founded the principal Welsh ruling house which was to provide in descent from him, however devious, a large proportion of the rulers of the Welsh princedoms up to the time of that Llywelyn the Last, who was killed so obscurely in the final bid against England's Edward I.

But it was not of the domestic significance of Cunedda that I thought that afternoon among the quiet Welshmen who were mourning their King. Cunedda's vigorous blood had played its part in the succession of George VI. Some of it had flowed into the veins of his daughter to make a bond between that distant Dux Britanniarum and the new young Queen of Britain.

In those grim days for Wales, when all independence at last seemed lost after the conquest by Edward I, the bards revived the old prophecy that a leader would come to bring freedom to the Welsh. His name would be Owain, and he would be descended from Cadwaladr the Blessed. There came Owain Glyndwr, and hope surged through the country, but Glyndwr's success was evanescent, as the meteoric usually is. Hope centred next on Owain Tudor of Anglesey, and, as is so often the way with prophecies, the hope was both justified and mistaken. It was not Owain who came to lead, but through him the leader did come. Owain's two offspring were Edmund and Jasper. Edmund died young, leaving his son Henry.

I wonder what clear-sightedness came to Jasper Tudor as he looked at his orphaned infant nephew. Perhaps he alone was gifted to see the future of the babe. Jasper had already fought beside Owain Glyndwr and had learned bitterly that prophecy had there run awry, yet in the grandson of Owain Tudor he was prepared to try again for fulfilment. Jasper later put Henry in Brittany, among the Celtic cousins of the Welsh, for safe-keeping, and when the time came he called him to Wales to rally his countrymen. The Welsh followed Henry, grandson of Owain Tudor, to Bosworth, not because they cared about the rivalries of Lancaster and York, but because the bards had kept alive the prophecy that through an Owain freedom might be won; that a descendant of Cadwaladr the Blessed would regain the lost Crown of Britain.

Henry Tudor's right to the throne of England was slight enough. Even though other more direct lines of male descent were extinct, his claim was magnificently impudent. He claimed through his mother, Margaret Beaufort, because his maternal great-great-grandfather had been the fourth son of an English king. The children of this maternal great-great-grandfather, John of Gaunt, had not even been born in wedlock. It is unlikely that this dim connexion with English royalty could have inspired much fervour among the Lancastrians, and, left to the English choice, York might have retained the throne.

The Welsh had a different idea. York or Lancaster interested them little. Henry Tudor was not important to them because of a wrong-side-of-the-blanket connexion with John of Gaunt, even though the issue was later legitimized, but because there was on his father's side a thin connexion with Cunedda. The bards felt justified in singing of Henry as a descendant of Cadwaladr the Blessed.

The window of history gives but a clouded view of one length of the descent of the Welsh princely houses from Cunedda. They can be traced positively only as far back as the accession of Rhodri Mawr, in A.D. 844. The misty gap is between that time and the death of Cadwaladr in A.D. 664. Records tell of too few kings who span this period of 180 years, and there are some who claim that the Cunedda line was broken when Merfyn Frych, an interloper, took, rather than succeeded to, the throne of Gwynedd in A.D. 825. The name of the lady Esyhllt, of the house of Cunedda, here becomes vital. Some historians say that she was the wife of Merfyn. If so, then she transmitted the Cunedda blood to her son Rhodri Mawr. But the most recent thought is that Esyhllt was Merfyn's mother, and thus that he himself was of the Cunedda stock. In either case the blood came through to Rhodri, flowed on to Llywelyn the Great and Llywelyn the Last, and sent also its potent force into the noble house of Tudor.

The thread which Henry Tudor personally carried from Cunedda to our new young Queen was thin enough, but he wove into it another strand by his marriage of policy to Elizabeth of York. Elizabeth was the direct descendant of Gwladys the Dark, daughter of Llywelyn the Great, by Gwladys's marriage with Ralph Mortimer. Thus, through his mother Henry VIII carried the Cunedda blood more strongly than his father.

Henry, grandson of Owain Tudor, landed at Milford Haven sixty years after the death of that other Owain surnamed Glyndwr. Through the land the bards sang the ancient prophecies; of how Henry was descended from the ancient British kings, and from

Cadwaladr, who, in that unfortunate battle, had lost the physical Crown of Britain to the invading Angles in the seventh century. Now, sang the bards, here was Cadwaladr's heir come to regain the Crown and to fulfil the predictions of the ancients.

Henry marched through Wales behind his personal standard, the Draig Goch, the British Dragon. The Welsh swarmed down from cwm and hillside to join him. Borderers such as the Herberts and Stanleys came in support.

Prophecy was fulfilled at Bosworth Field when British Dragon triumphed over English Lion. Richard III wore his crown throughout the battle, and at its fatal end the symbol of Kingship was taken from his cold brow and set upon the head of Henry Tudor. The crown of Britain, lost literally to the Angles by Cadwaladr, was as literally regained.

Thenceforth shrewd Henry saw to it that the Dragon and the Lion buried their ancient quarrel.

The House of Tudor raised all Britain to such heights that the people were loth to let the throne lose connexion with it, though they were not always fortunate in their search for Tudor blood.

James I was only brought to England because he was the great-great-grandson of the grand old man Henry Tudor, the first British king of England, through Henry's daughter Margaret. It was of no importance that James happened also to be king of Scotland. He might just as well have been a crofter.

Similarly, George I, the Hanoverian, succeeded because he was the representative of the only Protestant Tudor line, through his great-grandfather James I.

Thus, though the links with Cunedda had been more than once stretched, they had never snapped. To-day the new Elizabeth sat on the throne of Britain, deriving her right from her Scottish ancestor, James I, and her English ancestors, the Anglo-Normans. But her most ancient right to be Queen of Britain derived, not from Scots or Teutons, but from Cunedda and the British kings.

We stood that day in the snow of Moel Fferna and thought of the thin strong thread which joined our dead King with Cunedda, whose son Meirion had given his name to the county in which the mountain stood. Among the titles of the second Elizabeth was that of Countess of Merioneth.

Work began again in the quarry, and Willie Edwards handed me over to the clerk, John Davy Evans. John Davy was much more smartly dressed than I, in tweed cap and light tweed overcoat, but seemed quite willing to take me below ground. We took a candle lantern apiece and crunched through the crisp snow, now glistening in pale sunshine, until we came to the opening of the level which was here driven into the mountain. We bent our heads beneath the icicles which sparkled in the lantern light like glass pendants. Before very long I saw the burly figure of John Davy in front of me straighten from his crouched position, and I too stood upright. We were in a big excavation, cathedral-like, off which led passages whose openings showed only because they were darker than the dimness of our chamber. Two or three light-bulbs were struggling with the shadows, their life supplied by Jack Newnes and his Ruston engine far away in the sunshine.

John Davy led me to one end of the chamber, and, swinging aloft his lantern, showed me the great slate vein which the quarrymen had been following for eighty years. It was visible in its full thickness, for every now and again it was left intact to buttress the weight of Moel Fferna, which sprawled above our heads. The result was that the interior of the mountain was being eaten into until it was left like a honeycomb; a series of cells from which the slate had been extracted by patience and perseverance, joined by short levels cut through the thickness of the pillars which held up the roof. The design within the workings was, however, complicated by the angle of the seam of slate, which, dipping towards the entrance, conversely climbed away from the floor of the levels the deeper they penetrated. Thus after a spell of excavation the seam rose out of comfortable reach, and it would become expedient to drive a new level into it higher up. To give entrance to the new level, which would be high in the wall of the previous chamber, slate debris would be heaped in a steep ramp from the old floor to the new entrance. In effect, the workings rose storey upon storey within the mountain, and the lower and older cavities were partly filled by the waste from the higher and newer.

John Davy Evans wanted me to see the start of one of these new cuts. He had been moving about purposefully within the catacombs, me pressing close on his heels in case he darted up an alleyway and left me, and was obviously on ground so familiar to him that he did not realize my sense of direction was bemused. He pointed into the darkness to indicate where we were to go, and after much peering I saw a faint light through what seemed to be a hole in the roof of our present chamber. A great grey heap of slate debris spilled down from the hole like earth from a rabbit burrow high in a bank. John Davy began confidently to scramble up the heap, his feet dislodging lumps of slate which rattled away down on either side of us, or sometimes between my legs, into black depths which our candle flames shrank from showing. He told me over his shoulder that in the days before he became office clerk he had for a long time worked in the chamber to which we were climbing, and that he knew the area blindfold. This was, I thought, a fortunate qualification, for our pitiful lights did no more than emphasize the absolute dark which lurks below the earth.

Our slate heap led us to a small chamber, like a landing between flights of stairs, on whose floor rested the base of yet another pile. Somewhere at the top of this flickered the light which we had seen at the start of our climb. Muted human sounds echoed quietly down to us. This second heap was not fairly firm and settled like the first. Its materials lay at an angle which corresponded to the point of balance between rest and the pull of gravity. Some agency with a shovel was feeding the top of the pyramid and the surface, so delicately poised, was in constant motion downward. John Davy yelled, and the spectral hand was stilled. Not so the heap, however. As he plunged up ahead of me, floundering like a horse in a bog, the surface slid with increasing momentum until I was in the position of a man trying to ascend a 'down only' moving staircase.

The agency above us, still disembodied, produced a voice. John Davy relayed to me the information that there was a chain lying somewhere on the surface of the slate pile. We groped about, lanterns clattering, and presently disinterred the half-buried lifeline. All was now easy, and it was only necessary to dodge the really big slabs which John Davy sent tobogganing down. Our feet struck solid rock, and we found ourselves once more beside the deep seam of slate. The seam had been excised above, and a short passage had been driven along its flank a little past us. The rock-man who had owned the voice squatted beside a candle which was stuck by its own grease on the wall and talked technicalities to John Davy.

The seam, though twenty feet in depth, was made up in layers of much less thickness. The object was to drill through the top layer as far as the surface of the next, pack the hole with black powder, and set off the charge. Assisted by the downward slope of the seam, a neat flake of slate perhaps two feet by four by six, would slide off into the depths below; a labourer would stroke the detached fragment, hypnotize it, tap it with a hammer till it fell apart, and load the pieces on to a trolley ready to run along the tramway into the daylight, where the diamond-toothed saw waited.

Of course, this patient dismemberment, this carving up of the mighty bones of the earth deep beneath its hide, is not a surgery which can be learned from book and lecture. There must be instinct also to guide the knowledge of practice. John Davy and the rock-man discussed gravely the structure of the seam, the thickness of its layers, the direction in which it ran, and the faults which would occur in it at distances a year or two away in working time. They spoke with the certainty of surgeons making a diagnosis.

This instinct for the stone was older than the Welsh race. The Iberian migrants certainly had it, for on their long journey from beyond the Mediterranean they left behind as their milestones a chain of megaliths in Algeria, Spain, and France, and just as industriously they erected more up the western edge of these islands when finally they came to rest. Possibly too the Celts, who later came to mix with the Iberian settlers, were versed in the ways of stones. Their name derives from the ancient Greeks, who named them Keltoi, meaning, it is likely, the people who used stone axes.

And now, on this afternoon, under the bulk of Moel Fferna, I watched the Welsh rock-man as he squatted beside his seam of slate, paltry hammer and chisel to hand; I listened to him as he talked of it, speaking not as a conqueror of a victim, but as a good master of an old servant.

Presently John Davy and I slid down the slate heap, and he, calling into the darkness, provoked response from yet another chamber. We were in time here to watch the blasting of a slab from the seam. The hole was already drilled by the pneumatic tool whose air-pipe snaked away into the darkness through level and chamber back to Jack Newnes's compressor. The rock-man filled the drill-hole to the brim with black powder fron a conical container, tamped it firm with a brass rod, which could strike no dangerous spark from the rock, lit the fuse, and slid unhurried off the seam of slate. Black powder has a slow combustion and unleashes a thrusting force rather than a bursting one. Its function here was to shove the flake of rock off the seam, not to blow it into useless pieces.

The rock-man, John Davy, and I slipped through a level into the next chamber and waited until the dull concussion of the powder clapped past our ears. We went back to see the result and found a slab of about two tons weight neatly detached. The rock-man inspected the scarred seam, satisfied himself that the explosion had done its work cleanly, then advised us to leave. The fumes and smoke had risen high into upper parts of the workings, but would soon settle back, he said, so thickly that our present position would be unbearable. He himself was leaving the slab to work upon it next morning.

The quarryman has much latitude in his hours of work, and as we threaded our way back John Davy amplified my knowledge. The men work in teams, almost as sub-contractors, though there are a few men who are centrally employed by the management. Yet all are on bargaining rates—that is, piece-work. The bargain is struck on the first Monday of each month. The two rock-men of a team will go to see the manager. They will argue the difficulty of their immediate progress. They may say that they are due to cut a new level in order to tap the seam again at a higher point, and that therefore they must be given consideration for this preliminary task which is not immediately productive of slate; or that they are in a position where work is slow because movement is difficult. The labourers, two to a team, will state their case too; the debris may have to be shovelled and levered for a distance to a tramway. The sawyer, the trimmers, will have their say.

I supposed to John Davy that the men painted a very gloomy picture.

"Maybe they do sometimes," he agreed. "But the manager starts in then and tells them what fine advantages there are in front of them that month. In the end they always strike a bargain between them, and everybody's happy."

He said that up to the end of the First German War the men had worked entirely on piece-rates, but that a scale of basic pay had been brought in thereafter to safeguard them against the uncertainties of daily production. Yet even now a good pay-packet in a small quarry was rarely more than six pounds fifteen for the aristocrats of the craft, the rock-men and trimmers. I must have expressed surprise at this low return in comparison with the wages of skilled factory-hands, and wondered why it was that the men continued in this and similar quarries under the difficulties and hardships peculiar to their trade.

"It's in the blood," said John Davy. "I worked back in there for years until I smashed my leg up on a motor-bike. I couldn't manage underground after that, and went into an engineering works in Llangollen. I stuck it for seven years, but back I had to come, and I got a job here as clerk."

I said that I supposed he had found his working companions very different types in the engineering works.

"Yes, indeed," said John Davy. "Different they always are in the factories to us up here. I remember, when I was a boy starting in the quarry, how I used to listen to the older men talking in the cabin where we ate our bit of food. Educational it was. The way they talked would lift you up and make you want to learn. A man carries on very independent in this job. There's time for him to think about a lot of things while he's at his work. It's a sort of work that helps you to think too. Wrestling with nature it is. That makes a fellow think."

We reached the open air at last. The wind struck bitterly cold after the equable and perennially constant temperature within the mountain. I looked at the entrances to the workings and wondered suddenly why these men burrowed for their slate instead of digging down to it from the moorland, whose surface was not so far above.

"Do it that way we could easily enough," said John Davy, "but it's funny slate here. It's kept damp underground, but it dries in a few hours in the fresh air, and when it's dry it won't split for the trimmers. Awkward it gets, and they can do nothing with it. If a trimmer has some slabs left over when he comes to go home he puts wet sacks over them against the morning, or else they'll get the better of him."

John Davy took me in to a stone hut to see the manager, Thomas John Davies. John and I raised hats and shook hands. He was a small, spare man, in age well past the biblical span. He wore a bowler hat with a high, rather square crown, a navy-blue overcoat, and a purple woollen scarf. He began to speak to me of my father, who forty years before had interested himself in the village of Glyndyfrdwy, and had intended to develop a quarry a little farther back in the Berwyn Mountains. Thomas John Davies spoke of it as yesterday, pointing through the window at the track up which my father used to walk to watch the early probings after the slate seam. He gave extempore versions of their conversations, just as an after-dinner raconteur would tell of a happening of that very morning. It was almost a shock when he said: "Pity it was he died so young."

Thomas John Davies began to talk of difficulties. Quarrying throughout the country was suffering under the threat of silicosis. He himself thought there was very little of it, especially in his own quarry, where the dampness of the slate inhibited the dust. Just the same, recruitment was negligible. He could have employed two hundred men instead of thirty-seven. The slate was there. The market was there. His talk became a repetition of that of Mr Jones Flannel Mill when he began to mourn the loss of the craftsmen, the wheelwrights, the smiths, the village bootmakers and tailors, the carpenters and masons. The skill was slipping from the hand of man, and the machine children of his brain were robbing their parent. He spoke as if this disrespect for the old trades were a defilement of the memory of his ancestors.

I had told Thomas John that I intended to walk down to Cardiff. As I got up to leave he nodded through the window at the Eglwyseg rocks, whose parallel limestone strata were clearly visible beyond Llangollen seven or eight miles away.

"Look out for those rocks in the south," he said. "They crop out again down yonder."

He might have been saying: "Mind you go and see John Jones when you're down there. Always at home, he is."

I said good-bye to them all, and returned down the dead tramway in the chill of the late afternoon. I learned afterwards that John Davy Evans, the quarry clerk, was a Justice of the Peace. In Wales it is common to find men and women in ordinary jobs with uncommon attainments. I know of quarrymen with the degree of B.A. or M.A. and women with high musical honours who run village shops. The Welsh like to have knowledge and intellectual status, but they like to have it for its own sake, not for its commercial value. They lack what many nations call ambition. This is an Eastern characteristic which has remained with them. If, for instance, an Arab can live off six goats and three date-palms he sees no reason to work hard to obtain twelve goats and six palms. He would prefer to use the time saved for contemplation. The Welsh have much the same philosophy. They must work a great deal harder than the Arab to gain a living from their unwilling hills, but such leisure as they have they spend in discussion and the pursuit of the non-material arts.

Perhaps the Welsh err on the side of conservatism, but the sense of values of most other Western nations may well be distorted in the opposite direction. Perhaps the vaulting ambition of the others o'er leaps itself and falls on the other side of the point of balance.

CHAPTER THREE

Genealogy—Seven Famous Evanses—Great-uncle Huw and the bag of gold—Divorce and inheritance in the laws of Hywel Dda—A minister of the Church in Wales—The Holy Stranger—Nonconformity

I HAD an aunt who lived at Glyndyfrdwy. The old lady was well beyond eighty years of age, but her memory was clear as a filing index. I was talking to her one evening, and asked questions about my Welsh ancestry. Without a pause or a correction she recited to me a family tree which, when I counted up from my notes, contained a hundred and seven names. With the names I was given a concise description of the relatives, told who it was they married, how many and what sex were their children, and what success or failure they made in life. It was a prodigious feat effortlessly performed. I had to cry "Enough!" as my aunt, having finished with the stem of the tree began to work outward towards the tips of the innumerable branches.

All Welsh people have this interest in and gift for unravelling the twisted skein of genealogy. The old Welsh laws of inheritance had demanded that they should be expert. In England title and property descended in olden times to the eldest son, and so long as his legitimate birth was well established the other children were of less interest to the lawyers. Wales, however, practised divided inheritance; the law of gavelkind. There was an automatic entail on property. A father might not dispose of his lands save for his own lifetime, for on his death it must be divided equally among his sons. When that time came the youngest son marked out the patrimony in the necessary number of parcels, but the choice of parcels was made by seniority. This system of ensuring fairness was yet another example of an Eastern twist of mind.

When in due course the brothers were dead the property was

divided afresh among their sons, who would be first cousins to one another. On the death of the new holders redivision was made yet again among *their* sons—second cousins. And so, to the fourth degree from the original holder, relatives had a keen interest in the maintenance of a property and in knowing how many were entitled to share in each new division. The interest was the keener, and the need for intimate knowledge the greater, because natural sons had full equal rights.

This skill in genealogy, though no longer of financial importance, persists as strongly as ever, as my aunt demonstrated to me.

My aunt's house is close beside the Holyhead Road, and the roar of cars and lorries disturbed the quiet as we sat that evening by the flickering firelight without other illumination, as the Welsh so like to do. This love of firelight is old in them. In the ancient laws fire was a physical possession, its importance dating perhaps from the pagan festival of Beltane. A man was accused of stealing if he entered another's house, put a torch into his fire, and carried off a light to kindle one of his own. At one time tax was paid on each hearth, commercializing the symbolism of the hearth.

The old lady was gazing into the coals, reading the pictures there, and she harked back to the family tree, loth to leave the security of its strong association.

"I suppose now they've made the road," she mused, "you can soon get to London."

She spoke of Telford's Holyhead Road as though the labourers had only then removed their tools, and gone. Yet their passing must have been a hundred and forty years before.

"Grandmother used to say," she went on, "that in her day there was no wheeled traffic passing through. Travellers had to ride. Grandmother was a half-sister to your great-great-uncles, the Seven Famous Evanses. Their father, old Robert Evans, married twice, as I told you just now, and she was the child of the second wife, so her half-brothers were grown men when she was a baby. Old Great-grandfather Evans used to send grandmother to school in Essex. Once a year she used to go, and once a year she would come home. It was dangerous to travel all that way in those days, with the wild men and footpads about, so she always went when her seven brothers were going on their business to London.

"They used to shoe their cattle and ride horseback behind them to the great markets of the south. The women of the hired men used to go along too, knitting long wool stockings as they tramped, to sell to the houses beside the way. Many travellers would find out when they were travelling, and they'd band with them for protection on the journey. They used to do banking for people who couldn't spare the time to go, and they'd carry gold or drafts for them up to the London banks."

My aunt reminisced so quietly, in so matter-of-fact a way, as she watched the changing pictures in the hot coals, that I came under a spell which made time without meaning. She had heard relatives talk to her about events in which they had taken part during the Regency, and she in turn recounted them to me complete in detail of place and dress and quoted conversation.

She told me of how my great-great-uncle Huw quarrelled with his father.

"They never got on," said my aunt as sadly as if it were to-day's tragedy. "One early morning the lodge-keeper was woken by some one throwing gravel at his window. He got up and looked out, and there was Huw with a bundle over his shoulder. 'Well!' the old man said. 'Well, Master Huw! Where are you going like that?'

"Huw said that he and his father had had their last quarrel at dinner the night before. His father had got up from the table, and when he came back he flung a bag of a hundred golden sovereigns along the table, and told him to get out of the house for ever.

"'I'm going to Australia this morning,' said Huw, just as simply as if he was off to Bala market. 'I'll say good-bye to you, Bob.'

"'Good-bye, Master Huw,' said old Bob Parry, 'Good-bye. God bless you.' The old man broke down and cried, because he was very fond of Huw. But he knew it wasn't any use to try and persuade Huw or his father to talk things over again. They were very hard men.

"Well, Huw might have died for want of food on the ship, except for what his mother sent after him to the docks at Liverpool. A crock of salt butter it was, and it lasted nearly through the six months' voyage."

My aunt stopped, and gazed again into the fire while my imagination played with these inflexible forbears. I had thought the story done, but a Welsh story is a continuing growth, and my aunt went gently on.

"Twenty years later, when Bob Parry was a very, very old man, some one came into the kitchen of the lodge. Bob's eyes were bad by then, but he knew Huw's voice.

"'Master Huw!' he cried. 'Happy I am you've come back after all these years."

"'I'm on my way again, Bob,' Huw told him. 'I came to give my father back his sovereigns and the interest on them for twenty years.'

"And away he went for ever. He'd become a barrister in Australia, and a very rich man."

The stories rolled on softly and effortlessly.

There was the tale of my grandfather riding home from London, much gold in his saddlebags. In Shropshire two footpads leaped out at him. Grandfather spurred his horse over one of them, and brought his crop down on the head of the other. Then he dragged them on their backs behind his horse into Shrewsbury, and dumped them in the gutter outside the house of a magistrate.

There was the tale of Great-aunt Gaynor, who, like Huw, quarrelled with her family. She was eighteen years old, but she had money, and took ship for South America, where in due course she married a rich rancher, and, so my aunt assured me, lived happily ever after.

That a girl of eighteen could exercise this initiative in the year 1820 would be strange in another country. The old Welsh laws, however, were remarkable for their emancipated attitude to womenfolk. A wife was protected from arbitrary divorce, and had herself full right of petitioning against her husband. The laws were first set down on paper in the middle of the tenth century, during the reign of Hywel Dda, Hywel the Good. The good king called a representative conference to his hunting-lodge, Y Ty Gwyn ar Daf, the White House on the Taff, now marked by Whitland, in Carmarthenshire. There a long discussion took place on unification and codification of tribal law and custom. Most probably a small sub-committee—to use the modern term with which we are too familiar in these days of heavy government—then sat down and worked out the decisions on paper. The laws had been unwritten until then, for the Welsh had always stored the most intricate information in their minds. But perhaps the English passion for scribing had taken Hywel.

The laws of Hywel laid down minutely how property should be divided when a couple separated. Separation could legally take place by mutual consent at any time up to seven years less three days, when a woman could remove with her the dowry which she had brought her husband, her personal possessions, and her 'cowyll,' which was the gift given to her by her husband after the consummation of marriage.

However, if the couple bedded together only once after the seven years were three nights short, and there was separation by common consent, then their belongings were divided. In general the law gave the man the implements of husbandry and the woman the household goods. Such possessions whose future ownership was not specified by law were shared. Here again was the Eastern touch, for the woman made such possessions into two heaps, but the man had choice of heap.

Children were shared alternately between father and mother, the man taking the eldest.

A wife was empowered to extract a fine from her husband for his adultery, though for a similar mis-step she herself might be divorced with loss of her property rights. However, she could win divorce if her husband was afflicted with leprosy, bad breath, or impotence, and, having won divorce, could impose on her husband a fine for each act of adultery. After the vital seven-year period was past the allocation of goods on divorce was different. An equal division was made between the couple of all the man's wealth and property.

This equal share-out after the period of seven years less three days was directed against the man who wished to replace his present wife by a younger one. The most attractive young second bride came dear at the cost of half a man's goods. She might well have been referred to as his better half.

From the religious point of view, it is most curious that temporal law recognized divorce, although the Celtic Church recognized the supremacy of Rome, which would only relieve a marriage by annulment. Divorce was not so recognized in Catholic England until the Welsh King Harry VIII found his appetite getting the better of his piety. It is even more curious that the Popes of Rome did not put pressure upon the Welsh to abandon this part of their legal code.

These laws were maintained to a large degree intact until the Act of Union in 1536, when they were replaced by the English code, in which a woman was a chattel. The Welsh attitude to women, however, established by long custom, may here and there have persisted. At any rate, my old aunt did not think that Great-aunt Gaynor's excursion to South America was at all remarkable a hundred and thirty years before, in a period when women of some lands were struggling with the vapours.

The wheel indeed spins full circle. Slowly the law of England swings round to embrace the Welsh laws which it destroyed. The modern sponsors of the Acts dealing with married women's property, divorce, and illegitimacy are bravely winning back to the tenth-century code of Hywel Dda. The English are beginning to acknowledge that British was best.

My aunt's endless story-telling was interrupted by the parson, who often called upon her. He was a dark man who, dressed in robes and velvet skull-cap, would have passed as a Moor or Kabyle. The Welsh parson, like the Welsh minister, is in very close personal touch with his parishioners. He may be helped to come close to them because the Welsh social structure is almost classless.

Our clerical visitor that night was the son of a Merioneth farmer, product of Oxford and St David's College, Lampeter, which has a Theological Hall. The village had petitioned for a North Walian, for there is still quite a difference in tongue and outlook between North and South. Indeed, the North Walian has a saying about any outlandish fellow such as an African medicine-man or the Grand Cham of Tartary. He says of such that he is *tu hwnt i hwntw*, or "more foreign than the people over yonder." The people over yonder are the South Walians.

However, well over half the Northern clergy are from the South. Possibly not all of them are instinctively in sympathy with their parishioners, and these misplaced appointments may have slightly weakened the hold of the Church. Of these Southerners most come from Cardigan. Cardigan is a farming county well removed from industrial openings. If, therefore, a son shows academic leanings, it has become customary to put him into either the teaching profession or the Church. The College at Lampeter is conveniently waiting for those who choose the ministry.

There is a saying that Cardigan exports two animals: pigs and parsons.

My aunt's friend was a very lively sort of clergyman. I prodded him a little with stories of the archaic attitude of some clergy to modern problems. He robbed this sport of its excitement by capping my tales with far better ones.

The parson conformed to the Welsh pattern when I asked him whether the Disestablishment of the Church in Wales, in 1920, had been a good move.

"Yes, indeed!" he said. "At first we found difficulties, but we've got over them. For instance, on Disestablishment we lost our income from tithes, though the Welsh Church Temporalities Act did pay us a million pounds in compensation. But our first Archbishop was Edwards of St Asaph, and he started to collect a fund to replace the loss of tithe. To-day Welsh stipends come 80 per cent. from invested capital."

He looked down his nose, eyes gleaming, the picture of a Barbary pirate.

"Anyway," he said, "whatever we lost, we won independence from Canterbury. Canterbury used to like us to call the see the 'Holy Mother.' We have always called it the 'Holy Stranger.'"

The parson told me that the office of Archbishop of the Church in Wales was vested on the senior bishop, and was not tied to one of the five cathedrals at St Asaph, Bangor, Llandaff, Brecon, and St David's. Thus the Welsh insistence on fair shares, illustrated by their laws of divorce and inheritance, was again satisfied, for each of the five sees would every now and then have its turn at being an archbishopric.

I wondered whether the Church was making headway against Nonconformity. I was tacitly rebuked for my phraseology.

"We are not 'making headway,'" said the parson. "But we are certainly gathering in more and more stragglers."

This differentiation was delicate. It was as if my friend, in his piratical guise, had said: "We wouldn't dream of boarding a ship and kidnapping the passengers. But if we shift the lighthouse and the ship runs ashore, then we'll pick them out of the water."

At any rate, he saw signs that Nonconformity was less strong than formerly. He was a practical man.

"If churches and chapels are both three-quarters empty the churches can stand poor support better. They've more funds to tide them over bad times."

CHAPTER FOUR

Holyhead Road—Borrow and Owain Glyndwr's mount—Stones of the Brave—I approach the Keep of the Welsh Castle—I am commanded to a beauty spot—The dancing Ladies—The fairies and Tom Wern—The monster of Beaver Pool—Betws-y-Coed—I argue about trees and tractors

---

I SET off early next day westward along what my aunt would have described as that nice young Tom Telford's new road.

The steep slopes of the Berwyn Mountains were on my left hand, the Dee on my right. After a couple of miles I passed Owain Glyndwr's mount. George Borrow had paused here on his walk through Wild Wales, and had, true to his usual custom, told an old Welshman all about the hill. I wondered if the old man had humbly accepted Borrow's lesson tongue in cheek, for it is very unlikely that he would, with his long race-memory, have known less about the hill than the Englishman. Borrow discovered the profoundest admiration for the Welsh, and remarked his astonishment time and again at the intelligence and courtesy of the poorest of them, which, he said, was in strong contrast to the attainments of peasantry in other lands. Just the same, the Saxon touch of patronage would out from time to time as he explained the Welsh to themselves. He made amends though. A few days after he had passed the mount of Glyndwr he walked with his stepdaughter to the summit of Snowdon. Inspired by exertion and the sense of achievement natural to a Norfolk man who had reached the height of 3560 feet, Borrow quoted a Welsh poem, and, for good measure, paraphrased it in his own language:

> Such was the harangue which I uttered on the top of Snowdon; to which Henrietta listened with attention, three or four English, who stood nigh, with grinning scorn, and a Welsh gentleman with considerable interest. The latter coming forward shook me by the hand exclaiming:

"Wyt ti Lydaneg?"

"I am not a Llydanau," said I; "I wish I was, or anything but what I am, one of a nation amongst whom any knowledge save what relates to money-making and over-reaching is looked upon as a disgrace. I am ashamed to say that I am an Englishman."

Such an apologia would be considered handsome anywhere.

This part of the Dee Valley was a great stamping ground for Glyndwr. Though, as Borrow had remarked to his Watson, the old warrior had not raised the mount on which he had stood to watch for the approach of the English, who would follow the River Dee up from Chester. Most likely it was an ancient burial-place.

It is said that the old warrior was born at Glyndyfrdwy, though no one is able to give chapter and verse. Yet I remember, when a boy, as I was scrambling about the mount, an old farmer had shown me some long humps in the field below. They formed squares and rectangles, as if the crumbled foundations of a building had become grass-grown. The old man claimed that here had been Owain's palace. It must have been a very small palace, but one could hardly describe Owain's dwelling as a mere house.

Corwen too, some three miles on, gave a reminder of Owain in a hotel which had taken his name. Borrow did not overlook this. His interest coincided with his thirst, and he spent an hour within in order to refresh himself. It did so happen that his desire for beer would even to-day have come at an hour when the law considers it legitimate to be thirsty, but had he arrived, as I did, soon after ten in the morning, he could still have slaked the desert of his throat: not so me. "Thirst for another hour," said the modern law, "after all, there is always water."

At Corwen Telford's road leaves the Dee and rises gently over the cultivated uplands which fringe the Mynydd Hiraethog. The country here is bleak and windswept, and on this day was streaked with snow, which lent teeth to the wind. I plodded on, ever more conscious of the weight of my rucksack. I am used to packing a rucksack. Before I do so I make a heap of the articles which are a necessity for a journey, then, as experience has taught me is essential, throw aside half the necessities. I had done this before I started out on my present trip, but the knapsack began to grow heavy, for there was little of interest to catch the eye, set the imagination to work, and thus distract the mind. One of my disadvantages was the weight of a respectable suit which I had put into my pack. There were quite a few people on whom I wished specifically to call, and I was not sure that some of them might not set their dogs on the trampish figure which I usually presented. Indeed, the dogs might have taken action on their own initiative, for they are notorious snobs.

By the time Cerrig-y-Drudion was reached and passed, however, I had determined that the good suit should be sent back to the care of my wife. If its loss were to lay me open to attack by packs of pariahs, a cudgel would, I thought, be a lighter substitute for the suit's defensive value.

Cerrig-y-Drudion is a windswept place. Many was the time during my farming days that I used to attend its periodic sales of mountain sheep and Welsh black cattle. Because of its central position, accessible as it is from all four points of the compass in spite of its high altitude, the sale attracts many dealers. Dealers wear a uniform of polished boots and leather leggings, raincoat and bowler hat. They carry little thin twisted sticks. They are a close corporation, and among them something less obvious than a wink does for a nod. The body as a whole knows what its individuals have come to buy. There was no need, then, for the Cerrig dealers to stand throughout the sale exposing their fine garments to the elements, which used the bare moorland as a tilting ground. Instead they would repair to the inn, near which the stock-pens were, fortuitously perhaps, erected, for they could be certain that word would reach them when the ring held lots which interested them.

In any case, long experience had taught them the rhythm of a particular sale under a particular auctioneer. At such and such a place three lots would be sold to the whisky, in another brisker fair only two lots, in a really dilatory ring perhaps a whisky would span as many as five lots. The dealers knew therefore by a time-whisky horology just when to pop back to twitch a bid for some desirable barren heifers or draft ewes.

I, not so practised but eager to learn, had found this an expensive sale to attend, for my drinking would fall out of step with the lots, and thus I was often forced to gulp my liquor and rush out only to find myself too late.

For some reason even the native people spell the last part of the village's name 'Druidion.' True, there used to be a cromlech near by, but the place was not named after the Druids, but after the Brave. 'Cerrig-y-Drudion' it should read—'The Stones of the Brave.'

I lingered not in the chill of Cerrig-y-Drudion, but pressed on towards Pentrevoelas. Just short of the hamlet I breasted the unspectacular rise which is the highest point the road reaches between London and Holyhead. I felt the thrill which has never failed me here. From the crest I could see, still quite far away, the mountains of Eryri, the Abode of Eagles. Snowdon, Crib-Goch, Lliwedd, and Siabod were clear-edged against the sky, the browns of their lower slopes giving place to the white drapery of the summits.

I was in Gwynedd now, the Kingdom of Cunedda Wledig, Dux Britanniarum, King of the Britons, whose potent, persistent blood had dripped from century to century until it entered the veins of our young Queen newly upon her London throne. It was the kingdom of mighty men, of Maelgwn, Cadwaladr of the Long Hand, Rhodri Mawr, Hywel Dda, the Great Llywelyn, and the Last Llywelyn. From the fierce hills now before me had gone the constant summons to all Wales to resist the despoiler of British independence. Angle, Dane, Roman, Norman, the new-compounded English, all had beaten their mailed fists against these hard rocks and had won little but bloody knuckles. The original racial identities of the invaders had been mixed in a confusion of breed and language, but the British remained to that very day as little changed as the hills which had tried them in times of peace and sheltered them in trouble for the full two thousand years since the main strains of their race had blended.

There is for every man one place which speaks, above all others, to his inner mind. Those hills which then lay ahead had spoken to me from childhood. Their voice had reached me whether I was near or far.

Men talk of the atmosphere of a house, of whether it is a happy atmosphere or unhappy. It is recognized that what man builds and lives in, shares his emotions with, loves and dies in, must absorb some of the essence of the hopes and fears which has drenched the bricks and mortar. So it happens with these Welsh hills. They have been lived in to the full. There has been no unused room in the house of the Britons. These hills have from the first been woven inextricably into the ancient history and present life of the people who have lived among them so long that they are now not tenants, but freeholders. The hills influenced the Welsh to become what they are, then helped them with storm, bog, and precipice to resist encroachment on the preserves of custom and character.

The rucksack sat lighter on my back, and not all because the way now lay downhill. I came at last to the long grade which drops to Betws-y-Coed. I diverged to the left along the original course of Telford's road. The track runs along the steep side of a wooded ravine, where signs invite the tourist to view the falls of the infant River Conway and the Fairy Glen. There is a perversity in me which usually drives me to refuse such invitation. I do not want to be told that this or that has been inspected, disinfected, graded, made accessible, and passed by a Board as worthy of a twopenny turnstile, and that therefore I must have a look.

Once I was on a very strenuous Army course. My squad instructor would now and again shout, "Five-minute break! Smoke!" We would drop in our tracks and nestle thankfully into the wet earth, our lungs swallowing huge draughts of air, insatiably demanding the restorative power of oxygen. Yet such was the power of command that we produced tobacco and struggled with the smoke which just then we hated, until sometimes we were sick.

There is a similar authoritative property in the sign: "Beauty spot! Pay twopence!" Dutifully the tourist ruins his shoes over a rough track, glances, perhaps, at the wrong view, and struggles laboriously back to his conveyance, hating every moment of the excursion, but hating more to have to say later that he has not made it.

To-day in the off-season the Falls were mine. They were indeed beautiful when I looked out from the railed platform where I was tacitly directed to stand. But I saw them as beautiful against my will, which reacted against coercion to admire.

Opposite the Fairy Glen was a deserted attendant's hut. There was a slot in the locked door which said 'Pennies.' I prowled about the deep ravine until finally I came to a place where I could look up a long reach of rock-walled river. It was very lovely. To make sure that I realized it a bench had been erected at this place, backed by an old motor-seat against which to recline. Here was another invitation to view as directed, which I refused.

The track slid on downhill. As I walked I was interested to see two very gaily dressed women dancing on the grassy surface. When I drew near I saw that they were young. They were pirouetting in company with a cocker spaniel and a bullock. It was an intricate dance with a to-and-fro motion like a square set. First the girls would walk a few paces with their graceful backs to the bullock, and the spaniel in front of them. Then the bullock, with a-one, a-two, a-three, would skip past them until level with the spaniel, who would now retreat behind the ladies. The ladies then turned their backs once more on the bullock and reversed their direction in the wake of the spaniel. The bullock skipped past to the spaniel, who again retreated. The ladies reversed after the first small, black gentleman, the second gentleman skipped past, and the figure was repeated.

I watched this pretty scene during the time it took to fill and light a pipe. Then the less nimble lady spoke to me.

"Vy does not zis beast stop?" she inquired in a charming French accent.

I suggested that he might not yet be tired. There was silence during a couple more measures; then the lady said:

"He is fierce, yes? He is a bull?"

I said that their partner was undoubtedly fierce, and to casual outward appearance a bull.

"Make for 'im to go away," demanded the second lady imperiously.

I gave the bullock a reluctant slap on his flank, and he stopped his prancing to eye me reproachfully.

"You are ver-r-ry br-r-rave!" exclaimed the first lady. "A t'ousand, t'ousand t'anks."

I offered to see the maltreated aliens safely home, but both declined the necessity for me so to trouble myself.

"Remain to watch ze beast!" ordered the first one. "Ve vill save ourselves."

Regretfully the bullock and I ambled on down the track until finally we parted near a small, elderly man who carried a white stick and was guided by a mongrel dog, who took careful stock of me. The man said "Good day," and we began to talk. He lived, he said, in a small studio-cottage back up the track. He had lived there for forty-five years, and had painted the Glen in winter and summer, sunlight and gloom. His blind eyes no longer saw the beauty, but it was held clearly in his mind. From where we stood he pointed here and there with blind accuracy at this or that grove or rock or waterfall. He had been born near by at a farm named Yr Ynys —The Island.

"It is Crusoe I am now," he said, "for I cannot see the way to leave my island."

I asked about the fairies of the Glen, and my new acquaintance confirmed that they were light-haired. I suggested to him that their colouring in legend might be a race-memory of the blond Beaker people, who had built one of their tombs at Capel Garmon a mile or two away, and whose fairness must have been in contrast with the dark Iberian settlers, with whom they later intermarried. My friend agreed. He told me that he had recently heard a lecture which described the discovery of two tombs on the Denbigh Moors. Tradition had always said that a tall fair man had married a short dark woman thereabouts. When the tombs were opened they contained respectively a long male skeleton and a small female one. This tradition, he said, might have sprung from a race-memory of the mingling of the breeds.

The blind man turned his dark glasses on me, as if inspecting me thoughtfully, then addressed me by name. When I acknowledged that he was correct he introduced himself, for we had never met before. His name was Tom Wern.

I inquired about Tom Wern later that evening. He had indeed spent forty years of his life in painting the moods of the Glen, and five more in remembering its changing guise. Painter he might be, but his real art was carving. They told me that when Tom was a young man he had been asked to go to Germany to do his carvings on the screens and woodwork of a great cathedral. The top rung of fame was in his grasp, so skilled was he. Tom prepared to make the journey, but one evening he quietly unpacked his bags, and said that he would not leave his glen, that he preferred to remain an obscure artist in the place where he was born, and where he was happy, than to be acclaimed in a strange land. Tom Wern he was known as, according to the Welsh custom of naming a man after his occupation or the place of his work. His family name was Evans, his little studio-cottage Wern.

When I left Tom I hurried on towards Betws-y-Coed. I crossed the Conway by the beaver bridge, below which was a great, quiet pool. In times past a water-monster dwelt in these depths, the afangc, whose mischievous delight it was to cause floods the length of the Vale of Conway. At last, goaded by desperation, a band of men crept up beside the pool, and, picking their moment, flung chains about the unsuspecting brute. They hitched the chains to a team of oxen, and dragged the monster up the tributary river Lledr, and thence over the shoulder of Siabod between its summit and that of Cribau. The going must have been hard indeed up the long and steep slopes to the crest of the shoulder. It is soft and boggy to-day, and may well have been worse in those far-off times. One of the oxen so exerted itself that an eye fell out here, or perhaps was knocked out by the struggles of the monster. The spot where this happened is named Gwaun Lygad yr Ych: the Field of the Eye of the Ox. The poor animal wept so hard with the remaining orb that a pool grew from its tears, the Pwll Lygad yr Ych.

It must have been easier when the gang had crossed the crest and began to descend into Nanhwynen, but again was a long uphill pull to the sombre Glaslyn, the blue-green lake, close under Snowdon's shadow. Here at last was the exhausted afangc released, to vanish with a quick wriggle under the surface of the lake.

The Nant Conway men had been very cunning, for, if the afangc had not learned his lesson, he was beyond the Conway watershed, and his playfulness would now flood the vale of Nanhwynen.

Like so many Welsh towns and villages, Betws-y-Coed lies up against steep hills which screen it from the sun. Just the same, if it is a dull stone, it has a beautiful setting. I went to the Gwydyr Hotel, which I had known for many years. It is a hotel with a strong atmosphere of homeliness. It was built a hundred and thirty years ago by the Scottish grandfather of the present owners, and was turned into a place of rest and refreshment fifty years later when the railway came through to the village. The building has had continuity of family occupation, and is that much-advertised but very rare home-from-home.

The furnishings are so violently early Victorian that they stun the guest into acceptance of their heavy ugliness. But the brightness of the fires, the warmth of the welcome, and the robustness of the meals belong also to the age of the little old Queen and Empress, God bless her and them.

Much land about Betws-y-Coed has been leased by the Forestry Commission. There are diehards who deplore the woods of conifers which are growing slowly to maturity on the steep hillsides. But conifers suit this mountain country. They are Nature's raiment on mountains the world over, and Nature never errs in taste. In olden times, before tools came readily to the hand of man, these native hills had been wooded. True the trees had been largely scrub-oak, birch, and ash, of which a few stands still linger here and there, but I am not at all sure that the conifers which are now springing up on the graves of the old woods are not more beautiful.

For a few years after their planting the trees stand in regimented rows, except where rock, precipice, and stream break the alignment. But as thinning begins the rows lose their order and soon allow the plantations to assume a natural air. The Commission too does plant hardwoods where the soil is suitable, especially on points of prominence where such trees can lend their variety to the landscape.

On the whole, the Welsh do not like the work of the Commission. In the bar that night I prodded many old friends into voicing their opinions. They harked their memories back, as their race always does. They instanced farms now swallowed by the trees, and told of the sheep and bullocks which once had browsed there. To a Welshman it is the ultimate sin to dispossess a sheep or a sturdy black bullock.

I tackled a forester who was drinking without comfort on the fringe of the argument. He was English, young, and new to his work, but turned out to be well supplied with facts. He maintained that the Land Commissioners kept control of the Forestry areas, and that they allowed the Forestry so small a sum per acre with which to make their purchases that it was out of the question to buy any but the poorest ground.

The Welsh company gravely begged to differ. For a while they recalled farms and their long-dead farmers, and stated precisely how much stock such holdings had carried before the trees came. They mentioned the days of the early nineteen-thirties, when the best mountain land sold for a song, pointing out that, however tight the purse-strings, the Commission had at that time no competitor in the market, and had bought much land which could have been better employed in its original use. They spoke of the trees as if they had marched in serried ranks to take up occupation.

Our forester countered by claiming that, wood for stock, the planted lands would produce more in money's worth, and that any decent bits on the farms had been left untouched. These small parcels were let as holdings to foresters, who contracted to give not less than a hundred and fifty-six days' work a year to the Commission, in return, of course, for pay. He also said that the afforested areas were able to employ more labour than had been the case before the invasion of the trees.

The Welsh customers were not too sure about this. They recited by name the dispossessed farmers within a wide radius, the names of their children, and the names and characters of their hired men, if any.

I felt that the opposition was firing too much circumstantial ammunition at the Englishman, so I worked him out of the press until his back was in a corner. When I had him to myself I asked if the Welsh foresters had a way with trees, as has the Celt with stones. He said that he did not think they had a special flair, but that such skills did not grow in a year, and that only now were second-generation foresters being recruited.

But if the poor fellow had been rescued from the locals, he now came under a minor attack from me about the sort of land which the Commission planted. This time the complaint was in a different context, and was but one of many in a wider argument.

Briefly, the argument was that in a little over a hundred years the population of Great Britain had increased three and a half times. The increase began with the dawn of the Industrial Age. Until that dawn our islands had been more or less self-supporting for food, but afterwards, of course, it became necessary to buy more and yet more from other countries. There was no difficulty about this.

The international stores were well stocked. The shelves and meat safes were full, and our custom was eagerly sought at cut rates. On our side, there was plenty of housekeeping money. We had vast capital invested in all parts of the world; we were earning a handsome income because of our early lead in the industrial export race.

After the First German War the picture of prosperity began to fade. As a people we were a little tired; we had spent a little of our capital; the buyers of our industrial exports were beginning to make some of the goods for themselves, so that our income was becoming reduced; the shelves at the international stores were not quite so well stocked, for the populations of other countries were increasing and, in the New World, the fertility of the soil decreasing after generations of reckless exploitation.

These signs were plain to see in the nineteen-thirties. Trade statistics showed that we were spending twenty shillings and a penny, but earning no more than nineteen shillings and elevenpence. However, no one felt much alarm. True, industrial redundancy was felt, but we had enough capital left to pay the workless a dole, and to cover the gap between our earnings and our spending.

What was a slow run-down became accelerated into a headlong plunge after the Second German War. Our capital was spent within the space of those few fatal, splendid years. Most of our remaining customers learned the tricks of manufacture for themselves; peasant nations ate more of their food, and had less to sell. We borrowed from friends to meet the higher prices which the international stores demanded for such goods as they had on the now dusty shelves.

Finally, we had to eat less.

Our population, three times and more multiplied in just a century, was only justified by a great export trade. Now the trade had dwindled to a trickle, but the workers who had supplied it in the days of greatness still remained. They were unable to find nations who would take their manufactures and ship food in return for them. Our trade on the old scale was dead, and we had no capital left to live on.

There was, of course, only one remedy within our own control, and that but a partial one. We could try to shift some of our working emphasis from factory to farm. We could try to grow some of that portion of our food which the stores no longer had to sell, and for which, in any case, we would have been unable to pay.

Many complicated devices and incentives were juggled with to conjure more food from our own land. But nearly all these tricks were tried upon the well-established lowland farms, which had been in quite good heart under the care of generations of curators, and whose production was never much below its potential.

Now, the surface of these islands is made up of two almost equal portions of good land and poor land. The good land has always produced well enough, the poor land never. It is with the poor land that our conjurors would do better to concern themselves. Here there is a backward audience to respond with ingenuous delight when called on to the stage to assist in pulling an extra rabbit out of the hat.

I put it to my forester that sooner or later the nation would be forced to tackle the marginal lands, where lay the only areas not developed; that so far there had been no need to develop them, which was the reason for their present backwardness.

My victim had borne this harangue for the space of a pint, though with symptoms of restlessness. To my surprise he agreed with me. He too felt that trees should not be planted on ground which was workable for improvement, but should be grown on slopes too steep for implements or too broken by rock outcrop. A little more beer inspired us to coin a phrase or two. I said, "No trees in tractor country." He said, "Where the plough can go, no trees we'll sow."

I am sure that both of us were quite right. Before long the Government will have to bring the marginal lands into proper use. The University College of North Wales's farm at Aber and the Welsh Plant Breeding Station at Aberystwyth have both shown how to feed three sheep where two grazed before.

Somewhat restored, the forester faced another local assault. This time he was accused of harbouring vermin. I was glad to notice that he did not take this personally, nor did he deal brusquely with his accuser, but admitted that there was some right in the statement.

Hill farmers suffer very serious losses from foxes. In spring, when the foxes have cubs to feed, a hill farmer may well lose five lambs out of a hundred; not that the killer will remove all his murdered prey, for he slays for sport as well as food, and sometimes kills half a dozen lambs only to carry one away.

Now and then big fox-shoots are organized. These are dangerous to hunter and hunted, for the weapons are often heirlooms, the aim is unpractised, and the rocky ground lends itself to the sportive ricochet. Just the same, foxes are killed in numbers during these drives, when, bolted from their rock dens by scarred Welsh terriers, they face the fearful crossfire of the posse. Neither beast nor were-wolf could carry the lead which sprays the mountainside, and a fox, fortunately, will die from a pellet or two, for the wound poisons him. He is a wanton and cunning murderer and bears no one's sympathy.

The hunters well know the dens in the mountains, which is the major factor in their favour. However, the Forestry plantations are often impenetrable in their early years, and at no time give the field of fire to which the farmers are accustomed. The fox has realized that he is secure among the trees. He makes his lair in their shelter, and only issues forth on his forays.

The last I heard of the argument, the forester had been manœuvred into having to deny that the true but secret purpose of afforestation was to maintain fox sanctuaries from which to replenish the hunting shires.

CHAPTER FIVE

Llanrwst bridge—Trefriw Mill—Swallow Falls—Capel Curig —The peaks of Eryri—Pen-y-Gwryd and Mount Everest— The secret of Athole Brose—King Arthur—Davy Jones and Hydro-electricity—Beddgelert—Owain Glyndwr—Cranical indices—The landlord, the Normans and Taffy

I LEFT my rucksack at the Gwydyr Hotel and set out on a detour to Trefriw. I took the old road, which has the left bank of the Conway on one hand and a steep hillside on the other. The slope was tree-planted, and I saw with approval that it was not tractor country. My forestry acquaintance of the previous night had said that these trees were well established, and that soon the roadside fence would be taken down. A road through woods is transformed if it becomes unfenced. No longer is it a trunk highway which urges the traveller not to linger, but a magic-carpet strip off which he may at will wander into grotto or tree-circle, or find seat on rock or bank of stream. I remember that even the sooty con fines of the London parks took the public into their confidence when the railings were cut down for materials of war.

I passed the ruins of Gwydyr Castle, Llanrwst in the distance beyond. The town was reached by the perfectly proportioned bridge of Inigo Jones, which seems to have grown across the Conway as tree-boughs reach and touch above a lane. Plain the bridge is and functional, and there is all the secret of its loveliness. It is tragic that the Welsh who hear beauty with an ear which is never deaf are yet blind to it. They may not always have been blind, for there are other beautiful bridges in Wales, often hidden in remote valleys, and designed with unerring line by humble village masons. Simple and unpretentious too are some of the old farmhouses. Like Inigo Jones's bridge, many of these seem to have grown from the hillside, often standing in the niches from which their stones were hewn, and roofed with the slate whose veins lie exposed through the skin of the turf. But later the Welsh became self-conscious in their building, with awkward and terrible results.

The first wing of Gwydyr Castle was built in Henry VII's day, and was probably a symptom of the more secure feeling which Wales knew once the Tudors had taken the English throne. There is nothing so reassuring as to have your own general in command of the enemy's forces.

Sir John Wynn enlarged the place during the next reign, and told all and sundry that it was now the fairest house in Wales. Perhaps it was, but he need not have said so himself. At about this time Harry VIII was busy anglicizing the old Welsh families, and the remains of the house and garden as seen to-day are typical of the Elizabethan type of small English manor house.

I was going to Trefriw for some tweed patterns requested by my wife. There is here one of the small family woollen mills of which there are about a dozen in North Wales and thirty or forty in the South. Mr Williams, the owner, was an old acquaintance. He told me that he was no longer able to buy his wool from the farmers of the neighbourhood, who were now directed to sell direct to the Government. Instead he bought at the Government auctions. The system of the Wool Marketing Board was designed to protect the farmer from violent market fluctuations. In my own farming years I sold my wool at prices varying from fourpence to seventeen pence a pound. Now, however, in a good season the Government did not distribute all the auction receipts to the farmers, but retained some of the money to distribute in a bad one. I always, perhaps unjustly, suspect such schemes. As in a casino, a fair amount of the money must go to the house for administrative expenses.

No doubt the system is a good one; nevertheless, life is robbed of yet another little individuality. The countryman can no longer walk his farm wearing tweeds woven from the wool of the sheep his land had nourished.

Anyway, Mr Williams was happy, for he said trade was good. I asked about the Rural Industries Bureau, of which Mr Jones Flannel Mill had approved. Mr Williams thought, too, that the Bureau was useful.

On another occasion a mill-owner answered this query in a way which showed that he had a crafty mind.

"Not bad they are with their advice," he said. "But watch out if you've got good ideas of your own. Let them over the mill and they spot what you're up to, and tell your competitors they ought to work things same way. If you've got a bit of butter on your bread they spread it all over the other fellow's crust."

I parted from Mr Williams, the tweed patterns in my pocket, and set off again. Perhaps I ought to have sipped the waters, for Trefriw is a spa, but I prefer even poor beer to good sulphur. In the hills above the village are lead- and zinc-mines, which, the historians say, were known to the Romans. There is a fine track over the high ground, where lies Llyn Crafnant, to Capel Curig, but I had to go back to the Gwydyr for my pack, and also to stoke myself with their immense lunch on the principle of a camel at a waterhole before facing a desert of unknown facilities.

By mid-afternoon I had left Betws-y-Coed behind me, and was on the way to Pen-y-Gwryd, where I proposed to sleep. I passed the Swallow Falls, where a sign threatened me with the view. The turnstile was still at that early season, the charabancs and their uncomprehending freight absent. Lord Ancaster, who had owned the Falls, has put them in the keeping of the local Council, who use their very considerable revenue to ease the local rates.

Just the same, were I a householder I should feel that I was living on immoral earnings.

I had known Capel Curig, to which I soon came, for many years. It seemed to me now that its atmosphere had changed. It was always a village which took much of its character from its hotels, for the main source of its revenue was tourists. The tourists I remembered, however, were not the casual kind. Many of them had come once a year or more over a long period. They knew the villagers well. They came because they loved the place, and left because they must. They walked the hills, climbed the rock faces, and identified themselves with the country and the life of the people.

Now, I felt, it was different. Perhaps the changed financial balance had barred the old type of visitor from the hotels, and allowed in a new sort who made other demands. It may be that the hotels changed their characters to please their new guests, or else because they changed their characters the old guests no longer came even if they could afford to do so. Whatever the reasons, change there was.

There has been a notable Lancashire and Midlands penetration hereabouts in the hotel trade.

I passed through Capel Curig and turned from Telford's road up the long valley which points to Snowdon. The afternoon was fine. On my left the long hump of Moel Siabod tempted me to scramble to its summit. I crossed the footbridge which spans the young River Gwryd at its outlet from the Llynau Mymbyr, and climbed the long slope to Siabod's tilted ridge.

Moel Siabod is just lower than three thousand feet, but it is the finest viewpoint in North Wales. From lofty Snowdon the other hills lose their stature. But the few feet by which Siabod is lower than the bigger mountains enables a man on its summit to see all the Welsh Three Thousands in their right perspective. It was beautifully clear that day, and all the high ground was picked out for me by the gleaming snow. I think that I identified all fourteen of the Three Thousands; the five peaks of the Snowdon Group; the Glyders and their cousins, Y Garn and Elidir; and, peeping over the saddle east of Glyder Fach, the uncompromising rock-tip of Tryfan; beyond were the Carneddau, less determinate. Southward I saw Cader Idris, the wild Aran hills, and possibly Plynlimon.

The valley between Siabod and the Glyders was divided by the swift River Mymbyr. Built on a shelf high above the river's far bank was the grey stone house of my former farm, shrunk to the size of a child's toy by the void between us. On the near side of the river, close under the foot of Siabod lay Cwm Farm, crooked in the sheltering elbow of a ridge. It is the very farm of which Huw Menai wrote:

Some cool medieval calm hath settled here
  On this lone farmstead, wherein humble folk
  Still speak the tongue that Owain Glyndwr spoke,
And worship in it, too, the God they fear.
For to these perilous Ways, where rocks rise sheer,
  Their kinsmen came to curse the tyrant yoke;
  And here the proud invader's heart was broke

By brave and stubborn men year after year.
Unconquerable still! here birds but know
  The Cymric speech; the very mountains brood
O'er consonants that, rugged streamlets, flow
  Into deep vowel lakes . . . and by this wood,
  Where Prince Llywelyn might himself have stood,
Forget-me-nots in wild profusion grow!

What a storied land was this Kingdom of Gwynedd, and how indelibly had its inhabitants chipped their history on its rocks, the oldest known to geology! So clear-cut, so set with age, were the valleys and high passes, the outcrops and ridges and peaks, that my imagination could fill the valleys with the glaciers which had deeply scoured them; had left the debris of moraines which lies as if the ice had been a visitor of yesterday; and had grooved the very boulders which here and there stand poised just where they once were left. Down the Pass of Llanberis a great ice-river had poured in slow majesty, fed by its tributary which had gouged out secret, wild Cwm Glas. Another had slid down into Nanhwynen, reinforced by cold allies from Cwm Dyli and Cwm-y-Llan. Beyond the saddle of the Glyders had been yet another glacier, a thousand feet thick, which had frozen the Vale of Ogwen into a dead country above which Tryfan and the two great Carneddau had waited patiently for the warmth, and the coming of Iberian, Beaker man, and Celt.

The mountains which raised themselves about Siabod stood as an example of the influence of geography on history; an example of the beauty which gives inspiration to sing of it and die for it. For once, a romantic, violent, and often sad tale has a happy ending, for the Welsh still hold the mountains which they defended so fanatically for so long against such overwhelming assaults; they still have their language; they remain the Britons, whom neither Roman, Angle, Dane, Norman, nor Englishman could assimilate, could rarely subdue, and could never conquer.

Their sustained feat of independence against such odds is unique in racial histories.

It was very cold on the summit of Siabod. I hurried down the long, curving western ridge over which the afangc had been dragged, and dropped down to Pen-y-Gwryd, beyond which was the white highest peak of the Snowdon group, looking as Constance Davies wrote of it in a Triad:

> Y Wyddfa
> In the January snows,
> Immaculate as thought
> Made perfect in a mood of exaltation.

Here stood the squat hotel at the junction of the passes of Llanberis and Nanhwynen. I was just a little apprehensive of my welcome, and more of my appetite, for I was finding that hotels were changed in Wales.

The Pen-y-Gwryd Hotel is an unusual place. It is all alone on its road junction, poised above the head of Nanhwynen, frowned upon by Glyder Fawr and Lliwedd. The hostelry began as an ale-house at the very beginning of the nineteenth century, and catered for the rare travellers who struggled along the track up densely wooded Nanhwynen, or who required to imbibe courage before making the crossing of the Llanberis Pass. Because of its situation it was natural that the Inn, together with Gorphwysfa, a similar lone shelter at Pen-y-Pass, should become the first headquarters of British mountaineering.

Many were the men of notable character and, often, eccentricity, who used, and still use, these inns.

To my relief the atmosphere of the hotel was not changed. The present proprietor, though an Englishman, seems to have identified himself with the country and its customs. He is not a retired Midlands tradesman, unhappy in his new surroundings but too obstinate to leave, but an active mountaineer. No one sniffed at my rough appearance or sneered at my lightened rucksack, nor was the quantity of food which my appetite demanded made a cause for wonder.

The only other guests at that time were a young couple who surrounded themselves with a protective wall of whispers, so that after dinner I left the sitting-room and made myself comfortable in the bar in company with an attractive receptionist-cum-manageress—the proprietors being away—who ministered to me. The young lady had come there from the gentle atmosphere of a Cotswold hotel, but had fallen now beneath the spell of gale and crag and spraying waterfall.

I was prepared for a quiet evening when the outer door opened. There was a burst of hearty Scottish conversation, and three strong, rough men came in. They wore, between them, a range of garments which covered almost every known Western article of apparel: corduroys, breeches, plus-fours, jackets, wind-breakers, sweaters, woollen hats with bobbles, helmets with ear flaps, and, as a common factor, nailed climbing-boots. The three were entirely different in features, but identical in expression, wearing the cold, hawk-like look of the expert climber who relies on his skill for his life.

It turned out that one of the three had been a member of the recent reconnaissance expedition which examined the south approach to Everest. He said that he thought the route better than the hackneyed approach by the North Col. One of his companions added that, as a makeweight, the other led too near the Reds. Being a Scot, he liked salt in his porridge, but did not wish to mine it in Siberia.

Just the same, the first man said, at twenty-one thousand feet was an ice-fall contained between two unclimbable rock ridges. At the top of the ice-fall was a crevasse of the tremendous width of a hundred yards, and of great depth. This was caused by a sudden increase in the angle of descent of the glacier which lay between the ridges, and which cracked as it took a sudden plunge. If there was a way across by means of either of the rock-walls it would be hazardous to a degree, for the walls were swept by constant avalanches and falls of stone. It was conceivable that a summit party might have attempted a crossing, but several camps would be needed above the crevasse, and it would be on the daily route for porters. These must not be exposed to the dangers of avalanches.

I wondered how the Swiss party proposed to deal with this impasse on the forthcoming attempt which would precede ours. The newcomers said that there was some talk of firing guns to bring down the avalanches before each crossing.

The ex-reconnaissance man had insisted that he was drinking his beer unwillingly, and under pressure of his companions. He was, however, regularly persuaded. He began to plead strenuous plans for the morrow, and that he wished to wake with a clear head. His friends at once laughed heartily at the quaint notion that English beer was empowered to affect a Scot, and, being so reminded of this absurdity, began to put some life in it with chasers of whisky. The Everest man mournfully acquiesced in this innovation.

Whisky is a subject on which the Scots are fully informed, and in which they delight to reminisce. The mournful one had brightened after the chasers and apropos of nothing but their memory told how Athole brose had been made by his battalion of the Highland Light Infantry. Apparently they used to pour whisky into a tub part filled with coarse oatmeal, stir for forty-eight hours, add honey and fresh cream, strain through muslin, and drink the result. After an abortive attempt or two by the Mess to bring this consummation to fruition, the battalion commander himself dedicated two days to the stirring, and with great devotion produced the long-sought liquid.

The mournful man began to detail what followed from the tasting of the brew, but before he could do more than catch our interest and astonishment one of his friends interrupted. He jeered at so superficial a method. There was, he said, only one recipe for Athole brose, which he had had from the Macdonald in person.

You took a bottle. You filled it half with oatmeal. You added three-quarters of a bottle of whisky, which, by a divine negation of the principles of Archimedes, could still be accommodated in the half-full receptacle. Then daily for a month you shook the bottle and turned it. At the month's end you strained off into a bowl the liquid, which, further fermented by the oatmeal, should give off stupefying fumes. To the bowl you added a quarter-bottle of heather honey and a gill of fresh cream. You stirred for three days, and drank.

I remarked that I supposed once the cream was in the stuff would not keep, and should be disposed of quickly. The disciple of the Macdonald gave me a queer look, and said how would a man know if the brose was a good keeper.

The man in the woollen hat with bobble said that Athole brose tasted like vodka, only smoother and stronger, whereupon an argument sprang up. To settle it, the attractive receptionist brought out a bottle of vodka, and the three Scots practised various ways of drinking it, sometimes rolling it round the mouth to compare the flavour with the memory of brose, and sometimes taking a glass at a gulp to compare the paralysing effect.

Finally, the mournful Everest man stated that he was not in a mood for drinking, and that after a pint of beer to quench his thirst he would insist upon going. After their departure to the Climbers' Club hut, where they were staying, I too went to bed.

The hotel provided me with an enormous breakfast next morning, a monster meal based on porridge and egg, and with some sandwiches in my pack I set off towards Beddgelert, taking the old track which twists below the motor-road. Again the young day was beautiful. It was some months since I had seen Nanhwynen. This true name of Nanhwynen derives from the 'Vale of Gwynain,' a personal name, though now the valley is usually called Nant Gwynant. It was here that Medrawd—Mordred—plotted against his father, King Arthur. Near by, above Pen-y-Gwryd, is the Bwlch-y-Gwyddel, the pass of the Irish or Goidels, and down in the bottom by Cwm Dyli are the remains of Muriau'r Dre, the Goidel township.

I was here the previous summer with my elder daughter, when she was seven years old. She has always been a student of Arthurian days, and as we were on our way to Y Wyddfa, the highest of the Snowdon group's five peaks, she pointed out many features which she recognized by the descriptions of Geoffrey of Monmouth and the poesies of Tennyson.

I had told her of the strong Goidel hold which was upon the country before Cunedda came raging down from Cumberland to join the Cymry, compatriots of his, in their effort to clear the Irish out. When later we stood upon the Bwlch-y-Saethau (the Pass of the Arrows) we had looked down into the great hollow of Cwm-y-Llan in which had flourished the Goidel settlement of Tregalan.

My daughter was much excited to see the very country where the great warrior had met his end, and, indeed, at that moment she was standing on the ridge where the arrow had given him mortal wound. Below us, shrunk by distance, was Llyn Llydaw. Perhaps, we thought, some Druid priestesses had dwelt by its shore as anchorites, which sometimes they became. Perhaps down one of these springing buttresses which pillared the thin ridge of Lliwedd Sir Bedivere had stepped, his mailed feet ringing on "juts of pointed rock," and he "larger than human in the frozen hills." On that reed-grown marge of Llydaw he had paused and looked, and looked again at the jewelled hilt of the symbolic sword Excalibur. Twice he had failed, bewitched by gems and moonlight, until at the third time he hurled the sword in a flashing arc far over the waters.

Then slowly, painfully, he had fetched down his dying King to the Queens, the priestesses, who awaited him, their boat lying quiet on the sullen lake. On the great inscrutable face of Lliwedd they laid him in a cave, where still he sleeps.

"He'll come again," my daughter had told me, her eyes moist. "He said he would."

"I hope you're right," I said.

Henry Tudor had named his elder son Arthur, after the Celtic hero, and had invested him with the Principality of Wales. Arthur was a minor, and Henry reconstituted the Council of Wales, first formed by Edward IV for his minor son. Edward's son was murdered; Henry's Arthur died. Thus, although the Council functioned spasmodically until 1688, it never, somehow, achieved the status which consistent princely care might have bestowed, and which might have won much for Wales.

History has so often taken the wrong turn for the old British people.

This day, however, I was leaving Lliwedd and Llyn Llydaw to their secrets. I passed the North Wales Power Company's turbine shed down in Cwm Dyli, the great twin water-pipes sprawling down the hillside like a gigantic snake beside its sloughed skin. My breakfast still lay heavy, and I was glad to turn into a farm to greet an old friend. Davy Jones was in his kitchen. After greetings he asked what I was doing. I said that I was walking to Cardiff.

"Jesu!" he exclaimed.

Mrs Jones threw me a terrible look and vanished from the room.

Davy Jones was not quite himself that morning. A neighbour had been stricken with a sudden appendicitis late the night before and Davy had been called forth by two worried daughters to take the sick man to hospital for an immediate operation. He had not returned until morning, and had been over to the two daughters, now alone, to help out with the care of their beasts. He had only now completed his own early morning chores, and was about to breakfast.

"You'll have a cup of tea," he stated.

I thought I could just manage this, but no more.

Worse still for Davy, his hired man who had been so long with him was, as he put it, under the doctor. They had told him that he had what they called a 'tired heart.' I knew well that big farm of Davy Jones; the hillsides so steep that on the dry grass of summer the walker had to beware of a slip which might carry him down a thousand feet; the cruel scrambles up rock and scree; the wind which sometimes stopped a man from moving; the rain which fell in some years to a depth of two hundred inches. There was no gentle shepherding in these parts, no ambling after the flock with scrip and flute in hand. Even the great hearts of the local men sometimes tired.

From the kitchen door I looked out at the roof of the Cwm Dyli power-station, whose turbines hummed a few hundred yards away.

"Why don't you get the electricity here, Davy Jones?" I asked. "It makes a fine servant."

"Try I have, man!" said he. "Try and try again, but no use so far. For the Midlands it's wanted."

As I had, on my walk, drawn nearer to Eryri whisper had become louder and louder of a new power-scheme. While at Pen-y-Gwryd I had gone to see a man who had copies of the plan. I was aghast at its magnitude, for the scheme embraced all that ancient country between Cwm Penmachno and beautiful Aberglaslyn, between Dolgelley and the Vale of Conway. For twenty years the labourers were to work at scoring concrete leats along the flanks of these immemorial hills, at driving tunnels from one valley into the next; at piling up the dams in cwm and hollow; at building the power-houses; at setting up the steel pylons whose great strides would reduce the perfect proportion of this mountain scene.

True, beauty might fairly be prostituted for ease, and I asked Davy Jones how much he thought those parts would benefit when wild streams were caged in concrete.

"Unworkable some farms will be," he said, "with leats across where we want to drive the sheep. They'll be catching off the water which did ought by rights to come down to the lower slopes. Dry up they will under the leats, and soil erosion there'll be. Then what about the visitors? A big trade they are in North Wales, like Switzerland. Will they want to come and see works like they've got in their own cities? Trips of engineering delegates will be all will come. No, the hydro-electrics won't help Wales. Off to England the power will go to ease peak-load, and us with plenty of coal for power if it was left in Wales."

I had felt a cold fury earlier that morning as I glanced at the plans of the scheme; a fury that man was empowered to despoil the mountains which had endured all the shocks of the elements. But I had said nothing to my informant, an engineer, who saw naught but delight in translating a blue-print for destruction into the practice of ruin, for I felt that perhaps the power might smooth the rough road of those who gained a living here. However, Davy Jones was probably right: to Wales the ruin, to England the power.

Mrs Jones now returned to lay the table, and I was concerned to see that knives and forks for three were placed. I protested that I had very recently eaten unusually hugely.

"That's a good thing," said Mrs Jones, relieved. "I haven't much ready for you. Only a bite to keep you going, walking all that way."

She drew out a chair for me and put in my place a great platter of thick farm bacon, eggs, and fried bread. The quantity over-lapped the plate rim. Somehow I ate it all. I got away with no more than two cups of tea, but was, on pain of offence, forced to eat bread spread with farm butter and home-made marmalade.

I made hurried farewells, and laboured away down the track to Llyn Gwynant.

Hospitality has always been regarded by the Welsh as among the first virtues. In old times no traveller was formally asked in for entertainment, nor did he have to beg it. If harm comes to the guest of an Arab the face of the host is 'blackened' before all his tribe. In Wales the parallel continued as the young women gave entertainment with music, song, and dance, and when later the host and hostess waited at their guests' table and did not themselves sit until the strangers were replete.

I remember well the time when, if a wayfarer passed through a farmyard, a woman would hurry out with a glass of buttermilk to offer. For all I know this courtesy may now be an offence against the Milk Marketing Board.

That morning I passed the lovely shores of Llyn Gwynant, with

Aran, the fifth peak of Snowdon, towering beyond it. The use of 'Snowdon' to designate the main peak of the group, rather than as a collective term, is confusing, for the main peak has its own title of Y Wyddfa, the Tumulus. Under the debris of the summit King Arthur is said to have buried the corpse of the giant Rhitho, whom he slew in single combat. 'Snowdon' comes perhaps from early English 'Snawdune' of obvious meaning, and is therefore hallowed with some antiquity. So, it appears, is the collective derivative 'Snawdunia.' It is most unfortunate that the flavour of the modern word Snowdonia is so damned suburban. Old the term may be, but it is debased by modern association. I will not catalogue these five historic peaks together with The Beeches, Alwynds, and Bella Vista. The peaks have that name on which no English nomenclature can improve: Eryri, the Abode of Eagles.

Nanhwynen, besides echoes of King Arthur, tells a tale or two of Owain Glyndwr. The old firebrand spent some time in the wooded vale fashioning an army from the rough material of farm-lads, whom he drilled by the shores of Llyn Gwynant and Llyn Dinas. Glyndwr's inability to compose the differences of some of his influential countrymen was nearly his undoing here, for a local bigwig tried one night to seize his person. Owain slipped through his hands by swimming the Afon Glaslyn, in those days a tidal river. He made for Moel Hebog, threw off pursuit by a spectacular climb of the rock-chimney near the summit, and hid in the cave which is now called Ogof Owain Glyndwr.

Owain Glyndwr was an extraordinary man, part visionary, part warrior. He was inspired to action when the Marcher Lord, Grey of Ruthin, enclosed part of Owain's sheepwalk. Owain knew that England's Henry IV was no iron Edward I, and was unable to curb his barons of the border, who had for so many centuries had regal licence to improve their fortunes by robbery. He knew that he must make his own justice. With a scratch force he defeated Grey and sacked his castle lair. The Welsh, always ready to redress old wrongs, particularly over a sheepwalk, flocked to the standard of the Red Dragon. For four years bard and minstrel sang of the days of the House of Cunedda, and of its son whose memory was still fresh, Llywelyn the Great. For immemorial prophecy had warned the people to watch for an Owain who would come as liberator.

Like Llywelyn, Glyndwr stormed up and down the country with his army of half-trained shepherds. He forced Grey to make a treaty: he persuaded the Mortimers, who were directly connected with the House of Cunedda through Llywelyn's daughter, Gwladys the Dark, to ally themselves with him. He gained some moral backing from the Avignon Pope, and was sent 3000 men by Charles VI of France.

But the time was not ripe. The gains slipped from Owain's fingers. Yet much of what he fought for has been won. Henry, the nephew of Jasper Tudor, his comrade in arms, landed in South Wales just sixty years after Glyndwr's death. The Red Dragon fluttered the length of Wales as Henry Tudor marched from south to north gathering behind him those terrible Welsh bowmen whose fathers with Harry of Monmouth had broken the chivalry of France at Agincourt.

> And gentlemen in *England* now abed
> Shall think themselves accurs't they were not here,

said Shakespeare's Harry on the night before the battle.

Henry Tudor picked up the crown from the field of Bosworth, and Owain's dream of breaking English oppression was fulfilled. Owain also had wanted two universities in Wales—one North, one South. The University of Wales has more than achieved this. He had wanted freedom of the Welsh Church from the edicts of distant Canterbury, and had desired the Welsh Archbishopric so nearly won by Giraldus Cambrensis. This too has come about. I daresay old Owain's bones at last lie easy in their unknown grave.

A mile or so short of Beddgelert an elderly lady stopped her Ford Eight to offer me a lift. This was the first time that anyone had ventured to come to terms with my rough appearance, and I accepted as far as the village. My driver's English was not very good, but she began without prompting to speak of the hydro-electrics.

"Work! Work! Work! Morning to night! There's a farm for you! What for must they potch with the water? Flood, the valley does. What matter if they make it flood worse or flood better? Different it will be and the animals and us got to learn it all again, as if there isn't enough without it."

Experience runs at least equal in the race with academic theory. My driver feared for her low meadows and her wells, whose dangers and habits she knew. The academic geologist could not with truth tell her how her land would be affected once man upset Nature's careful arithmetic of watertables.

Beddgelert is known for its legend of the noble dog which defended the child against the wolf. This touching tale was invented in 1801 by the first landlord of the Goat Hotel, a South Walian named David Prichard. It proved so helpful to his business that, with the aid of the parish clerk, he discovered the grave of the dog Gelert and erected a headstone. Beddgelert also was the seat of a monastery, one of whose priors sustained Owain Glyndwr with food when Owain was hiding in the cave on Moel Hebog.

Anthropologists say that Beddgelert shares with Rhayader in having the largest percentage of population in Wales with Iberian skulls. One would expect to find here a preponderance of the dark, sturdy type of Welshman, who would not have the ebullience of the true Celt. It was a little embarrassing both for the people and me, but I had a good look at their heads. At the end of it all I was not in a position authoritatively to state the cranial index, but certainly the general impression was of dark, small people.

I had been wandering without much purpose this day, and before going far from the village I went into an inn to telephone Clough Williams-Ellis, best known as an architect, for I realized that I was near his house, Plas Brondanw. I had not met Williams-Ellis, but he asked me without hesitation to stay the night with him. He added that he was living at the hotel which he had designed at Port Meirion, near Portmadoc, but that he would pick me up at Brondanw, which he would be visiting by car in late afternoon.

I asked for a glass of beer to recompense my inn host for the use of his telephone. The little bar was empty, and mine host enveloped in an aura of depression. At sound of my English voice he brightened a little. He had, he said, retired the summer before from the butchering trade in Staffordshire, and had bought his inn. No! He did not get on with the Welsh, who were a backward people, as I would find out if I tried to do business with them. I waited for the word 'clannish,' and out it came. Furthermore, what could you expect? The old rhyme had already said it all:

Taffy was a Welshman,
Taffy was a thief,
Taffy came to my house,
And stole a leg of beef.

I thought that, for his own sake, I would do my host a kindness by showing him another viewpoint. The beer had not uplifted me to great heights, and I only managed to rhyme impromptu:

"William was a Norman,
William was a thief,
William came to my land,
And drove off all my beef."

My host was a little puzzled, wondering, I suppose, who this chap William, or Norman, was. I saw that I was up against a barrier of non-comprehension, and did not have the energy to try to burst through it with no assurance that there was fertile ground beyond. I paid for my drink and left, sure that I would find a new landlord when next I returned.

The jingle about Taffy is infamous, and demonstrates how mud, flung by the hand of the hooligan, will cling.

The Welsh border raids were, of course, provoked by William of Normandy. After his conquest of the English at Hastings, in 1066, he was hard put to it to find enough land in England to reward his followers, who had come with him only so that they might share in the loot of a freebooting expedition. England was soon parcelled out among the more vociferous, and those at the end of the queue began to clamour. William set up three baronies on the Welsh border, at Chester, Shrewsbury, and Hereford, and gave their holders licence to win what they could from Wales. There was no pretence at legality, or even of right of conquest, for the Normans had not come to fight the Welsh, but the English. The Normans did well for themselves in their first onslaught upon the country which the English had learned to leave alone. Within twenty-five years of Hastings most of Wales had been overrun, taken by surprise at the onslaught of trained, well-equipped Norman soldiers, except for Gwynedd and Deheubarth, the kingdom centred on Plynlimon.

At first the two races got on well. They mutually appreciated one another's culture, each finding the other's companionship agreeable after contact with the English. Through Geoffrey of Monmouth the Normans eagerly assimilated Celtic literature, and disseminated it through Europe with profound results. Almost all European literature stems from one of two sources: Græco-Roman or Celtic.

The newly circulated Celtic tales of that day had a remarkable effect in modifying European ideals of behaviour, for many of the stories told a moral of the quality of mercy. This quality had not previously been conspicuous.

But after a while the inhuman excesses of the Normans in their merciless punishments spurred the Welsh to action, for their own laws and customs had been based on a humanity unknown elsewhere in that dark age. It was Griffith ap Cynan who largely freed his country. He had fought as a boy against the mounting Norman tide, but had been driven into exile overseas. Now he returned. He was in direct line from the great Cunedda, a giant of a man, fair, blue-eyed, Celtic to the backbone.

Griffith first broke the Normans in their usurped Kingdom of Gwynedd; then, while they reeled under the blow, swiftly he united all Wales behind him. The prince Bleddyn of Powys became an able ally, and swept the Norman from the easier southland of Powys and some areas of Dyfed. At last in 1136, a year before his death, Griffith and the free association of Welsh princes with him met the Normans at Cardigan in a major trial of strength, and there defeated them.

In England William was known as the Conqueror, to the Welsh he was William the Bastard. As such they cleared his followers from most of Wales, and had remarkable success in denying re-entry to his successors for a full two hundred years.

Griffith's son, Owain Gwynedd, and the sons of Bleddyn of Powys, completed the work of their respective fathers, and Wales, except for the southern coastal fringe, was freed of the Anglo-Norman invaders.

The echo of this forcible recovery by the Welsh of their rights and lands had rung that very morning in the bar of the inn near Beddgelert. Yet how distorted had it become by the impact of the centuries!

CHAPTER SIX

Llanfrothen—Clough Williams-Ellis, the burned mansion, and Port Meirion—Evolution of architecture—More hydro-electrics —Madocks' embankment—Portmadoc

I HAD started out from Beddgelert on the Llanfrothen road. I passed under the remains of a bridge which had carried the defunct Welsh Highland Railway, a narrow-gauge line which must have been a delight to travellers; crossed the lovely Aberglaslyn bridge, where the hydro-electric planners now proposed to build a power-station; and followed along the road which skirted the reclaimed land of the Traeth Mawr. Indeed, it was William Williams, a forbear of the Williams-Ellis whom I was now going to visit, who had had a hand in building the embankment across the tidal estuary opposite Portmadoc. The dyke had reclaimed from the tide about fifteen hundred acres of land. Nevertheless, a hundred and forty years after Madocks completed the project, the meadow-flats look sodden and are overgrown with gorse and rushes. When the tide was in this estuary must have had great beauty before the days of the dyke, with the sea-water bathing the feet of the mountains, and the formal peak of Cnicht forbidding further ingress.

At the beginning of Llanfrothen I bore left up the back drive to Plas Brondanw, which road, besides being nearer, was more in keeping with my appearance. As soon as the house came within view I could see that something was very wrong with it. Looking up through the windows, I saw sky. The outer walls stood, but the gables were roofless.

A gardener was at work on a terraced lawn sheltered by yew hedges, and eyed me warily. After explanations I learned that tragedy had come to the house which had been for five hundred years in the Williams family, and that not two months before fire had taken hold and gutted the inside. The gardener talked as if he had lost an old friend. He led me to an outhouse where he showed me a flake of wall-plastering which he had rescued from the debris within the house. He ran his fingers over the plaster, and spoke in that declaiming voice which the Welsh use for old things and people. He pointed out the construction: how oak uprights had cross-pieces dowelled into them, each section from floor to ceiling looking like a runged ladder; how reeds were woven in and out of the cross-pieces; and how the lime plaster was worked between and over the reeds.

"Gone is the art of it," he said, more to himself than to me.

Just then there came a clatter in the yard, and a little sawn-off lorry skidded to a stop. I saw Clough Williams-Ellis for the first time. He was a very tall man with a shock of hair and a fine beak of a nose. He wore a wideawake hat, an ancient jacket, and tight breeches without strappings, below which were displayed fine Regency calves. He introduced me to his wife, told me to go up to the tower on the hill to see the view, and to holler when I came back. He disappeared into the skeleton of the house.

I went up the hill to the tower. It was, I knew, a ruin constructed by Clough Williams-Ellis himself. I had to agree that if no one else had built a tower there in ages past so that it might crumble into picturesque decay, then Clough Williams-Ellis had been right to catch up backward with time, and do the job himself. The spot was another of those low viewpoints, like Moel Siabod, from which the surroundings loom the more impressive.

Eastward was the inside of the mountain rampart which had for so long protected the flat lands of Lleyn and Anglesey, the granaries of Gwynedd. The curtain wall of mountains was strengthened by the towers of Moelwyn, Cnicht, Aran, and Y Wyddfa itself. To the west lay gentle country lapped by the waters of Cardigan Bay.

I strolled back to the house, but was spared the effort of hollering. Clough Williams-Ellis met me and took me inside the skeleton. The walls were sound as ever, but nothing much else remained except the oak staircase, which had been too hard for the flames. Already the estate men were at work. Timber and slates of great antiquity were arriving from old buildings demolished to restore the beauty of Brondanw.

Restored the house would be, but the fire had destroyed five centuries of family keepsakes; the silver, the pictures, the furniture, so patiently and lovingly accumulated.

In the yard we found the little platform of the lorry loaded with carpets, plants in boxes, and other flotsam which was being ferried to Port Meirion for storage. I made to climb on top of the load, but was forestalled by my host, who, with a flourish of his fine legs, sprang aboard like a mountain goat. His wife took the wheel, and I the passenger seat.

We drove through Penrhyndeudraeth, no uglier than the run of Welsh towns, but seemingly the worse in contrast to the beautiful surroundings. We came to the entrance gates of Port Meirion, and here Mrs Williams-Ellis drew up at the Castle, now converted into flats. She remained behind there, and my host sprang off the platform and twisted his long self in behind the steering-wheel. He communicated much of his agility to the venerable vehicle, and within a few hundred yards I too felt venerable. We travelled like a startled jack-rabbit, flaunting first this wheel up a bank, then that one; whisking the scut of our tail-board round corners as if tucking it out of the way of a charge of shot; finally darting up a burrow through the trees, and sliding with a squeal into a shed whose side we clouted as we stopped.

Port Meirion is very unusual. The land is a part of the Brondanw estate, and here juts in a bold headland into the tidal estuary of the Traeth Bach. The coastline is rocky, climbing back from the sands to abrupt, wooded heights. Next the shore, on a shelf of rock, is built the main hotel, and scattered round it wherever there is lodgment are the cottages of what might be an Italian village. I have heard people take Williams-Ellis to task for bringing a part of Italy to the Welsh scene, but undoubtedly the place is attractive. I suppose the architecture of a country can be too uniform. The well-dressed woman usually throws one piece of contrast into a matching outfit. Port Meirion certainly breaks the uniformity, and, seen from across the estuary, lends the coastline a dashing air.

Since the disaster at Plas Brondanw the Williams-Ellises were living in the cottage on the topmost rock pinnacle of the settlement.

During the evening we talked steadily about Wales. In my host and hostess I had two people who were unusually well informed on their country, and I felt like a man, thirsty for knowledge, who is turned loose in a great library, and does not know at what shelf to begin his education.

I knew that Williams-Ellis was best known as an architect, and began by demanding why the Welsh touch in building was so fatal to beauty.

There were several contributing reasons. First, Wales had been a very poor country, and there were few manors and dwellings of the richer folk to set a pattern. Until quite recent times, too, buildings had been impermanent, for the Welsh had retained a trace of the nomadic customs of the East. In winter the family lived in a sheltered valley in the 'hendref,' or old homestead, with their flocks and herds secure from the elements raging about the high ground. In summer all migrated to the 'hafod' up in the mountains, and the stock spread upward to the summits. The hafod was a temporary sort of building, built of mud and wattle, and thatched.

This impermanency of Welsh domestic life was given to it not only by the touch of the nomadic, but also by the endless fight to retain independence as race after race attempted to subjugate the country. At every threat—and they were many—both courtier and shepherd would jump to arms and swarm about the enemy in the traditional harassing tactics which bled so many a proud army to death. The women and children and old men would abandon the houses, and drive their beasts deep into the hills.

Solid houses would have satisfied an invader's lust for destruction; their ravaging would have been a heartache for their owners; their rebuilding a burden. For the same reasons the Welsh were encouraged to develop those arts of song and verse which needed no shelter for their practice, and of which no looter could rob them.

I asked Williams-Ellis whether the coming of Nonconformity had had an adverse effect on architecture, and instanced to him the design of Welsh chapels. If the cult of beauty is a sinful vanity and a road to hell-fire, then the Nonconformists need have no fear to enter their places of worship. I complained that many a chapel was not left in plain ugliness, but was bedecked with embellishments, like a hideous old woman in the trappings of a girl.

"I know what you mean," commented Clough; "God's box into juke-box."

In former days there were few townships, for the small centres of population established themselves in scattered communities, rather than tight settlements. Thus, as Wales began to take on a more static way of life, and industry grew up alongside the old pastoral existence, the Welsh had to learn how to reorganize their dwelling-places. It was unfortunate that early Victorian England became an example for their architecture and the planning of their industrial towns.

It is said that a mild form of children's German measles, if it becomes epidemic among a race which has never before had contact with it, may kill off adults as certainly as the plague. Wales, unused to solid building, was infected with early Victorian architecture, and her simple, inoffensive native style died a horrible death.

Warmed by a pleasant burgundy with my dinner, I broached hotly the subject of the hydro-electric scheme. My host was in the forefront of the defending ranks. He made at once a comment on the plan which typified Welsh disgust at vulgarity.

"Ansyberwyd!" he said bitterly of the English proposal to destroy by science what they had failed to destroy by force of arms. 'Ansyberwyd' is not readily translatable, but 'gross behaviour' comes near to its meaning. It appeared that the gross behaviour was also stupid behaviour. The people who were fighting against the scheme had at their command some of the best industrial and financial brains in the British Isles, for not only the Welsh, but other races under the name of British were strongly opposed. These advisers claimed that after twenty years under construction the completed network of power-stations would only produce energy equal to one half of one day's production of coal from the British mines. What a value of beauty which had inspired history was to be put into irredeemable pawn to win a pittance.

And, as had commented the old lady to whom I had been indebted for my car-ride near Beddgelert, in twenty years' time we might well have atomic-bomb power.

Clough Williams-Ellis and his wife were baffled by the mentality of a race which had by Parliamentary action named much of the Kingdom of Gwynedd a National Park. The flags which had been waved at the opening had hardly ceased to flutter, the echoes of the fanfare still sounded through the hills, but already the trail of defilement was being laid. 'Ansyberwyd' was the word for it.

I spent the night in a room beneath a studio which had been prepared for Augustus John, and slept well in the shadow of great company.

Clough Williams-Ellis escorted me round the cottages of the hotel before I moved on next morning. He had hit on an ingenious method of construction, though it seemed to have some of the impermanency of the hafod. As far as I could find out by peering behind the scenes, the buildings were wooden framed. A material of German origin was nailed across the uprights. It was bituminous and came in sheets, deeply corrugated, and so provided its own damp courses. The outside was plastered, and washed in pastel pinks, blues, or greens.

The surroundings formed a natural garden of shrubs, trees, and rocks, and was so sheltered that the lushness was sub-tropical. Indeed, a local man had once told me that Clough Williams-Ellis had diverted the Gulf Stream in a loop round the shores of his headland.

We said good-bye after my host had accompanied me some distance across country towards Portmadoc, he leaping over walls and ditches, I moving more soberly because of my rucksack.

The day before I had had unquestioning hospitality from two strata of Welsh society, at a time inconvenient to both the givers. On reflection, I do not think that the strata were so very different after all. For they had in common the same profound racial consciousness as fellow Welshmen, and the same interests as country-dwellers.

As I crossed the headland the whole of the Lleyn peninsula lay spread like a sunlit map in front of me across Tremadoc Bay, and off its seaward tip the island of Bardsey floated, for once, on a quiet sea. This point of land has a terrible history of shipwreck, and the burial grounds thereabouts are as full of strangers as natives. Bardsey itself is peculiarly holy, and at one time its tariff of virtue was such that three pilgrimages thither equalled one to Rome. However, when Rome became the mother of the Christian Church in England Bardsey maintained British independence, and many a staunch upholder of the old tradition fled there for shelter.

I crossed Madock's embankment across the Traeth Mawr, paying a penny for the privilege, and quite glad to be reminded that here the coin could still justify its minting.

From Llangollen I had been working west-south-west, but now I wished to go north, far off my direct line to Cardiff. I had no hesitation in taking a bus from Portmadoc to Bangor, beside the Menai Strait.

CHAPTER SEVEN

Bangor—The barman and the bottle—A discussion on curfews, sins, and smugglers—Elusive Druids—Speculations on their cult—Roman severity towards them—A theory on the Anglesey monoliths—Druidic parallels in the Old Testament

IN Bangor I had wished particularly to learn something of the Druids. I went first to the Normal College, where in the common room I was hospitably received by several of the learned staff. I think Sir John Edward Lloyd's newly revised *History of Wales* had frightened people off the subject of Druidism. He had dealt brusquely with these old Magi, and even more brusquely with writers on the subject.

Disappointed, I left the College and prowled through a book-shop or two. I had thought it just possible that here, in a university town and an episcopal see, there might be some old tomes written about the religion whose citadel had been Anglesey, across the narrow strait. But again I was disappointed.

I went into an hotel to telephone an antiquarian who lived in ancient Mona, but he too failed me.

"You won't find any real traces," he said testily. "The sacred oak-groves have all been cut down."

He spoke as if a local timber merchant had been at work. But it was about A.D. 60 when Caius Suetonius Paulinus ferried his legionaries across the Strait to massacre the priesthood and destroy the mystic trees.

I was really despondent by now, and went down to the hotel bar for a drink. There was no one else present except the barman. When he had served me he sat on a stool and began, I thought, to polish an empty *crème de menthe* bottle. He went on for so long, and his cloth made such curious noises, that I asked what he was doing. He told me that he was drilling a hole in the side of the bottle in order to insert electric flex for a lamp conversion. This was a feat which I had more than once wished to perform myself. The barman told me that it was quite easy with the help of a Swedish file. You bought the round tool not for its filing value, but for its hard steel. In fact, you nipped the end off the file to leave a jagged grinding edge. With your hand wrapped protectively in a cloth you ground and ground. At the very end you tapped through the film of glass with a nail. The barman said that he had done dozens. Sometimes he coloured the inside of the bottle with a fluid of which he was not anxious to divulge the secret. He had worked out the formula with the help of a hospital pathologist.

I asked if he sold the lamps.

"Diw, no! For fear of Board of Trade. There's purchase-tax if they're sold."

One lamp he raffled to buy a season ticket for the football ground for an eighty-year-old customer of his. The present one was to be sent as a bedside light to another customer's small girl who was ill.

Bottles varied. Dimple Haig was popular, but the barman found this sort difficult to drill. The concave dimple was too thin, and was liable to splinter, while the ribs between the dimples were very thick. To illustrate this he came round the bar and showed me a Haig bottle-lamp on a shelf. I noticed that it had a very well-made shade on which was painted the arms of the City of Bangor.

"Funny how some is ignorant who ought to know better," mused the barman. "A big official of the city was in one day, and saw this shade. He gave me a quiet warning not to use the city arms. Penalty up to six months' gaol, he told me, if I didn't have permission. Then he said anyway I'd got the arms wrong. 'Right, they are,' I said. 'You go and look in the Town Hall.'"

The barman slid back behind the counter to deal with a customer who came, swallowed convulsively, and was gone in a flash.

"Back comes the big noise another night," he went on, reminiscently, "and sees me with another shade."

"'Don't say I didn't warn you,' he said.

"Well, I had to put him right, didn't I?"

I said that I supposed so, and the barman looked at me speculatively.

"Fancy him not knowing! There's only three lots of arms is

registered in Wales: Beaumaris, Caernarvon, and Wrexham. If arms isn't registered there's anyone can use them.

"Well, then he said he hadn't been able to check I'd got the arms right, because they couldn't find the original drawing.

"'I've seen it,' I said, 'so you needn't worry. And I'm not telling who's got it, except it's not me. My copies are right, but most of those Presents from Bangor you give licence for in the shops are wrong.'"

The barman drew me some more beer, and refused one himself.

"There was a man with the big noise who started talking about St Asaph, which he called his own city. Well, St Asaph isn't a city, although there's a cathedral. There's three things make a city: a cathedral, a fire engine, and a probate register. St Asaph's only got a sub-probate register."

I agreed heartily with the barman that the sum of human ignorance was startling when you really came up against examples of it such as this.

"Well, he's not the only one," said the barman, anxious to be fair. "Once I was talking to a retired engineer in a big way. He said wonderful it was that Telford had built the tubular bridge over the Strait without any workmen killed. Made a study of the bridge, he had, and still didn't know. Nine there was killed. You go and look under the bridge on the far side, and what'll you see but a rock with a steel core going down through it. That was the anchoring for the base of the crane they lifted the tubes with. Floated to the site they were. One day what happens but the crane tumbles, and nine was killed. Their graves are on the island for anyone to see."

The barman paused to give attention to the *crème de menthe* bottle, which had reached the tap-with-a-nail stage, then continued:

"A wonderful bridge. Every joint made for expansion and contraction. Flues above to draw off the engine smoke. They used to send little boys to crawl through them to shift the soot. Old Telford would get a surprise if he was to see the Irish mail going through at sixty-five mile an hour."

I asked the barman how he managed to gain such curious bits of knowledge.

"Father was a printer's compositor in the city," he explained. "Keen he was on the history of the place, and I got the same way.

Then except for the War I've been in the hotel twenty-one years. I remember you when you had your sheep-farm. You meet all sorts here."

I did not know how to take this, but was reassured when he added:

"His Highness Prince Philip stayed a few times when I was doing night porter. I expect I knew about who he'd marry before most people. Give me letters to post he would sometimes, addressed to the Princess Elizabeth.

"Yes, the history of the city is interesting. There was a professor in one night from the University. Just before eight it was when he was ready to leave. I asked him if he was hurrying off home before curfew. You wouldn't believe it, but he didn't know what I was talking about."

I did my best to look aghast.

"One time when the English was here the curfew was started. The townspeople got restless, and the English had to have them in their homes by dark. The cathedral still tolls at eight every night. Well, the professor didn't believe me, nor a lot of others in the bar, and them born and bred here! Out they all went and listened, and sure enough it was tolled. The professor was very excited.

"'Did you listen for the date?' I asked him when he came back in. He hadn't waited to listen, and back he came next night to hear it. There it was after the deep bell of the curfew, a little light bell tolling once for each day of the date in the month."

I felt that I ought to have another glass of beer to justify my presence. The barman went through a door behind his counter to draw from the wood, and while within the cellar called me to come in. He placed a crate against the wall under a small trap, and directed me to open the door and look through. I saw a passage which disappeared on either hand.

"The electricians put the trap there," the barman explained. "It's handier than tearing up the road every time. This passage goes under the Cathedral and comes out by Bangor pier. It was me told the electricians they'd find a passage. I knew about the smugglers' way up from the Strait, but no one knew where it ran after the Cathedral, until I guessed a few years ago when there was some workmen doing alterations in this cellar here, and they knocked a hole in the foundation wall. There was a bottle of old, old spirits back of the hole, and so drunk they got—strong stuff—they were carried home in a lorry."

We left the cellar to its secrets, and returned to the bar.

"Very interesting, the Cathedral," the barman said. "You'll see the gratings in the wall where the lepers were allowed to listen to the service. Then hung up inside are pairs of great long tongs: there was a time when a lot of mad dogs was running around the town, and now and again they'd get into the cathedral, and they'd be caught by the tongs."

I was stuffed with information, and was about to rise from the feast of learning, when the barman said that near the War memorial was a lopped-off tree with seats round the trunk. He said that it was known as the Reform Tree, having been planted to commemorate the displacement of wickedness by an upsurge of piety within the town some centuries back, but its benches were now used after dark by courting couples.

Thus the wheel turns full circle.

I found the Reform Tree, its seats untenanted at that public hour, but when I went to look at the Cathedral I could discover neither mad dogs nor tongs. I prowled round the outside, but the only leper-gratings seemed to me to be connected with ventilation.

Since I was depressed by my failure over the Druids, I did not want to be disillusioned about any of the exhilarating stories told me by the barman, and forbore to ask questions of anyone. It had begun to pour with rain. I had friends near Valley, in Anglesey, and decided to go to see them. Mist and rain obscured the windows of the bus in which I travelled, but I saw enough to be reminded of the bleakness of this low, windswept island. It is an island with a character all its own, with even, here and there, remains of an individual, simple architecture shown in occasional one-storey cottages which crouch before the wind, clawing a hold in the soil.

I would have remained in the bus as far as it could take me towards my friends, but was finally dispossessed by a small female child which took a fancy to me between bouts of sickness. I was afraid that one of her periodic approaches to me would coincide with a bout, and reluctantly left the vehicle some way short of my destination.

The coast was not very far away, and the wind, rain-laden, swept in unchecked from the Irish Channel. I was not very sure just where my friends had their house and was misdirected when within a stone's throw by a man who turned out to be an idiot. However, I did at last arrive, and my low spirits were raised by restoratives.

This house, alone on the edge of the sea, was a splendid place in which to let the imagination play with the past. The Afon Alaw flowed into the sea close by, and there had once been a monastery on the estuary. Immediately in front of our garden was an old fish-wall, exposed at low tide, inside which the monks would drive fish to be trapped with a net behind them. It was easy to picture the monks securing their Friday repast, wading through the shallows with their habits tucked up through their girdles; the younger ones splashing each other, the older intoning prayers and petitions for a successful haul; the fish fleeing in silver streaks into the trap, startled by the threat of bell, book, and candle.

But before the time of the monastery and its fellow Christian communities on the island there had been Druidism, a remarkable and powerful religion to have left so few traces. It is possible that it has left traces which are unrecognized. It may be that Druidism was not so much exterminated as translated into Christianity.

Anglesey was the focal point of the cult, its leadership and guidance being accepted by the Continental order. It seems to have become the fashion to impute little that is good to the religion, and to dismiss its practice as bloodstained barbarity. This is done because there is no evidence of humanity in the creed, and therefore it is guilty because it has left no record of its innocence.

It is possible that a form of the cult came to Wales in prehistoric times with the Iberian migrants who had left their trail of megaliths across North Africa and Europe. These early people believed in the immortality of the soul, and their megaliths may have been memorials to the vital parts of the body which were buried close by them. More primitive man had laid his dead away with spear and cooking-pot to hand against physical rebirth, but the Iberians expected no miracle of bodily resurrection. They believed in the transmigration of the soul. It is probable that successive waves of migrants accepted, and perhaps slightly adapted, the religion which they found in being, until finally the Celts added to it the religious-cum-secular cult of minstrelsy, bardism, and lawgiving.

The Celtic Druids believed in the immortality of the soul, and in the one invisible God. These were remarkable tenets to hold in a pagan world. The oak-tree, which covered large areas of Mona in those times, played a part in their ceremonies. I believe correct those writers who say that the oak and the mistletoe which grew upon it were treated as symbolism of God, the strong supporter, and Man, the weak, who clings to Him.

Symbolism is easily misconstrued by later ages. Were Christianity to die out leaving no adequate records, later researches might well disinter a cathedral window and decide that Christians were a pastoral people who worshipped a lamb as the token of fecundity.

Human dismembered remains have indeed been found buried by Druid monuments, but it is possible that these were portions dedicated to the preservation of the vital essences whose virtue would descend to the next generation. A noted spear-thrower might, perhaps, have his right arm thus preserved.

Not so many years ago the body of Thomas Hardy was buried in Westminster Abbey. But first they cut out his heart and interred it in the churchyard of his own Stinsford, in Dorset.

The Druids had an all-embracing hold upon the Celts. They directed their religion; they taught their culture; they gave and administered their laws. In spite of the massacres of their priests and priestesses, and the destruction of the sacred groves by Suetonius and Agricola, it is against all the probabilities that the strength of the cult was sapped away to nothing within a few years. It is curious, then, that Christianity was so readily accepted by the Celts within living memory of the old cult, unless Druidism was fertile ground.

The cult was a philosophical one, and the Druids great debaters. The news of Jesus came early to Wales by the western trade routes, and His teaching was rapidly adopted. At that time the Roman legionary was still a last-ditch pagan, whatever his Emperor might profess. Scarcely a century after St John's death Tertullian wrote that places in Britain not yet visited by Romans were subjected to Christ. Furthermore, the Celtic Church was subjected through the teachings of St John, not, as were the Romans, through those of

St Peter. The beliefs may have been adopted so easily because their inspiration was little more than an advance on the older practice.

After all, the one invisible God was already venerated by the Celts; the immortality of the soul was already a tenet. If, indeed, the Druids had practised human sacrifices, now they were told that the sacrifice to end all sacrifices had been offered at Golgotha, that the sins of man were finally expiated, and that no more need suffer to wipe clean the record of past evil.

Had Druidism been a savage and inhuman profession Christianity surely could not have been so quickly and so effortlessly imposed upon it. Nor again could Welsh law, as set down on paper in the reign of Hywel Dda, have been so humane in an age of barbarity unless there was a tradition of mercy behind it.

It has been implied by some historians that the Romans put down Druidism because they must have been horrified at its savagery at a time when they themselves were learning the elements of humanity. Whatever else the Roman was in the first century, he was not allergic to savagery. He was a merciless, ruthless imperialist, a conqueror rather than a colonizer, who would murder with every circumstance of contrived legality when it was expedient, who exploited to the full the deterrent value of cruelty and torture, and whose major peace-time relaxation was the gladiatorial circus.

The legionary was a professional killer, a savage veneered with the material civilization of the day. It was obviously on no moral grounds that the Druid priesthood was massacred. Ordinarily the Roman bothered little about the religion of the countries he conquered just as long as they gave him no trouble politically. But here was a different religion. Here was a god who could not be burnt on a bonfire should it become necessary; could not be put under the vigilant eye of a centurion. The Romans were afraid of this god they could not see, as they feared the God in the Temple in Jerusalem. The hard legionaries recoiled when first they confronted the Druids in the shade of the sacred groves, and only their disciplined blood-lust spurred them later to put aside their fear. But most of all they feared the secular power of the priesthood.

I have a feeling that the priests of the oak have been maligned, and that within the limits of those early days they were enlightened men.

The Romans themselves paid tribute to the learning of the Druids. Julius Cæsar and Pomponius Mela both testify in similar terms to their astronomic knowledge, their understanding of terrestrial phenomena, and the scholastic wisdom which they imparted to pupils.

In connexion with the Druids or, maybe, the pre-Druids William Evans makes some very fascinating speculations in a book called *The Meini Hirion and Sarns of Anglesey*. Meini Hirion means Long Stones, and a Sarn is a paved trackway. Evans discounts the garbled ideas about the standing stones of the island: that they mark burial places; that they have a sacrificial past; that they were erected for cattle to alleviate the itch.

He begins by showing that the ancient trackways of Anglesey ran parallel to one another from north-east to south-west, crossed at right angles by a set running from north-west to south-east. These tracks, therefore, divided the island into squares. He gives one exception to the rule: the road from Garth ferry, on the Menai Strait, to Porth Trwyn, some three miles north of where I was staying with my friends near Valley. This, he says, was a Roman road built for the Irish route, and superimposed upon the elaborate system of much earlier trackways.

Each of the squares bounded by the grid track system were, he claims, trefs, or townships. The boundaries of each were just over one mile, the extra length, as laid down in the laws of Hywel Dda, allowing for road-widths and the Diffaith Brenin, or King's Waste, which was a strip left for forest and game preserve.

As William Evans points out, Canada to-day is surveyed on the block system, which has given it a basis of land-tenure similar to prehistoric Anglesey.

He then gives a reminder that Giraldus Cambrensis stated that in Anglesey there were 343 trefs. Evans to-day locates 343 of his track-bounded squares.

That these had no Roman origin he proves by showing that the flank of a block, after the legal deductions laid down in old Welsh law, was 1760 yards. The Roman mile was only 1666 yards and 2 feet. It seems, then, that the statute mile used to-day by the English is not Roman after all, but British.

The monoliths of Anglesey, says Evans, are of three heights:

nine feet, six feet, and three feet respectively. The smaller the stones, the less is the distance between them. In other words, the smaller stones mark out smaller squares, the biggest stones very large squares made up of several little ones. He instances the big monolith above Cadnant, near the Strait. From this starting-point he traces the lines of similar large stones set at four and a quarter miles apart—the old quarter absorbing the cumulative deductions for tracks and King's Waste—which mark the corner boundary of superblocks which, even my arithmetic tells me, each contain sixteen of the one-mile-square plots.

This theory, if correct, shows that a high degree of surveying skill was present long before the arrival of the Romans. But Evans goes much farther in his claim. He says that Sir Norman Lockyer spent some time on the island while seeking to show that the cromlechs of Britain had no direct connexion with burial rites, but were scientifically oriented temples. After all, megalithic man had contrived to divide the Zodiac, and to calculate the equinox and solstice.

Lockyer took the azimuth of the Summer Solstice on a line passing through his headquarters at Llangefni, and found it to be N. 46° 40′ E. This line was parallel within five hundred yards with the Malltraeth—Llanddyfnan row of giant monoliths, whose azimuth is N. 43°. As Evans says, in language no layman could equal, "Thus, allowing for the difference in the obliquity of the Ecliptic, since the time the system must have been incepted, we obtain an index to its glorious antiquity."

The preoccupation of the modern Britons, or Welshmen as they are called, with the stone is inherited from both major strains in their ancestry. The Iberian ancestors would have brought with them the veneration with which the early Egyptians regarded the stone, and did indeed leave behind their trail of megaliths up Western Europe and along both shores of the Irish Sea. The Celts, who later fused with them, had in remote times a connexion with the ancient Greeks, whose earliest form of worship took great account of stones. Pausanius, who lived at the time of the Roman Emperor Hadrian, was interested in the history of early Greece, and wrote that almost every temple had its fetish stone; that the oldest idol of the Thespians was a rude stone; that one was placed beneath the pedestal of Apollo in Delos; and that in Achæan Pharæ there were thirty squared stones which each bore the name of a god.

It is easy to understand, therefore, how the Celts came to accept, and possibly adapt, the stone worship which, on their arrival in Britain, they found to be already flourishing among the Iberian settlers.

I suppose we moderns must sneer at this primitive reverence which found its highest expression in Druidism. Yet we may sneer, perhaps, only because we do not know the symbolism which inspired it.

After all, mythologists five thousand years hence, if written records were absent, would make great play with the ceremony of Holy Communion. Of the Protestant branch of the Christian faith they would say that it worshipped bread and wine, as the fruits of Ceres had previously been worshipped. The Roman Catholic belief they would stigmatize as consecrated cannibalism.

Such histories of the Druids as have been written are now mostly discredited, and the professors seem mainly to rely upon the oblique writings of men like Julius Cæsar, whose knowledge of the priesthood, although he was a contemporary, was just as secondhand. There is, however, a history taught to all modern Christians, whose descriptions of religious rites may well lift the veil of silence. This history is the Old Testament.

Chapter twenty-eight of the Book of Genesis describes how Jacob, after his vision of God, set up a pillar of stone, and poured upon it a libation of wine and oil. Stones are said to have been found in Wales with a cavity in their top, and a runnel down their side as though to receive and dispose of a liquid. Jacob named the site of his pillar, and of his altar, Bethel, or God's House. Here it was where later died Rebecca's nurse Deborah, and was buried under an oak. The copse was named Allon-bachuth, the Grove of Weeping.

The stones of God, most of them secreted within their sacred groves, litter the pages of the Old Testament. As often as not, the Deity Himself had commanded their erection. At Gilgal He ordered Joshua to set up twelve stones out of Jordan to commemorate the passage of the twelve tribes, one of which was sprung from the sons of Ham.

It was Moses who ruled that the altars of God should be "of

whole stones, over which no man hath lift up any iron." Perhaps there is an explanation here of the deliberate crudeness of the cromlechs and megaliths.

I have an old book titled *Mona Antiqua Restaurata*, by Henry Rowlands. My edition is dated 1723. I suppose that we have all learned so much since then that we do not take Rowlands seriously, but nevertheless his theses are interesting. Archæologists may yet progress until their paths at places touch his. He says 'cromlech' is probably a rendering of the Hebrew 'Choerum-luach,' a consecrated or devoted stone. Alternatively, the word might derive from 'chema-luach,' a burning or sacrificing table.

Certainly there was no lack of sacrificing among the Israelites. Abraham was prepared to offer up his son. The priesthood was fed upon the flesh of sacrificed beasts. In the Book of Numbers God directs Moses most minutely on the formula for sacrifice to Him. Chapters twenty-eight and twenty-nine tell of nothing but sacrifices of lambs, rams, bullocks, and kids; and of offerings of beaten oil and strong wine. The Druids are said to have been much addicted to sacrifice on their unhewn stone altars in the shade of the oak-groves.

The scenes and the smells within the groves of ancient Mona must have been very similar to those of Bethel. Similar too must have been the secular convocation called by the Druids, just as the Israelites used their sacred places as forums.

The Druid priesthood exercised the same judicial rights as did the priests of Israel. Samuel went yearly in circuit to Bethel, Gilgal, and Mizpeh, hearing causes in those places. Just so did the Druids make their circuits to carry justice.

It is accepted now that the Iberian strain came north and west from a home on the shores of the Middle Sea. The parallel between the religious practices of the Israelites and those of the Druids, so far as we know them, is not, therefore, remarkable.

There is in Wales another echo of the East, though most chroniclers hear the echo only from the sixth century. I think that it comes from much farther back along the road of Celtic history. The dim tale tells that King Vortigern had proposed to bury a youth named Merlin at the foundations of his castle, in order to get over some difficulty about subsidence. The budding magician and soothsayer fortunately outwitted the ruler, who was, perhaps, not to be blamed for following an idea of Joshua. The Israelite had cursed ruined Jericho, and had proclaimed that he who rebuilt the town must lay its first course upon his firstborn, and erect the gate pillars upon his youngest son.

Archæologists have found that in early Celtic settlements, such as Skara Brae, in the Orkneys, and Woodhenge, on Salisbury Plain, humans had been buried under walls and under sanctuaries, presumably that their spirits might uphold the buildings.

Merlin survived his proposed architectural career to suggest that the dancing-stones put up by ancestors from Africa should be transferred to Stonehenge. By 'dancing-stones,' as we construe him, he did not mean that the rocks were animate, but that they were the Hebrew 'bowing stones,' the sacred pillars erected to God, and to which the worshipper bent his head. In the Chaldean such are referred to as Even Maschith, a Stone of Bowing. The Book of Leviticus tells how man, lacking vision, transferred his reverence from the symbolism of the stones to the stones themselves, and how at length an angry God forbade them to "set up any image of stone in your land, to bow down unto it."

I wonder had the sons of Ham begun their long trek before the Israelite religion had lapsed into idolatry, and before Moses came to reform it. I wonder if they brought to Britain the untarnished symbolism, and so maintained it until the later teaching of God's Son was so easily imposed upon it.

At any rate, legend and recent archaeological discovery blend. It is conceded that the Iberians came from Africa, Egypt, and the general area of the Mediterranean basin; that they set up their stone circles as Merlin claimed they had. The groves, altars, and sacrifices on the Isle of Mona were probably identical with the groves, altars, and sacrifices at Jacob's Sichem.

The Romans seem to have seen dangerous similarity between Druidism and the Israelite profession of faith. They crucified Jesus in Palestine, and in Mona they massacred the priesthood which maintained a religion so very akin to that once practised in Palestine in reverence of Jesus's Father.

The early megalithic migrants probably brought with them the rites of Judaism, which the later Celtic Druids adapted to the usage of their hierarchy on Mona. The Celts may have expected the Messiah. The legendary Art, who is told of many centuries before the Normanized Arthur depicted by Geoffrey de Monmouth, is said to have anticipated Christian belief, while his brother Condla was instructed by a heavenly being to rule over the plain of honey in the Land of Promise. The Druids may have been conscious caretakers of the best faith of which they knew until such time as stronger hands came to give direction.

When the Israelities began to abuse the symbolism of stones, God said: "Thou shalt not plant a grove of any trees near unto the altar of thy God which thou shalt make thee, neither shalt thou set up a pillar which the Lord thy God hateth."

I wonder if those men of the stone circles who came to Britain migrated because of the increasing dessication of the Mediterranean fringes; or were they Pilgrim Fathers, fleeing from the reforming zeal of the Israelite prophets, who sought to enforce God's command that the stones be forgotten?

All is speculation. The only certain knowledge of the Druids is that they existed.

CHAPTER EIGHT

Anglesey—The farmer, travel and Beethoven—Owain Tudor and Sweet Kate—University College of North Wales—History and functions—Future of the Welsh language

I FINISHED my week-end by the shores of the Irish Sea, and took bus back to Bangor, where I wished to talk to the Principal of the University College of North Wales.

There were no children on this bus, and I shared a seat with a farmer. He was a small man, but I am not. He remarked to me in Welsh that two human seats more than equalled one bus seat. I understood him, but was not equal to replying in his own language. As soon as it was apparent that I was a foreigner, he turned on me sharp eyes and a pointed, inquisitive nose, and began to question me.

Yes, I had been to Wales before. No, I was not staying in Anglesey. As a matter of fact I was walking to Cardiff, in spite of being at that moment in a cramped position on a bus.

We were bowling along Telford's road, and my companion pointed to a distant house, tree-surrounded. Did I know its name?

I said that I did; that it was Plas Pen-y-Mynydd.

My acquaintance was pleased.

"A lovely place it is," he said: "old Owain Tudor's house. I know the people who've got it now."

He might have been saying: "Owain's not there this minute, but I've met the tenants."

I dreamed for a little as I looked through the window at Plas Pen-y-Mynydd, where Owain Tudor, grandfather of Henry Tudor, had lived as squire. So handsome had Owain been that he was known as the Rose of Anglesey. His bravery in Henry V's Continental wars had been such that the king had enrolled him in his personal bodyguard.

I dreamed of the scene where Henry, after the success at Agincourt and the Treaty of Troyes, went to woo Catherine of Valois, Shakespeare's Sweet Kate. Love-making in those days was a public recreation, and more than likely the Welsh youth, Owain Tudor, was in close attendance on his king. Were the eyes of Kate quite dazzled by the monarch of England, or did they stray to the incomparable beauty of the Rose of Anglesey? That Kate and Owain struck fire from one another is almost certain, and there must have been heart-burning when the royal marriage of policy took place.

But they were not long separated. Henry of England died not much more than a year later, and for once a boy and girl romance came to fruition when all had seemed lost. Owain married the young widow secretly, and their son Edmund was father of the great Tudor dynasty.

I regained interest in the present when my farmer companion asked where I was staying. I told him that I was going to visit my family in rooms at Conway before I plunged southward into the hills of Deheubarth.

He liked Conway. It was a fine old town, with its castle and its wall all round. It was like a town in the south of Italy where he was on a walking-tour last year: a town called Mottola. He did not expect that I had ever heard of it.

I did in fact privately remember Mottola. I had first seen it in the light of the dawn of September the 10th, 1943. The Germans were ensconced on the ramparts and gave us a brisk skirmish before we made our way in. The mayor had handed me the keys of the town, and his wife a garland. The Germans had taken most of the wine.

This year, my companion said, he proposed to go to Spain, and was busy learning the language. He had been a dairy farmer, he told me, but had found dairying a great tie, and had now changed to beef cattle, which he could more readily leave.

We talked a little about Wales, then about foreign travel, and presently I was invited to return to the farm and spend a night or two so that we could talk some more. My friend said that he would not be long in Bangor. He had a viola on the luggage-rack and was only attending a rehearsal of Beethoven's Violin Concerto. Would I like to come and hear it, then return with him in time to feed the beasts? I regretted that I had an appointment at the University, and later was expected by my family. A pity! He had some eggs in with his viola in the case. They were really for a fellow musician in the orchestra, but I must take them. They would be all right in the rucksack if I did not sit on it. Here, too, was his address, which I must visit when next on the island of Mona.

As I said good-bye at the Bangor bus terminus I noticed an Anglesey policeman who was evidently visiting the City. His uniform and peaked cap were modern. But in the centre of the cap-badge was embossed the sacred oak of the Druids.

The University College of North Wales has been built on what the realtors could, in truth, call a commanding position. By sloping paths and flights of steps I reached the lower storey of the building. I had approached, perhaps, from the wrong direction, for the incline of the site was against me, and when I entered by an undistinguished back door I was in the bowels of the College. From scurrying students I gained vague information from time to time, and presently infiltrated to a part where there was less noise and more dignity. One student denied that the Principal had a room within the College, and as I turned away baffled I saw a door marked 'Principal.' I was early for my appointment, so, the door pin-pointed, went out into the sunshine.

Surroundings influence the frame of mind. Were I a Welsh student this College would inspire me. At one side, close under the foot of the hill on which the building stands, are the waters of the Menai Strait, and across the narrows lies the wooded shore-line of Anglesey. In front the little cathedral town is strung along under low foothills. From the eminence of the College I looked out over these hills and saw beyond them the towering mountains of Eryri. Old Owain Glyndwr had dreamed of colleges for Wales, one North, one South. Here was the college of the North secure behind the mountain rampart which had so often in the past taken the shock of invasion, with Anglesey, the granary of Eryri, in support. This was the college which served that Kingdom of Gwynedd, which had always been the citadel of Welsh independence.

The College was built of dressed Cefn stone: a plainly handsome erection, which gained grandeur from its massive frame.

The Principal, when the time came for me to see him, was most friendly. My impression of Mr Emrys Evans was that he was all the better as a pedagogue for being first a humanitarian. He was more interested in living people than inanimate abstractions. With this quality one felt that he held the balance between the warmth of live knowledge-seeking and the cold facts which would feed it. He has since been knighted.

The structure of the University of Wales, to which this College belongs, is a good example of the Welsh independence which prefers decentralization and a large degree of autonomy. There are four colleges in the University of Wales, placed roughly within the ancient kingdoms. They are at Swansea, Cardiff, Aberystwyth, and Bangor. The broad curriculum is common to all colleges, but each caters especially for the needs of its area. Bangor, for instance, has a strong agricultural side, which specializes in upland husbandry and which maintains its own farm on the Aber hills. It also teaches forestry. Aberystwyth, too, is strong on agriculture, having as its offspring the Welsh Plant Breeding Station. Cardiff and Swansea, serving the highly populated commercial and industrial South, cater for specialist needs in their area, such as mining and metallurgy.

Each college is governed by its own senate under the Principal, guides its faculties of arts, science, and theology, and has its own registrar. Over all is the University Academic Board, which fosters the educational life of the four colleges, and the University Council, an executive body which looks after material affairs and allocates funds to the colleges. The funds are wisely distributed on a five-year basis, so that the colleges have latitude to plan some way ahead.

A large number of students eventually find their way to the teaching profession or some denomination of the Church. These have ever been regarded as desirable goals for the Welshman who is thought by his family to be too clever to cart out muck or feed bullocks. At Bangor the Theological Faculty is non-denominational; a powerful cocktail of dogmas; Methodist, Baptist, Church in Wales, and the rest. It is a practical demonstration that many roads lead to God, and that how one travels is unimportant. The great thing is to arrive.

The Registrar joined us for tea, and I was quickly filled with facts and bread and butter. The College was opened in 1884 with fifty-eight students. To-day there were 900, of whom a third were

English. In 1884 the first Women's Hostel was opened, as was the Agricultural Department, then the only one of its kind in Great Britain. From the nineteen-twenties onward more and more extra-mural work was undertaken in the farming and quarrying countryside.

Like most institutions, the College was ever in search of money, and it was remarkable how many subscriptions came in from poor people. To help towards the cost of the main buildings Anglesey, for instance, subscribed at a rate which equalled thirty shillings for every household on the island. The quarrymen of Llanberis and Bethesda were continuous supporters of the funds. Quarrying is a philosophic occupation, and breeds an elegance of the mind which is uncommon in manual trades.

I had had enough of figures, which are an indigestible diet, and we began to talk more generally. The Principal was a South Walian who had lived for quarter of a century in the North, and was well qualified to make the inevitable comparison. He agreed that there was a divergence, particularly in outlook; that the North Walian was conservative to a fault, but retained with the fault the virtues; that the Southerner was more liberal in the mind, but was therefore the more readily contaminated with such vices as were to be found in commercial and industrial expediency.

It was obvious that the impact of business had brought change and modification to the South, and that economic forces were at work to widen the divergence. In the North the men still wrestled with the stones and rock, and still herded their stock on the hillsides as they had done two thousand years ago.

The Principal also was interesting on the Welsh language. He could remember, he said, when the young lads of Bangor, playing about the streets, spoke nothing but Welsh. To-day that was much less apparent. However, he was convinced that the educated classes were using their mother tongue to a greater extent than formerly.

This was interesting, because it had been just these educated people who had taken to the English tongue when the Welsh Tudors sat on the throne of England, and had taken pains to anglicize the leading families of Wales. Then it had been the peasantry who maintained the native speech. Now the rôles were changed.

There is a danger that the Welsh will become self-conscious about their language. If they do so it will indicate that the tongue is a museum piece. That which is embalmed is dead. I have noticed that the signposts and notices at the National Eisteddfod are all in Welsh, without a translation. This seems to me to be the height of self-consciousness, and on a par with the childishness of the Southern Irish. However, the tongue is still virile, and in spite of the observation of the Principal, I believe that quite enough small boys at play in street and field speak it, and that for another generation, at any rate, there is little danger of a marked decrease in its use.

The Principal said that if it were desirable it would be difficult to give instruction in Welsh on technical subjects. I said that the Welsh language must manufacture its own new terms if it were to remain alive and not repeat the English in a Welsh accent. As soon as I had spoken I realized that I had tumbled below the level of my companions. The Principal put me right very quickly, and his lesson was, of course, sound. A language remains a living growth largely by borrowing from other tongues, and adapting the words taken. English is an outstanding example of borrowing without much acknowledgment. Even the manufactured words, so common in the sphere of science, are mostly compounded of Greek terms. There is, then, a common source for many of these technical expressions, and it is as open to the Welsh to say 'telephone' as to the English.

One advantage which the Bangor College holds over those of Cardiff and Swansea is that it is situated in a small town. The College colours the town, and is not swamped by the other activities around it. The life is intimate, with the students living in a close community in hostels or rooms. At Cardiff, and indeed at many civic universities in Great Britain, students commute between residence and work. They travel in to their lectures and disperse afterwards, and so lose much of that value of communal life and thought which a university can provide.

I left the College impressed with its vigour, and sure of its importance in modern Gwynedd.

CHAPTER NINE

Conway—Edward I, Queen Eleanor, and sweet peas—Village school—A good landlord—The Welsh shaggy dog—Maelgwn Gwynedd—King John—Plas Mawr, the British Dragon, and the two Elizabeths

MY wife and two daughters had been in rooms at Conway during my stroll through the country. After my visit to Bangor I felt that I ought to find out how they did in this foreign land. It seemed to me that they were doing well. My daughters were attending a village school on the outskirts of the town. They liked their fellow pupils, and had found no difficulty in settling into the nearly classless Welsh social structure. I think my wife was right when she remarked that their manners had much improved after daily contact with the village children. The elder, who was eight years old, was particularly happy because her insatiable demands for knowledge were always met. Too often a forward child is fobbed off by its mentors with the injunction that it will be told the answer when it is older. This means that the teacher is either idle or ignorant.

Her younger sister, Johanna, who was not quite six, was turned into an adequate reader and writer by the end of the term. But, then, the Welsh standard of education is very high. The pre-War Spens report showed that where in England from 4.2 per cent. to 26. 4 per cent. of elementary schoolchildren passed into Grammar Schools, the comparable Welsh figures were 17.7 per cent. to 55 per cent.

Conway is very charming, and is the first comparatively unspoilt and unbastardized coastal town as the traveller moves westward from England. The barrier of the River Conway makes a frontier between the town and the world of change, and it is influenced by the immemorial mountains of Eryri, which loom above its back door. Across the river the coast is degraded by tripper traps and pustulated with a rash of permanent caravans and impermanent shacks, but from Conway westward there has been a certain immunity from the diseases which holiday visitors leave behind them.

My daughters were especially pleased with life in a bastide town, the only one in Britain whose walls were still unbroken, and through whose narrow arched gateways the traffic was constrained to creep in single file. They delighted to prowl about the castle itself, Edward I's favourite of all, and to picture his Queen Eleanor in her garden on the battlements, far removed from the climate of her native Spain, tending the first few sweet peas which these islands had seen.

The hand of the foreign breweries lies heavily upon Conway too. But at the Erskine Hotel I found at last a manager, a Somerset man, who had taken the trouble to learn something of the Welsh, their ways and customs. This unusual man had been a Corporal-of-Horse in the Household Cavalry, and as a fellow Guardsman I saw a lot of him during my visit to the town. He was a remarkable mimic. During an impecunious period at the beginning of the War, when he had been a recruit, he had, so he told me, put his imitative gift to good use. Near his barracks in London had been three public-houses run respectively by a Scot, an Irishman, and a Yorkshireman. My new acquaintance told me that he fell into a routine, when walking out, of visiting these hostelries in turn. There was at each a hard core of regular customers who came from the same part of Britain as that particular landlord. Taking care to use the appropriate accent and turn of phrase, my Conway acquaintance told me that he was speedily accepted as a fellow-exile in the Scots inn, the Irish inn, and the Yorkshire inn. For quite a time it was unnecessary for him to pay for a drink in any of the three houses of refreshment.

One evening my friend had entered the Scots inn, and had, as was customary, been greeted with:

"Hallo, Jock! Ye'll tak' a dram with me."

As the dram came up it was the worst of mischances that two customers who were *habitués* respectively of the Irish and Yorkshire houses should enter, exclaiming simultaneously:

"A fine evening to ye, Mick, me bhoy! Can you manage a drap of the creathur, now?"

And:

"How do, lad! Tha'll sup a pint of ale for t'sake o' Wensleydale."

Trained, as is a Guardsman, to show initiative, my friend became a Pole the following evening and commenced to operate in Soho.

In the bar of the Erskine Hotel one day I heard an indigenous shaggy-dog story. I had my daughters' Welsh Corgi with me, and she effected an introduction between a very mountainy farmer and myself. The talk turned on the intelligence of dogs, and the old farmer mentioned a sheepdog named Toss, who had belonged to a neighbour of his.

Toss was, even for a sheepdog, unusually gifted, and was a great friend of Gwilym, the only son of the farm.

"Well, old John Jones done well in the '14 War, isn't it? And what must he do but give Gwilym education? Down to the South to school he must go—paying for his place! Diw! Off goes Gwilym to a grand school with gentry and all, and before long he's putting in a letter about more pocket money. Well, old John Jones send him a bit, not liking for him to be short before the others, isn't it? More letters come, and more pocket money, and when it comes time for holidays old John Jones is getting worried, because he's paying plenty without all the pocket money. He tells young Gwilym when he comes home that he's got to go steady next time at school, and not spend all that money.

"Young Gwilym say it be hard for him not to spend among all them nobs, but if he can take Toss with him he can make a bit. Old John Jones won't part with Toss at first: useful on the mountain the dog was. But Gwilym say in the South they've got a professor can teach dogs to talk, and that some of them fancy animals like spaniels recite poetry and such.

"Old John Jones gets upset and say if them sort can do it, Toss can beat the lot of them, being clever like he was. In the end he lets Gwilym take the dog back for one time. Well, Gwilym had talked to the lads a lot about Toss. There wasn't nothing the dog couldn't do—working with sheep, and tricks, and everything. He'd had bets with some of the boys, and Toss won a lot of money for him.

"Some time before he was to come home again for his holiday one of the boys' fathers wanted to buy Toss. He offered Gwilym a big price for him, and in the end Gwilym let Toss go. Well! Frightened he was all the way in the train what he'd say to his father! He daren't face the old man, see! Instead of changing trains at Llandudno Junction, and coming on to Conway on the railway, Gwilym comes from the train at the junction and walks while he thinks over it all again. It isn't no more than a mile, but he gets a good idea.

"Old John Jones was waiting at the station at Conway, and first off he asks where's Toss. Gwilym tell he have a serious thing to say about the dog. He say Toss learn fine how to talk in the South, and could do his recitations in English and Welsh better than all them fancy animals. Pity it was, but he got full of his cleverness, and got spoilt properly. Well, what happened as they was coming from the train over Conway bridge, but they met the minister. The minister asks how was Gwilym, and how did Toss do at the school, and Toss began to blackguard the man. The dog hadn't never liked him, and what was worse, he started to tell what he'd heard old John Jones say about him.

"Gwilym said to his father that he'd felt terrible shame to hear Toss repeating things like that, said confidential at home. He tried his best to stop the dog, but no use. In the end there was nothing for it but to give him a shove with his foot, and over into the river with him.

"Old John Jones patted Gwilym on the head.

"'You done right, boy!' he said. 'You done right! Shame on him blackguarding the minister! If he was to go repeating every little bit anyone said about the neighbours, no friends we'd have, especially with him knowing two languages.'"

The reciter of this moving tale had but little English, and appeared in public but once a month from a fastness deep within the range of the Carneddau.

Conway is identified with one of the most colourful of the sons of the house of Cunedda, a king named Maelgwn, a tempestuous, mischievous, and clever man.

The life of Maelgwn, Prince of Gwynedd, is well documented, for he was a contemporary of the writer Gildas. Maelgwn was the son of Cadwallon Lawhir—the Long Hand—who was the son of Cunedda himself. Gildas disapproves of Maelgwn in an old-womanish sort of way, but a reluctant admiration creeps between the lines.

By the time power had come to Maelgwn it is likely that the Goidels had lost their influence in Gwynedd. No doubt the intractable had been slain or driven out, and the rest absorbed. There was no great danger from England, which was then a melting-pot of petty jealousies, disturbed constantly by raids from the north of the Continent. In fact, even the hostile Gildas names Maelgwn "Insularis Draco," the Dragon of the Isle of Britain, though some authorities say that Anglesey was the island. At any rate, there was no power strong enough to disturb Maelgwn, who spent much of his time at Deganwy, on that side of the Conway which would have been vulnerable had there been an opposition to fear.

One evening I was walking to Conway from Deganwy, and just before I reached the bridge across the river I saw an inn-sign which at first I took to depict Canute. The sign showed a crowned king seated on a chair which was befeathered, and about which lapped the waves of the sea. The inn was named the Maelgwn Hotel.

The picture recalls a scene on the Dovey estuary. It seems that Maelgwn's accession to leadership was not unopposed, and that it was decided to settle the matter by contest between him and other claimants. It was to be a trial of ingenuity rather than battle-craft. Each contestant provided a chair in which to sit upon the sand and await the flowing tide. He who floated longest was to be approved. Maelgwn won and the others came nowhere, for he had his chair stuffed with hollow goose-quills, which gave splendid buoyancy. To-day boat-builders sometimes use celluloid table-tennis balls for the same purpose.

I wonder if there is an echo here of the idea behind that other Celtic tale of the winning of Excalibur from the stone. The principle of cunning rather than brute strength is similar. The Welshman of to-day still prefers to use ingenuity instead of force.

Maelgwn was a great man for bards, and twenty-four of them were quartered on his Court at Deganwy. The spiteful Gildas says that they "spat out bacchanalian ravings" to please the king, and implies that what he calls the lying quacks composed nothing but sycophantic verses. If they did, it is possible that Maelgwn heard them tongue in cheek, for he persuaded the poets and the harpers to compete in a swimming-race in full kit. They were to cross the river at a point near the present village of Aberconway, and to perform their arts immediately afterwards.

This may have been the original battle-course. In the recent War it was customary to make men race across a number of obstacles, among them often a water-hazard, and while wet and breathless at the end of it to fire competitively at a target.

In this earlier event Maelgwn must have had it in mind to humble the harpers, for their instruments were ruined by the water, and produced the most discordant sounds when the strings were plucked. The poets, however, clearheaded after their dip, versified splendidly.

Maelgwn lived with considerable licence, but at the height of his pleasure, and of his glory too, for he was a very great king, he retired to a monastery. Probably he looked on this spell of austerity as a gourmand and wine-bibber looks on an annual cure at a watering-place. The gourmand disciplines himself for a couple of weeks in order to make it possible to indulge all the more during the next fifty. Maelgwn mortified his desires for a period in order to return, as he did, with sharpened appetites. Still, it indicated self-control and the holding of a long-term policy.

During his life he conflicted frequently with the British saints—Brynach, Cadog, Cyby, Padarn, and the rest—but again this may have been out of mischief, for in the end he gave them all substantial help. He died of the yellow plague about A.D. 547.

The land across the Conway, so secure in Maelgwn's day, was to become a disputed tract. It lay at the end of the easy coastal route from Chester to the ramparts of Eryri, but end it did on the lip of the Conway, which washed like a moat about the mountain wall. It was a tract to which the scorched-earth policy often applied, for on the approach of English armies the people would ferry their beasts and possessions over the water, and make their way up into the hills, while the fighting men disputed the passage of the enemy. In Llywelyn the Great's time his father-in-law, John of England, was held up on this river-bank, and was forced to retreat for lack of food, his army bleeding from the harassing tactics of the skilful Welsh. But by the end of his reign Llywelyn had made this land secure, and he died in the Cistercian monastery of Aberconway, one of the greatest sons of the house of Cunedda, just seven centuries after his ancestor Maelgwn Hir—The Tall—had organized his bardic swimming-race from that very village. He died Lord of Snowdon, Prince of Gwynedd, master of all Wales, on equal terms with the King of England. The power which Llywelyn had won for his country declined little by little, until it reached its nadir at the time of England's Edward I. But a little more than a century later than Edward the marriages of Llywelyn's house bore fruit, and Wales was released from subjugation by Henry Tudor. The hand of the great Prince of Gwynedd had reached across the years to upraise Henry and to break the bonds of Wales.

One of the tourist traps of Conway is the Elizabethan house of Plas Mawr, the Great Hall, which was built by Robert Wynn, son of the John Wynn who built Gwydyr Castle near Llanrwst. There are the usual little pleasantries to delight the sightseer: a haunted room; a window for every day of the year; a turret which makes a fine watch-tower. But the most interesting feature, and the least remarked, is the Royal Arms in the Queen's Room, executed under the cypher E.R., Elizabeth Regina.

The Arms are supported dexter by the English Lion, sinister by the British Dragon. History tells how strong were these supporters of the Arms of the first Elizabeth. It was the feckless James VI of Scotland (James I of England) who presumed to banish the Dragon and usurp its honourable place with the Unicorn, despite the fact that his only claim to England's throne was through a Welsh great-grandmother. The superstitious might believe that there is a fetishist power in a heraldic figure, for the Unicorn of the Stuarts was unable to hold aloft the Arms of England in the high position to which the Tudors and their Dragon had upraised them in the world. They were near enough lying in the dust of world opinion when another ruler of Welsh extraction, Oliver Cromwell, a great-great-grandson of Morgan Williams of Glamorgan, picked them out of the mire, and earned respect for them again. The only pity is that Oliver did not bring the Dragon back from exile.

It would be a fine acknowledgment of historic achievement if Queen Elizabeth II, ruling these British nations, which are now forgetful of their past, were to call back the British Dragon and the inspiration of its symbolism.

The Dragon is very very old. There is a host of theories to

explain its significance. Most likely it came from the Far East. Before that it may have lived in Eden, the serpent in the early garden of man's memory. It was not necessarily an evil serpent, though it made the mistake of teaching man too much too soon, just as have the atomic scientists of to-day. Man probably put the blame for his downfall on the serpent, because he has always shewn great ingenuity in excusing his own shortcomings. The rowan-tree may have grown in the garden of the serpent. It is a member of the pyrus, or apple, family. Among the Celtic peoples it is the fairy tree, and they still do not divorce it from the serpent-dragon who sometimes slumbers beneath its red berries. For the serpent-dragon-water-monster legend has always had a place in Celtic story-telling.

The British Dragon is no ravaging monster, but more of a watch-dog; a beast who guards the children; a kindly old thing until he is roused to defend his people. It is unjust that he should be banished from his rightful place.

CHAPTER TEN

Quarry office at Port Dinorwic—General manager—The quarry—Teams, bargaining, and Big Pay—System of promotion—Theories on retirement—A pattern for industry

THE time had come for me to complete my detour from the journey to the South, and to rejoin the road where I had left it at Portmadoc. On the way down I went to visit the vast slate quarry at Llanberis. I called first at the main office which is above the little dock at Port Dinorwic, on the Menai Strait. The general manager, Mr Williams, had, I knew, been with the quarry for sixty years, and manager for seventeen. In appearance he might have been a high ecclesiastic, a man of law, or a man of letters. He was of medium height, strong built, with thin silver-grey hair, and a fresh-coloured face. His clear-cut features wore an expression comprised of honest shrewdness, inflexibility, and humanity. It was a typical quarryman's face. He was chairman of the Bench, and as such would give fair trial, exposing duplicity, but tempering the wind of justice.

I find people of greater interest than the inanimate, but such an interest is a generalization, for very often the inanimate moulds the people who live with it. Slate moulds men. Quarrymen have a stamp set upon them, and it is a stamp which leaves a good impression.

My conversation with Mr Williams dealt much with men, but with men who had grown similar through generations of sharpening upon a common grindstone. The great Dinorwic quarry at Deiniolen, near Llanberis, is worked on much the same traditional lines as the little concern at Moel Fferna, in the Berwyn Mountains, with whose workers I had mourned the death of our King, but the scale of operations is far bigger. Fifteen hundred men work at the quarry, which is the largest in the world. As one quarryman said to me:

"Was you ever in America? There be no quarries there, man. Only little old holes in the ground, isn't it?"

The bargaining system applies. On the first Monday in the month the bargain settlers approach the teams of two quarrymen, a slate-splitter, and a trimmer. These teams are often family concerns, and in many cases have worked the same rock-face, a stint of about twenty-one feet, for generations. In fact, they regard themselves as tenants of their piece of rock just as much as a yeoman farmer is tenant of his farm. They feel in it a private interest according to the length of time their forbears have worked upon it.

The elder of the team will say that one more month like the last and he and his mates are finished. The price must alter. The bargain settler consults his book. He declares that the team have not done so badly, that if they demand any more for their work the central facilities of the quarry will suffer. In the end, without fail, the bargain is struck and sealed with out-stretched palms; the lease of the rock-face sold as a cow is sold.

Here at Llanberis the men on the face and the men in the shed are a unit. In some quarries they strike separate bargains. In these cases the error of human nature creeps in. The quarrymen do not worry very much about the handiness of the slate they send off to the sheds, for they have finished with it once it leaves them on its little trolley, and the trimmers may have to cope with awkward material.

Mr Williams was not anxious about the immediate slate market, but was not absolutely happy about the long-term prospects. These are days of expediency. A cheap house with a life of fifty years is more desired than a dearer one with a life of two hundred. Roofing tiles may last fifty years, and a tile roof is half the cost of a slate one. So uncertain, however, is physical and economic life to-day that a man does not build for his son and his son's son, but for the span of his own life. So often are the words said:

"It's not up to much, but it'll see me out."

This policy hurt Mr Williams, I could see, not entirely because of its probable effect on his industry, but because the old order was changing, and not for the better.

Quarrying is an unusual industry because of the lack of nepotism. It is, in a sense, a self-governing democracy, with recruitment within its own ranks to the positions of authority. A clever industrialist from without cannot with advantage be brought into a trade which depends for its efficiency upon a specialized inherited skill which has developed into instinct. Because the management at the top has sprung from the apprentice at the bottom, and because the quarrymen are as much sub-contractors as they are employed men, there is a long history of freedom from dispute. The quarrymen respect overseers who have reached their positions through being outstanding quarrymen, and the management have too much sympathy with their underlings, from whose ranks they themselves came, to perpetrate gaffs.

Mr Williams had a maxim: "Treat them like men, and there's no trouble."

Men the quarrymen are, and men of exceptional intelligence. It pays well to discuss with them the problems of the business. Because it is done, real disputes are almost unknown. Mr Williams, in all his time, had only had real danger of trouble once. When he took over management he insisted that a clocking-in system be adopted. The quarry was spread over eight hundred acres of open mountain, and round its fringes were the villages and smallholdings where the men dwelt. They could go to and from work without a possibility of being checked. This had not mattered in the days before the basic wage, since a man was paid only for what he produced. In effect, he sold to the quarry the slate cut from the rock he leased: if he did not work he had nothing to sell, and the quarry nothing to pay out. But when the basic wage came in it was essential for the quarry to obtain a basic production. Production over and above the basic ranked for the monthly Big Pay or bonus.

The independent quarrymen would not stomach the time-clocks, and determined to remain at home. But at later than the eleventh hour a final meeting convinced them of the fairness of the proposed new system. They saw at last that they could not have it both ways. They could not have guaranteed minimum pay without they themselves guaranteeing attendance.

This settlement of disputes and complaints is made easy because the manager meets the men frequently to discuss such matters. There is little or no Communist influence to prostitute the good will of either side. Nor does there seem to be animosity between management and the quarry section of the Transport and General

Workers' Union. In this industry, at any rate, the Union fulfils a useful function as an honest broker.

When I asked Mr Williams about silicosis he put on his legal air and looked at me from hooded eyes like a judge at a dubious witness. Perhaps he thought I was a mischief-maker who would add my small weight to the score. At length he said that, as a manager, naturally he would decry the risk. Just the same, he said, it was negligible. Offhand, he thought that there were about eighteen cases in the quarry industry of the whole country in 1951. Quarries now were taking great trouble over dust-extraction, and at Llanberis there was also a regular routine X-ray examination which would enable the disease to be diagnosed before it became serious.

Mr Williams suggested that I go up to the quarry itself to look round. There was no quarry train scheduled just then, and I made my way to Llanberis by bus.

From Caernarvon one approaches Llanberis from due west, coming to the lower end of the long, narrow Llyn Padarn. On either side of the lake are steep mountains, and beyond its upper reaches the precipitous ridges of the Glyders and the Snowdon group rear up against the sky. Organized quarrying was begun in earnest, though small earnest, in 1788. Up to this time local men, most of them small-holders, had made up teams to work slate on their own initiative. Naturally enough these men felt themselves dispossessed of what they had come to regard as a right when a company laid claim to the minerals under the turf where their sheep grazed. For some while there was difficulty, but gradually the men transferred their labour to the quarry company. Most probably the team-system which is now a feature of the industry is no more than an adaptation of the early method when a few neighbours banded together to work a vein of slate.

In those days transport was a grave limitation on production. The slates were ferried by boat to the west end of Llyn Padarn and thence carried by cart to Port Dinorwic or Caernarvon. Not until 1824 was a horse tramway built from the quarry to Port Dinorwic. After that production increased immensely, and to-day a steam railway supersedes the tramway.

I have passed by the Llanberis quarries many a time, but always view them with a mixture of admiration and horror: admiration at the limitless patience of man, who is eating the carcase of Elidir Fawr; horror at the relentless cancer which is killing the great mountain. Elidir is over 3000 feet high, yet slowly, remorselessly, the quarrymen are carving it away, on the south flank from Llanberis, on the north from the Penrhyn quarries, at Bethesda. It is a death infinitely drawn out, a death of a thousand thousand cuts. The mountain lies prostrate, humped and grey like the carcase of an elephant, and man is the petty maggot which will consume it.

I crossed Llyn Padarn by a causeway. In front of me the workings rose in terraces, each towards a hundred feet in height, until they scarred all but the topmost hump of Elidir. Tramways ran along the terraces—fifty miles of rail—and here and there steep cable-ramps connected terrace with terrace.

In the office I met the local manager, Mr Jones. He had worked for well over forty years in the quarry. As always was the case, the talk turned at once on the human element. He repeated what the general manager had said, that the executive positions were earned by the best quarrymen, and that when higher posts fell vacant examinations were held to fill them. He too did not attach much weight to the suggestion of unhealthiness in the industry, and instanced the number of aged retired men who, unable to forget the quarry which had been a fascinating life interest, returned now and then to have a talk.

Mr Jones praised the team system. Apart from stimulating output, it left the men room for manœuvre. A man who began to feel his age was in a position to relinquish to his son or to some younger member of his team the more strenuous work, and to go himself to the skilled but physically lighter work of the trimming-sheds. The team-system also ensured a continuity of special local rock-lore. The recent Socialist Government had felt that the quarrying industry was backward. A fact-finding team was sent from London to report upon it. It was some time before the team admitted that slates could not be cut by the inflexible tool of mass production. Each vein differed in character, and again differed within itself from one cubic yard to the next; and again the weather imposed overall variations. The geologist of the party, however, a large-minded man, stated at once that he would not try to compete in local knowledge with the men who lived with the rock, and whose fathers had lived with the rock as closely as deep-water seamen live with their ships.

Mr Jones confirmed that the Union was helpful. After all, the men struck their own bargain for wages, and knowing, as they did, so much about the business were satisfied that they were being dealt with fairly. They knew that a bargain has no value unless both sides gain from it. There was, therefore, little scope for the trouble-maker. These men knew too much to be misled.

Many of the men work on beyond the years of sixty-five and even seventy. Age penalizes skill but lightly. There are, in any case, many light labouring jobs in a quarry, such as maintenance of the tramways, for which an old man is suited.

Mr Jones said that the quarryman does not thrive on retirement. When he looses hold of the strain of work he overbalances into the pit of death. Jones said that he advised retirement in the spring. The man himself would announce that he would stick one more summer, when the good weather was a help, but that before winter came he would be in snug retirement in his cottage. To his cottage he would go. The evenings are short in winter, the weather outdoors uninviting. The old man naps by his fireside, bereft of his interests and cut off from old friends. Without stimulus the bodily machine runs down and presently rolls to a gentle standstill.

If, however, retirement is made in spring there are the lengthening light evenings which encourage traffic with friends. There is the better weather, when there is much to do in field and garden. By the time that winter lays cold hands over the valley the old man is entrenched against it, secure with new interests and acquaintance.

About one-half of the quarrymen at Llanberis are small-holders. In the early days of the Dinorwic quarry the Assheton-Smiths, who own the estate in which it is situated, leased parcels of land to the men at a peppercorn rent on condition that they built their own cottages. This system brought much rough land to higher productivity, kept the labour force more stable, and satisfied the land-hunger which gnaws at every Welshman.

I said good-bye to Mr Jones, and before leaving the area took a walk round the nearer parts of the workings. There was not much activity on the rock-face because the end of the quarry month was near, and when the day of Big Pay draws near 'doubling' goes on—that is, the whole team turns to the work of clearing up the piles of slate already blasted out of its stint so that it can be trolleyed to the splitting-and-trimming shed for the final handling. It is important to the teams to put out all they can at this time in order to climb into the bonus range for which they have bargained.

There is one disadvantage to the management of the guaranteed minimum wage now operating. If a team's production lags for any reason of bad weather or sickness during the beginning of the quarry month, it may not be worth their while thereafter to try to catch up. A deficiency may be too great to be remedied in order to bring output above the point at which bargain-rates apply. The team, therefore, does no more work than is needed to keep up appearances. The Old Adam will out, even among quarrymen.

I was interested to see that the quarry did not use the diamond-toothed saws of which the little Moel Fferna concern had been so very proud. It had reverted to the steel saw, which, though it cut much more slowly, was cheaper in upkeep. Although all splitting was done by hand, some of the trimming was done by machinery. Even so, there were plenty of hand-trimmers at work, for not all the slate was suitable for the machines.

The purple Caernarvon slate is not so susceptible to humidity as other natures. It will respond to the tools even when dry. Nevertheless, it works better if moist, and production suffers in summer weather.

I often wonder if there are insuperable barriers of custom or organization which forbid the quarry system of working to be applied more generally in industry. It is obvious that incentives are necessary; that the good man welcomes a monetary recognition of his excellence; that only the poor workman is not interested and, dog in the manger, decries the right of others to benefit. I daresay that there are few factories or heavy industries where this team and bargaining system could not be introduced, and where the management could not lease the facilities to the workmen.

CHAPTER ELEVEN

Caernarvon—Publican, preacher, poet, and undertaker—The Mayor and the Prince of Wales—The national capital—The siting of castles—Reformation of a guest—Portmadoc again—Barmouth—British inns—Finest estuary in Europe—Dolgelley—A Bishop and Bull story—Englyns and a full belly

AFTER my visit to the Llanberis quarry I was making for Portmadoc, where I had left my walking route to go for a few days to my family at Conway. However, the afternoon was wearing late, and I thought it best to stay overnight at Caernarvon. Although my farm had been within twenty miles of the town, it was not a place I knew well, and I could recall only one hotel by name. This establishment was near the Court House, and I had been introduced to it by my fellow-jurymen during a three-day case at the Assizes some years before the War. One of these midday visits had culminated in an act perilously near contempt of court, for we had allowed time to slip by unmarked and in our haste to anticipate the judge took a wrong entrance and filed heavily into the dock.

My host at the hotel which had nearly been my undoing on jury service was very hospitable. He was a man who looked more like a preacher than a publican, and was dressed in a solicitor's black jacket, striped trousers and a stiff white collar. He had the iron-grey hair of the legal profession. His clerical appearance was due to the fact that he was a lay preacher. I noticed in the hall, opposite the bar-hatch for secretive drinkers, a considerable framed correspondence with Buckingham Palace. On inquiry I learned that my host, Jack Roberts, was something of a poet, and from time to time forwarded apt verses to the Royal Family, who punctiliously replied.

There was a farewell to King George V sent on his death, in 1936; a welcome to the new King and Queen, who visited Caernarvon in the following year; a joyful address to the new-born son of Princess Elizabeth, in 1948; and a black-bordered ode dated the 6th of February 1952:

KING GEORGE VI AT REST

Britannia, you are sad to-day,
   You grieve, and feel forlorn.
You weep in sorrow for a son,
   And with the masses mourn.

We lived in hope of better news,
   We prayed, and hoped in vain,
But cruel destiny decreed
   "There ends a glorious reign."

How proud we were to have a king
   Who loved us all so well.
How, in response to this great love,
   The famous fought and fell.

So now we say farewell to him
   Most honoured and the best.
May he obtain eternal peace,
   Tranquility and rest.

Britannia, wipe away your tears,
   Brave in the past you've been,
And harken to your people pray
   "God save our gracious Queen."

As a corollary, perhaps, of his interest in the Church, my host ran also a taxi business, and was naturally enough often in demand to convey persons both to wedding altar and funereal pit. I was interested to hear that marriage was a less impatient business than death. Possibly a bride or groom might not be unwilling to hesitate, and indulge in second thoughts, but a corpse never. At any rate, there was a terrible to-do if the deceased was late in arrival.

Another trouble with the conveyance of remains was that it was unusual to obtain a return load.

Apropos his verses, I remarked that, where England might constitutionally have a queen, Wales might not have a Princess. The title 'Prince of Wales' is invested only in a male heir-apparent to the throne. To the day of death an English ruler, blessed only with daughters, in law may procreate a legitimate male child, and the title must be kept open. Jack Roberts said that once, while taking prayers in Church, he had, unthinking, mentioned the Princess of Wales, but, far from thus establishing a precedent, had been mildly rebuked by his vicar. While on the subject of religious practices, my host stated that one old lady of his acquaintance never stood for the English national anthem, but knelt. She argued that the sentiments therein were in the form of a prayer, and should be expressed in the correct posture.

I wandered out into the town to discover the Mayor, Mr Richard Davies, who, so I was told, was often to be found in the branch of the Co-operative Society. I went into the store, and was pleased to hear a lady customer address the head of Boys' Wear as Mr Davies. Several other ladies were awaiting their turn to buy vests and other articles, and I took my place. I felt that my competitors regarded me with disfavour: a great big man after that little boys' stuff; soft, it was.

At the end of my waiting I found that I had besieged the wrong Mr Davies. He offered to find the Mayor, but when I gave my name postponed his search to talk farming with me. This delay at the counter was embarrassing, for one female with an umbrella was slapping Boys' Grey Flannel Knickers on the counter in an intimidatory manner. Mr Davies Boys' Wear went at length for Mr Davies Mayor.

Mr Richard Davies was a dark, keen-faced man, and was, I think, a little wary of one who might commit to paper some unconsidered comment of his. In the end I think I reassured him that my interest was more general than reportorial. He answered me that he had, with the backing of the town, forwarded to the Queen a petition that her son be soon invested Prince of Wales, and that the ceremony might take place as tradition urged at Caernarvon Castle. Mr Davies seemed already to have heard from some secret source that the loyal address had been well received. The Mayor told me that the Welsh people were anxious for an early investiture; that they wanted once more to have their Prince.

There is an old story which has come down from more reluctant days. It is said that the Welsh notabilities were dubious of Edward I's offer to give them a Prince of his choosing. At length he said, "I offer you a Prince born in Wales, who speaks no word of English."

The assembled elders murmured approvingly at this, and Edward presented to them his new-born son.

I can remember being shown when a boy the room in the Eagle Tower of Caernarvon Castle where this first Prince of Wales had been born, but this was most likely a pleasant fiction. It is now believed that the foundations of the tower were not laid in that year of 1284, and that most likely the babe was delivered in a temporary wooden building.

I asked the Mayor whether there was great rivalry between Caernarvon and Cardiff in the fight to be regarded as the capital of Wales. He said that, on the contrary, the two places enjoyed the most friendly relations.

It is difficult to know how best to choose a capital for Wales. At the moment such bodies as the executives of the Llangollen International Eisteddfod, the National Eisteddfod, and the council of the University of Wales meet at Shrewsbury. Such are communications through the country that this is the centre most readily reached from all parts of Wales. Aberystwyth has some claims to suitability in that it holds the National Library and the oldest of the colleges of the University of Wales. The town is about midway between north and south. But even so it is a more difficult place to reach by public transport than is Shrewsbury. Neither has it a hotel to compare with the Raven, which is a factor to be considered carefully by men who travel from home to attend cultural functions. The internal north to south communications both by road and rail are extremely poor in Wales. Since the country became tied to the English economy the concern has been to give east-west facilities, so that England might have access to Welsh slate, stone, coal, and agricultural products.

I said good-bye to the Mayor, and on the way back to my hotel renewed acquaintance with the castle. It is curious how, except for the tactically stagnant period of the First World War, the system of area defence rather than linear has persisted. Early man certainly made his crude fortifications at points of military value; at river-crossings, mountain passes, and track junctions. The siting was by no means haphazard, but was dictated by the lie of the land. It is not surprising, therefore, that successive occupiers of a country have erected their own construction on the identical sites which had been used by more primitive peoples. To-day the military staff colleges teach the same doctrine as the ancients. They do not advocate the building of fortresses, for modern siege-weapons make short work of them, but they do teach that ground is best held by establishing troops on mutually supporting islands of tactical value. These islands are known as 'vital ground.' If an army were to defend Wales to-day modern soldiers would find themselves digging in behind the crumbled breastworks of Stone Age defences, for vital ground then is vital ground still.

Caernarvon Castle is built on the site of a Norman motte, and that, quite possibly, had succeeded an earlier work. Edward I captured the town in 1283 from Prince David, brother of Llywelyn the Last who had been killed obscurely the year before while raising the border against the English. Edward's first action was to raise walls round the place as a protection for his workmen. However, before he could begin work on the castle Prince Madoc ap Llywelyn made a successful attack and burnt walls and town, so Edward had to begin over again. The bulk of the castle was built by 1301, and the finishing touches put to it twenty years later.

I do not like its octagonal towers so well as the common round ones. Also, perversely, I feel the exterior to be too well preserved. It is not ruined enough. Clough Williams-Ellis, had he built the castle recently, would have given it a more interesting air of antiquity. However, its constructors knew something about striking firm foundations, for the weight of those tremendous curtain-walls and massive towers is prodigious.

Later that evening I repaired to a private room in my hotel to talk to a grown son of the house. He was teaching French to a younger brother. He spoke with fluency, and the tinge of Welsh accent and emphasis was most musical. He had, he said, while in the Army been stationed in Paris at the end of the War, had quickly learned the language, and been made an interpreter.

He was at the moment very busy, for as well as helping with the hotel and the taxi business, he was studying to become a doctor.

He told me that his father, who had succeeded Grandfather in the hotel, was proud of his dual licence to preach and draw beer, and found the two callings compatible. Before the War an eminent man of art had come to live at the hotel. This guest had a reputation not only for art, but drink, and imbibed immense quantities of spirits. The poet-preacher-publican was shocked at the slurring of a great skill, and set to work to regenerate it, even at the cost of the bar-takings.

The guest rarely ate, and never did more than lie fully clothed on his bed at night, descending unshaven in the morning for a breakfast of rum. First, the host and his wife talked to their guest like grieved parents, and all three wept. Indeed, the guest was so upset that he drank several bottles to cheer himself up. However, by subtle means the thirsty brand was slowly extracted from the holocaust of alcohol. His pyjamas were conspicuously laid out for him, and at bedtime he began to substitute the jacket for his tweed coat. As he slept his shoes were removed and cleaned. One red-letter morning the chambermaid was able to report that the guest had been found in bed fully undressed, wearing both halves of his pyjamas, and had accepted a cup of tea which he had drunk conscientiously, if without enjoyment.

It was now possible to remove the man's clothes at night for sponging and pressing, and in his new magnificence it was pointed out that he was too good for the tap-room, and should drink in more elevated company. Now he was introduced to beer, admittedly the strongest in the house, but nevertheless not so paralysing as spirits, particularly as the man was of an age when his bladder demanded frequent relief. Thus the element of exercise was introduced. Slowly he was weaned to weaker beers, and finally took such a distaste to these poor liquids that he became virtually a teetotaller.

Thus may all publicans treat sinners!

I moved on to Portmadoc the next day, picking up the thread of my tour where I had left it, and headed for Dolgelley by way of Barmouth. Barmouth had little to say to me, and nothing to offer to eat, though I was there soon after two in the afternoon. I thought back with envy to the days of George Borrow, when mine host of the inn was willing and able to serve the traveller according to his resources. To-day it is agreed that it is not easy to be able, but there can still be a pretence at willingness. The British inn holds a unique place in the life of these islands. It is the rich man's club as much as the poor man's, and in country parts, at any rate, is a fine social leveller, a place where ideas are exchanged on equal terms, and where one strata of society keeps touch with another without embarrassment. The parlous service which most of our inns so grudgingly offer is more damaging to the structure of our national customs than is appreciated by many.

Much of this deterioration must be blamed on the brewers who operate the tied-house system. A brewer's manager is not the same man as the tenant or owner of the rare free house. Often he strikes me as a harassed and depressed fellow who is nervous of his employers. If he wants to show initiative he is not always encouraged. I know of one Welsh inn where, as is customary, the manager has the job because he is married. He is given a salary which takes no account of his wife, although, without her, he would not have been considered. This particular brewery insists on a very full staff being maintained through the nine months off-season, and as a result charges are prohibitive, though probably the draining of profits is not the brewery's loss, but the Chancellor's. At this hotel the manager suggested to his employers that, were he to dispense with a proportion of his idle staff in the off-season, he could reduce his room prices by very nearly half, and that if ever there was a rush of bookings he and his wife would lend a hand. This initiative was snubbed. However, when the chef at one time left the establishment the manager's wife was expected, unpaid, to do his work, since it was one of the terms of agreement of her husband's employment that she should see that the food reached the table satisfactorily cooked and served.

An employer cannot take without giving. Life is a balance sheet. But it is the public who suffer from the brewers' lack of consideration.

A mood of gentle melancholy had been induced in me at Barmouth by repeated rebuffs during my search for bread and cheese. I pottered along the sea front, semi-derelict at that time of the year, and sniffed the hungry salt air in lieu of lunch.

There was little to be seen on the beach except amusement sheds.

I thought back to the little old Welsh lady who kept the pleasant inn I had chanced to find in Llangollen, and of how she had remarked that people dare no longer live within their own resources, but must dig deep in their pockets to buy the forgetfulness of vicarious entertainment.

Without more delay I left the town in the direction of Dolgelley. I had left Barmouth with the plumes of my sense of propriety ruffled by the calloused hand of hunger, but within a couple of miles my savagery was soothed. The road ran along the right bank of the Mawddach estuary. On the left the Rhinog group of hills swept down in steep slopes to the very water's edge, and the road twisted between rock and estuary as best it might. The tidal river was a mile or more wide, and on its far bank Cader Idris stood lofty, playing with cloud and sunlight. The Mawddach drove inland, pointing like a wavy-edged sword at the barrier of the Aran mountains. I had many times followed up the estuary, and now, as before, told myself that it showed the most beautiful view in Europe. Soon I was given another, more handsome, opinion. I came upon a couple who leaned over a low wall, intent upon the scenery as are lovers upon each other. We gave greeting, I with English purity of diction, they more nasally.

"Say!" said the man, "Likely there's a better view in the little old world, but I ain't seen it, and I reckon I've bin all over."

"Homer's goin' to settle!" warned the woman, a plump and *passée* blonde, speaking as if her husband were a wasp. "Homer's in the market for real estate. God knows what we'll do in this neck of the woods, but I guess there's always liquor and some one to come help drink it."

"I guess," I agreed.

"There's only one view licks Dolgelley to Barmouth," affirmed the man truculently, "and that's Barmouth to Dolgelley."

Again I agreed, and moved on, leaving the man to his militant partisanship, and she to her dreams of 'goin' thro' the rye.'

I came to Dolgelley as dusk fell. It is a queer, grim, stone-built little town, overborne by mountains which jealously jostle the space where it stands. There is no particular arrangement of the few short streets, and one wanders more between houses than along alleys. I claimed a room at the Royal Lion Hotel, and was given it in spite of my rough look and the fly-by-night appearance of my rucksack. The Lion is a very good hotel indeed, a free house run by the ex-cavalry son of the man who had previously been owner.

Once Wordsworth had stayed here. He is a poet who bores me, but on this visit he had been inspired to versify more to the point than usual. The epitaph of his stay hangs framed in the hall.

> If you ever go to Dolgelley
>   Don't stay at the Lion Hotel.
> You'll get nothing to put in your belly
>   And no one will answer the bell.

The management to-day are secure enough in good service to exhibit this opinion upon their predecessors.

During dinner I had noticed a rather farouche man, elderly, with a wiry mop of iron-grey hair, a legal face, and a young, sinewy figure. He accosted me after the meal and introduced himself as the former bishop of a major English see. We talked of mountain scrambling in the Snowdon district, then the bishop told me of an alarming experience which he had undergone that very afternoon.

He had taken his lady secretary with him up a path which led to the lower slopes of Cader Idris. When part way across a big ffridd in which a bunch of black cattle grazed, it became apparent that one of the beasts was taking an unusual interest in the pair of walkers. Presently this animal detached itself from the herd and was disclosed as a bull.

The bishop and his companion did not run, but, pretending that they were not in fact there, walked at a fast rate towards a point in the ffridd boundary where the path entered a sunken lane which was protected by a single strand of barbed wire. The lady diverged presently on a route which she fancied more, and the bishop, in the rôle of red herring, crowded on more sail. By now the bull was trotting, so the bishop, not to be outdone, did likewise. The bull broke into a brisk gallop, which new pace the bishop matched, at the same time making a nice calculation of angle and relative speed in connexion with the bull, himself, and the sunken lane. He bethought himself of his lady secretary, but, when he glanced round, could see no living creatures but the bull and the distant group of his cows.

The bishop's mathematics were excellent for a classical scholar, and he slid under the strand of barbed wire as his pursuer ploughed to a baffled halt behind him. The lane was no sanctuary, for it was unfenced save for a thin screen of gorse and hawthorn. The bull ranged up and down this flimsy barrier bellowing devilish threats at the man of God, but inhibited by some bullish fixation from tearing through the pitiful hedge.

Lower down the fence became substantial, and the bishop paused to consider the whereabouts of his companion, who had disappeared so inexplicably in the midst of the open ffridd. Quite soon she came unhurried down the lane, having reached the wire barrier while the bishop was acting decoy. Asked where she had taken shelter, she replied that she had joined the bunch of cows, who had displayed no animosity and little interest.

I saw the bishop again next morning, and was surprised to hear that he felt more fit than he had done for years. It appeared that his retirement from the Church had been occasioned by low blood-pressure, and that he was at that moment undergoing a course of adrenalin to counter the condition. His doctor had already told him that a severe fright daily would have the effect of releasing his own natural supplies of adrenalin, but that it was outside the scope of a practitioner to arrange frequent shocks. The encounter with the bull had, therefore, been most beneficial, and I left the cleric toying with my suggestion that if the bull could stand the pace he should repeat the dose daily.

In the hotel bar that evening the proprietor introduced me to the editor of a small Welsh paper named *Y Dydd* ("The Day") which was printed in Dolgelley. The editor, Mr Griffiths, was a notable baritone singer, as well as being, so I later discovered for myself, a practical engineer and a prime force in keeping alive a small paper.

He told me something of his particular difficulties. *Y Dydd* was a co-operative venture sponsored by a few prominent local Welshmen. It dealt with purely local news, and it was difficult, therefore, to sell advertising space, especially as the circulation was under three thousand copies. However, there was a good deal of poetry published in the paper, and to that extent it was a valuable outlet.

My own guess was that the paper itself could not possibly pay its way, but that its sponsors were men who put its moral value above its financial. It was likely, of course, that the other activities of the little printing-works showed a balance on the favourable side of the ledger.

Mr Griffiths presently made me acquainted with Mr Jones, the representative of *Y Cymro*, a much larger journal of national scope which was printed at Oswestry. Mr Jones was a small, dark man, wearing a dark suit, a black Foreign Office hat, and black-rimmed spectacles. The effect was a little sombre, but he himself perfectly cheerful. We soon became a quartet with the addition of a very burly, tall, fair man with cherubic cheeks, who was Gwilym Lloyd, a noted competitor for poetic honours at the National Eisteddfod.

My three companions had a common interest in words, particularly Welsh ones, though Mr Jones Cymro took a provocative line in the discussion. I had been gathering opinions on the strength of the Welsh tongue, and Jones Cymro, looking mutinous behind his glasses, remarked that it was of little economic value, and that a Welshman must rely for his living on a knowledge of English. Griffiths y Dydd and Gwilym Lloyd leapt metaphorically upon him, and cried out that a Welshman's language was a part of his being, its continuance against all the odds of the many centuries being a symbol won at great cost. Were he to turn from his language he would lose an irreplaceable spiritual value.

Jones Cymro stubbornly maintained that a full belly was a fine counter to spiritual loss, and that many Welshmen must seek a living over the border. He himself had begun his working life as a quarryman in the underground chambers of Blaenau Ffestiniog, and had early decided to study the English tongue. This he had done in off moments by candlelight within the interior of his slate mountain, and had in the end bettered himself by taking a job in England.

The other two pounced at once. Why, then, did he not stay there? What had brought him back to Wales? Jones Cymro ceased to be convincing, and I am sure that he had been arguing tongue in cheek, for he had to admit that the tie with the land of his fathers had been too strong to break.

At this Gwilym Lloyd knocked off a couple of apt englyns and Griffiths y Dydd, fumbling in a pocket-book, produced and read another which Lloyd had given him for publication.

"A fine thing is an englyn," declaimed Gwilym Lloyd, in a

magnificent, rolling, platform voice. "A beautiful, polished thing, neat and exact in form, with the consonants talking to each other, and a punch in it. *Multum in parvo*—Much in a little," he translated for me. "A mighty atom."

The other two assured me that Lloyd was a master of verse, and stood high at the National Eisteddfod.

"In the mines I started," Lloyd told me. "You don't know the miners? They're lovely people. There's only one word for them—lovely."

He gave me the address of his brother who still worked in the Rhondda, and told me that I would find friends in the blackened valleys; that the men who rarely felt sun, wind, and rain upon their cheeks had taken a fancy to my book about my mountain farm. He himself had left the mines to go to sea in the First German War, and had never resettled in his home district.

At closing time I strolled out with my new acquaintances, and we stood and chatted in the street. Griffiths y Dydd pointed out an ironmonger's shop and said that Owain Glyndwr had held a Parliament there. He spoke as if the old patriot had asked the present occupier to move out for the occasion. I had meant to leave next morning for Dinas Mawddwy, but Griffiths invited me to see his printing works, so I arranged to go there after breakfast. We parted in the square, and I walked back through the whispering shadows to my bed.

CHAPTER TWELVE

Y Dydd—Linotype machines—A lesson on type—Drift of youth —Bob Owen, Florence Nightingale, and Betsy Cadwalladr—A lift with Mr Jones—Origin of Welsh surnames—Dinas Mawddwy—Bracken menace—Problems of a co-operative woollen-mill—Hospitable hotel—Red-headed Bandits—Darts, penillion singing, and englyns—Dinas a century ago

NEXT morning I found the home of *Y Dydd* in an old tannery up a narrow alley. Griffiths introduced me to his staff of twelve, some of whom held artistic honours, one lady possessing no less than five bardic chairs, then took me into the Linotype room.

I had never seen a Linotype machine before, and found it an invention of fascinating complexity. There were three machines here, one of them sixty years old, and Griffiths had rebuilt them himself, an extraordinarily able feat. In a magazine above the body of the machine was a quantity of brass plates, each the width of a type character and measuring 1¼ inches long and ¾ inch wide. The plates ran at twenty to each letter of the alphabet. The operator sat at a keyboard and typed his copy. As the keys were pressed the selected letters dropped down a slide and ranged themselves in order in a slot, from which they were pushed along until opposite a container of molten metal alloy.

The letter which each plate represented was recessed deeply into one edge; thus when a series of plates was pressed up against a point where the molten metal was dispensed, the letter recesses formed moulds, and complete column lines were produced in strips of the rapidly hardened alloy.

A genie within the machine plucked the brass letter-plates away as soon as they had formed the type, and whisked them back to the magazine at the top. Each plate was keyed differently according to its letter, and as they slid along behind the magazine, was tripped off into its proper section ready to be called upon again by the man at the keyboard.

Griffiths certainly had the financial angle clear in his mind. He told me the percentage of loss in the use of the molten alloy, the cost of the brass plates, the sums to be charged against power, operator, paper, and overheads. It was an impressive performance.

With the Welsh utility is not an end. There must be satisfaction as well for touch, ear, or eye. Griffiths was, therefore, very interested in type. He had changed to a sort known as Times Roman, of whose form he approved. He gave me a little lecture and demonstration which brought out points of which I had never thought.

It was not the body of a letter which was most important, but the head or tail, the upstroke of 'h' or downstroke of 'y.' It was by these that the eye differentiated. He preferred, therefore, a type where the body of the letter was small, thus leaving space for an exaggerated stalk above or below the line.

He showed me several examples of type which he said would, in a long reading session, produce eyestrain and headache.

On the ground floor of the former tannery were printing presses, a guillotine for cutting wads of newsprint, and an ingenious American machine which folded the pages of a paper. There had been deep pits down here, used once in the curing of leather, into which Griffiths had had tipped some eighty tons of rubble before he had been able to concrete the floor.

The concern had a friendly air about it, and the employees seemed content and interested in their work. The pay was good, the operators earning from seven to nine pounds a week according to overtime.

The morning was getting late, and I hinted that I must be off on the road to Dinas Mawddwy. Griffiths y Dydd, however, had other plans. There happened to be several committees meeting that day at the Rural District Council offices, and he insisted that there were some interesting people to meet. As to Dinas Mawddwy, he would see that I was given a lift by car. To arrange this we went to the office of the National Farmers' Union, where the representative telephoned to the farms about Dinas until he learned of some one who had come to Dolgelley to attend a meeting. Griffiths y Dydd then went out to pass a message of instruction to the visitor, that he might not depart without me.

On the wall of the N.F.U. office was a map of the new hydro-electric scheme which was so upsetting every one. The N.F.U. man, who would have welcomed power and light in the remote farms, was dubious of the value which would in fact accrue from the plan. He too was nervous of changed water-tables and the barriers of open leats. Yet against disadvantages and disfigurement there might be something to slow down the depopulation of the mountain lands.

Griffiths y Dydd came back, and whisked me away to where knots of committee-men had emerged to chat on the pavement. I met first Mr Jenkins, the Youth Employment Officer. He told me that his purpose was to study the capabilities and inclinations of school-children and to direct them on leaving to suitable employment.

"Yes!" exclaimed Griffiths. "Direct them away from their own country."

Mr Jones Cymro had appeared from nowhere, and chimed in.

"They'll go where they can get a full belly."

I had to put in my own oar at this. I supposed that the young hopefuls drifted off to such jobs as light engineering in the centres of Liverpool, Manchester, or Birmingham. Mr Jenkins Youth Employment admitted that so many did. Inspired by the flights of allegory with which Gwilym Lloyd had coloured his winged words the previous night, I remarked that the more who crowded upon it, the sooner would the industrial ship sink; that within a decade these Welshmen would come walking home to the hills and cwms which had supported their fathers through many an economic storm.

Jenkins Youth Employment did not disagree. However, his purpose was to find his protégés work now. An argument began at once. Griffiths y Dydd gave warning of the misery which grew upon a rootless Welshman, and affirmed that his countryfolk were happier at home in poverty than straying spiritually among the gold-paved courts of the foreigners. Jones Cymro reiterated his piece about the belly; I said that there was no need to be poor in the Welsh hills if the land were properly farmed; and Jenkins Youth

Employment said that perhaps the land was improperly farmed, for there was a marked drift from the upland valleys.

Quite a crowd was collecting as it does in Hyde Park about the stands of the orators, but Griffiths y Dydd shepherded me away to meet Mr Bob Owen of Croesor, near Llanfrothen. Bob Owen Croesor, who, like so many Welsh intellectuals, has a quarry background, holds a unique place in native esteem. He is poet, historian, protagonist of the weak, and champion of grand causes. He is a small, nimble man with fiery eyes beneath projecting tufts of brow. I decided at once that I would prefer to be on his side than the other. He was unfortunately in a hurry to return to his mountain valley, but had time to disagree violently with one or two pro-English sentiments mischievously expressed by Jones Cymro.

I admitted that the English were liable to take to their own credit virtues which other nations neglected to claim. Bob Owen glared round our circle. As a parting shot he demanded whether any of us had seen the film about the life of Florence Nightingale. His eyes flashed, and his eyebrows quivered.

"Florence! Florence!" he cried, in a great deep voice which came up from his boots. "Betsy Cadwallader from Bala it was did the work, though English Florence took the credit."

Griffiths y Dydd introduced me to Robert Jones of Tyn-y-Braich farm, Dinas Mawddwy, who was willing to take me in his car. Jones Tyn-y-Braich was a little upset because some one from one of the committees had taken his hat. I hoped Mr Jones had been left with a better.

"Dash it, no, man," he exclaimed, "or I wouldn't be grumbling."

Tyn-y-Braich had been farmed from father to son back to a time fifty years before William of Normandy defeated Harold of England at Hastings. So long had been the association of my new acquaintance's family with the place that one would have expected a surname more high-flown than Jones. But Welsh surnames do not give credit to the antiquity or standing of the bearer's ancestry. In the old days the Welsh did not use the surname, but the Christian. If Davydd, son of Huw, christened his new infant Gruffydd the child would be identified as Gruffydd ap Davydd ap Huw. If by chance there was danger of confusion because of the similar nomenclature of another boy in the locality, the genealogy would be carried back until a divergence of ancestral name appeared.

The system might have been unwieldy, but it had merits. Under the law of Hywel Dda payment for 'galanas' and 'saraad' was made by transgressor to transgressed to compensate for a wrong done. 'Galanas' was the crime of homicide, and 'saraad' was a less determinate trespass, such as an attack on honour, privileges, or rights. The laws very logically joined payment for saraad to the payment for galanas in cases of murder, for when a man is killed he loses his worldly rights and privileges together with his life. The compensation was made by the one family to the other. The guilty family was mulcted to the ninth degree of relationship from the actual criminal. It was very necessary, therefore, for every one to have his tree well in mind.

The ninth degree was considered a legal limit of relationship in the ancient law set on paper by Hywel Dda a thousand years ago, and in this very twentieth century Welshmen still remind a court of the limit. If a witness is asked whether he is related to a defendant, he sometimes replies to-day; "Dim perthynas o fewn y nawfed ach" ("Not related within the ninth degree").

This practice was all very well under Welsh law, administered by Welshmen, but when Edward I began to superimpose his Anglo-Norman system the foreign magistrates must have been sorely perplexed at the string of So-and-so ap So-and-so ap So-and-so's thrown at them. In his book *The World of Wales* Edmund Vale speculates with much probability that one day some harassed judge threw down his quill-pen, scattered his papers all over the court, and proclaimed an adjournment until all seekers of justice took their fathers' Christian name as their own surname. Thus Gwylim ap John ap Emrys ap Davydd ap Owain ap Hywel ap Rowland ap Rhydderch ap Gruffydd returned to the stand next day shorn of the dignity of lineage. He was no longer Gwylim, John's son. He was Mr Jones.

However, English bureaucracy confounded its purpose of bringing clarity. By the turn of the sixteenth century Wales was parcelled out between Williams, Jones, Davies, Owen, Howell, Rowlands, and Griffiths. It was quite possible for accused and accuser, together with the witnesses of both parties, also the court usher, all to be named Jones. Thus, Gwilym ap John ap Emrys, the defendant, became Mr William Jones of Gwern-y-Gof Uchaf to distinguish him from Mr William Jones of Hafod yr Escob Isaf, the plaintiff. I doubt if the English lawyers found the new system any simpler.

As I drove up the hill out of Dolgelley with Mr Robert Jones Tyn-y-Braich rain began to fall. It was the second rain only which I had encountered on the road since my journey began, and now I had thwarted it with the help of Jones Tyn-y-Braich's car. The road at last began to drop into the valley where lay Dinas Mawddwy. It was a narrow valley drained by the head-waters of the River Dovey, a valley whose walls were so steep that the billowing tapestry of turf and heather threatened to slide off them. Forestry plantations clung precariously to some of the slopes.

Mr Jones said that bracken was spreading inexorably. There were now machines which would cut it, or, better still, crush it—for bracken dies most surely by bleeding—but on these impossible hillsides no implement could be worked except the scythe. In other days there had been plenty of capable scythes-men in the uplands, and time was of less consequence, so that the bracken had been kept in bounds. It is probable, too, that the more plentiful cattle of that period had had an effect. But now the battle was going against the farmer, and good grazing was being invaded by the fern.

Mr Jones was chairman of a co-operative woollen-mill which had recently been started in a disused quarry shed in Dinas Mawddwy. That day he himself was in a hurry to attend a farm sale, but found time to run me to the mill and hand me over to the foreman before we said good-bye.

The foreman was young, a native of Dolgelley, who had had much experience in other mills. At that moment the concern was being reorganized, and I had the impression that there had been teething troubles. The original plan had been to provide a direct outlet for local wool without resort to dealers and middlemen, and some seven hundred farmers, mostly in Merioneth, had banded together. Unfortunately the Government wool-scheme had been born at the same time as the mill, and the co-operators were forced to sell the wool from their flocks direct to the pool, and to purchase from it what raw material they needed for the mill. However, they carried on with their scheme, though under some difficulties.

The great obstacle was lack of labour. Since the bus service was inadequate, and the branch railway which had served the now derelict quarry was being ripped up to provide steel scrap, labour could not travel to and fro daily from any small towns near by. It must come from the valley, and little enough there was to spare. The few operatives who were found were taken on untrained, and taught from scratch. This must have been a formidable task, for, unlike diluting skilled labour, here the entire mill began diluted.

When, for the first time, a large number of amateurs have fingers in an industrial pie, there is always a good deal of interference with the professional cook. This must have happened at Dinas. I pitied the manager who had had to please seven hundred masters, each possibly demanding that the looms should weave for him a cloth just like grandfather's. Bearing such difficulties in mind, I thought the designs which the foreman showed me very good. In fact, in my imagination I could picture some of the quilted bedspreads and coloured blankets in the gift departments of the most expensive London shops. The only factor against these products in such emporiums was the price-ticket. The amount on it would need to be doubled to persuade the customer that the articles were worth buying.

Ventures of this sort are of the utmost benefit to country areas. This was no artificial industry brought in to provide employment and to halt the drift to the overcrowded towns. It was an industry natural to the district, using a raw material which the district grew. It was a culmination of an agricultural process. Whether or not this and other similar enterprises succeed depends on Welsh adaptability. The Welsh in the North are an ultra-conservative people. Again and again one reads in the history books anecdotes of a North Walian's reaction to this or to that. The reaction to a given situation was the same fifteen hundred years ago as it is to-day. There is virtue in this constancy, but vice in the obduracy which sometimes grows from it. The Welshman needs to learn to accept not necessarily change but evolution. In the design of tweed, for example, it is of no commercial value to stick faithfully to the Sunday blacks of a century past. Nor does such constancy serve the cause of beauty.

I had not far to walk from the mill to the Buckley Arms Hotel. The rain was now driving in spinning needles of grey athwart the lowering hills, and the valley was in mourning for the day reft too early from it. The hotel seemed deserted and gloomy. Behind it, brooded over by dark firs, the river coursed swiftly, silently, the broken water in haste to flow away.

In the empty hall I hammered for attention, and finally from down a passage a small bearded man approached. I asked for shelter for the night and such refreshment as he had. Perhaps the small man was nervous of me, despite the young bull-terrier who came to reinforce him. He disclosed himself by his voice as English when he told me that he was at present alone except for a daily help then on the point of going home; that no beds were aired; that there was no fire except in the bar; and that there was no meal prepared. I must have looked as immovable as I felt, for after a little hesitation my host said that he would see what he could do. Having made his decision, he became most courteous. He was, he said, sleeping in each bed in turn like a human warming-pan, and that he would let me have his present bed, and he would do his duty by the next on the roster. He then offered me roast beef and Yorkshire pudding. This I declined both for sake of the trouble to him and the delay I foresaw for my hungry self, and said that I would be well pleased with something simpler.

Within the hour I was eating eggs and bacon beside the bar fire.

Propped against a bench were some long strips of plasterboard and parchment on which were painted colourful designs. My host told me that these were for use as summer fire-screens and such like, and that his absent wife was the artist. One in particular I admired, and learned that it was copied from some embroidery with whose needling Mary Queen of Scots had whiled away her time between plots and lovers in the dour castle of Loch Leven. As I ate I stared at the design, picturing the prisoner whose fingers had worked that pattern; had turned that scroll and hesitated over the eye of that bird; picturing the gentle movement of the soft fingers, and the quick, unbalanced thoughts mirrored in the introspective eyes. I imagined, too, the white, bent nape of neck which was so soon to bow again before the headsman.

I shivered, and turned my eyes to the cheerful fire. Dinas Mawddwy is a place where grim thoughts are easily evoked. It hides secret and unchanging behind its mighty curtains of hillsides and towers of peaks. Here used once to lurk the Gwylltion Cochion

Mawddwy, the Red-headed Bandits of Mawddwy. Four hundred years ago less two, it was, that Baron Owen, Sheriff of Merioneth, surprised the band at their feasting on Christmas Eve. He captured eighty men and hanged them from the trees of a wood near by as obscene Christmas decorations. An old crone, the matriarch of the tribe, spat threats at the Baron as he looked at the strange fruit which swung from the wintry branches. She waved her gnarled talons in his face, and swore that one happy day those hooked fingers would wash themselves in his heart's blood.

Within a twelvemonth the Baron was ambushed close by the scene of the hanging; his retinue massacred; and the old woman laved her hands in his warm blood.

My thoughts were taking so unhealthy a turn that I was pleased when the outer door was opened and a number of men clumped in, glistening with raindrops. My host entered from the passage and took stance behind the bar. This formidable phalanx was the Dinas Mawddwy darts team, who awaited the representatives of a rival inn from away down the Dovey valley. Among these warriors was a figure who took my mind straight back again to the Red-headed Bandits. He was a fair man, but with, I thought, a tinge of red about him. He was built strongly like a chunky welter-weight, but with that barrel of a chest I was not sure he might not rate a class heavier. He had handsome, very clear-cut features, of so determined a cast that I was relieved my name was not Owen, like the Baron. I put him down as a boxer from the booths.

The enemy from an alien inn arrived, and hostilities began at once. The Dinas team, it was soon apparent, were poor performers. They hurled the futile darts with the scorn of spearmen rehearsing a parlour play. How had the mighty been reduced from murderous sport on mountainside to the delicate prick of the treble twenty. One of the few who showed a little skill, was, surprisingly, the blond bruiser. Every now and then, between turns, he would stand back among the press and carol a snatch of song in a pure voice so beautiful that it might have been the pæon of a visiting angel. I asked my host who the singer was. He was a local man, a county council roadman, and a leading member of the village octet and quartet of singers. He specialized in Penillion singing, and with his team-mates had swept the board at competitions the length of the country. Even up to London the roadman had been to charm savage English breasts.

The word 'Penillion' stems probably from 'pen,' the head. The words sung are kept in the head, not on music sheet or in note-book. Just as the bards sang impromptu to their patrons two thousand years ago, so to-day does the roadman of Dinas Mawddwy match his words to the music of the harpist. In competition each team of singers stands in line or circle. The harpist decides upon his air and plays the first few bars to which the singers, unwarned of the tune, listen intently. Then the first singer strikes in with a stanza, the second answers him, then the third and fourth, until the turn comes round again to the originator and he winds up the song, ending with the last note of the harpist. The harpist is free to introduce variations to his theme, and to substitute an entirely different air when the first round of singing is completed.

The adjudicator takes into account not only the quality of the singing, but mesur, acen, cynghanedd, amser, and tenyddiaeth—that is, measure, accent, harmony, time, and intonation. Also he judges whether or not the subject of the song agrees with the tune; whether a heroic tune is matched by heroic sentiments; a plaintive one with delicacy; whether the story is epigrammatic. Most villages or districts have their Penillion singers—shepherds, labourers, shopkeepers, and the like. The tradition has been maintained, in this case, not only against outside influence, but also internal. There was a time when the bards fell into disrepute in the halls of the great, due to the defection of the Welsh nobility to English ways when the Tudors reigned, though it is true that this House introduced Welsh liberality of thought and love of the arts to the English. Driven to seek appreciation from the peasantry, the bards maintained themselves precariously until even the lowly sanctuary of the bothies was invaded by Nonconformity, which crowded them out. Somehow they survived, and are now firmly re-established.

My host introduced me to the singing roadman, whose name was Hughes. He was pleased to speak with a barbarian who showed interest in, if not understanding of, the bardic arts. He explained many musical matters to me, and tried to give me a lesson in the value of cynghanedd in verse. I wondered if Wordsworth, during his stay at Dolgelley, had ever been taught the principle.

Gwynn Williams, the musical expert at Llangollen, had given

me a book which he had written. This showed examples of three types of cynghanedd, but I could not then remember them to impress Hughes roadman. Looking it up later, I studied the lines Williams gave.

One, written about the year 1500, was:

Gwelant oll   galon eu tad
g l nt ll   g l n   t d

The last syllable of each line is accented, and in each half the consonants answer one another in order.

Then there was from a poem of about the year 1370:

Hual gofal a gefais
g f l   g f s

This line divides into three parts. The two syllables 'al' rhyme, and the consonants of 'gofal' are answered by those of 'gefais.' However, lest this seem too simple, Gwynn Williams points out that there are two sorts of this type of consonance, according to the number of portions into which the line is divisible, and the order of the rhyming and harmonizing periods.

A third class of consonance depends on internal rhyming. The example given is:

Y ferch dawel   wallt-felen

In this case the unaccented 'el' of 'dawel' rhymes with the accented 'el' of 'felen.'

Hughes roadman rattled off a few englyns in Welsh, and I fumbled with an attempt to produce a line of consonance in English. Whereupon Hughes roadman gave me a verse by Owen Arran of Dolgelley:

Fishing is not a fashion—in winter,
  What's wanted is mutton.
Reel your line, leave rod alone,
  In summer we'll have salmon.

The value of the consonants was clear enough to me in this, and Hughes followed with a fragment from Ellis y Berth:

A spitting, spiteful spitter—is the tank,
  And a stern Hun killer.
In battle nothing better;
  Fire away now for a war.

He quoted a piece about a donkey:

> So sweet he sang his solo—in a field,
> With a full crescendo.
> And in the end, as you know,
> A tender ralentando.

And finally he declaimed one whose precise meaning baffled me, but whose consonance, at any rate, was clear:

> Pussy in her profession—is a maiden.
> She knows the mouse's direction.
> Saucy when in possession,
> She'll eat a rat later on.

I rather liked this, which had a Peter Pan flavour.

I turned to the bar to have my tankard refilled, and behind my back heard Hughes roadman discussing something with a friend.

"And what did they say about the lad," he was remarking impressively, "but he'd got the finest left hand ever they'd seen!"

My mind was, I suppose, still connecting Hughes roadman with the art of fisticuffs rather than music, and I imagined that he was hailing a new Jimmy Wilde. Not so, however, for a moment later it became clear that he was eulogizing a boy's touch upon the harp.

The part of Merioneth centred on Dolgelley was certainly much taken up with verse and song. I had spoken to a good many people of differing occupations thereabouts, and most of them were connected by an interest in or the practice of the immemorial art of the bards. I had spent much of my life in Wales, but, living too close to the people, my view of their attainments had been out of focus. Much travel during the War, and a home in England after it, was enabling me now to see the Welsh people in clear perspective, and to compare them with other nations. It would be more true to say that now I failed to compare them. There is in Wales no equivalent, for instance, of the English yokel who is traditionally played on his own national stage by a man in a billycock hat with straw in his hair, who grunts to converse. There is no parallel with the inarticulate, almost animal, peasantry native to so many Continental countries. I doubt whether there is a race in the world with so high a general standard of quick intelligence and lively interest in diverse subjects.

I remarked to Hughes roadman on my observation of particular musical aptitude in and round Dolgelley, and he told me that there were thirty-four regular attendants at the music class in Dinas Mawddwy. In Welsh villages such gatherings take the place of what in England would be entertainment in a billiards hall.

The time came for the bar to close. Hughes roadman and I were now firm friends, and he made a tentative suggestion that I accompany him to his home. He proposed to send a messenger round the valley to assemble his octet of singers for a 'noson lawen'—a musical evening. But it was late, and the rain still beat against the windows, and I felt that the vocalists, their enthusiasm not fanned by beer, might be unwilling to tramp through the wet night to sing before a stranger. Instead, Hughes roadman agreed that I might visit him at another time to hear in his mountain cottage the performance which had entranced a white-shirted and bejewelled audience in a London hall.

Before I went to bed I discovered the secret behind my host's ready offer on my arrival of roast beef and Yorkshire pudding. Off his own electric-light plant he managed to run three deep-freeze cabinets, in which was stored a stimulating variety of ready meals. Pastry, of course, is improved by subjection to arctic temperatures before cooking, and I regretted that I had declined a Yorkshire pudding which would have puffed up to feather lightness.

The only man I had happened to see in Dinas who might have had in him the blood of the ancient plunderers had turned out to be an exponent of the gentle art of song. The village, as I saw it, was quiet and respectable, despite the eeriness of the valley which fascinated as much as it repelled.

Borrow, a hundred years before, had found a different atmosphere. He had reached the place from Bala over the Bwlch-y-Groes. The coming of night must have touched his mind with gloomy fingers, for he says:

> Dinas . . . is at present little more than a collection of filthy huts. But though a dirty squalid place, I found it anything but silent and deserted. Fierce-looking red-haired men, who seemed as if they might be descendants of the red-banditti of old, were staggering about, and sounds of drunken revelry echoed from the huts. . . . I was glad to leave it behind me.

CHAPTER THIRTEEN

Welsh bus crews—Machynlleth—Owain Glyndwr's Parliament—Two Welsh Grenadiers—Dafydd Gam—Fish from the Boca Grande—How the Grenadiers fared in the Army—Aberystwyth—The exiled Englishman—Unchanging Welsh character

---

THE valley of the Dovey which runs south from Dinas Mawddwy is cut between steep scarped hills, showing in the sharp edges of ridge and *arête* the toolmarks of the glaciers. There is considerable afforestation on the slopes, and, whatever else the merits of the planting, the trees do provide employment in a place where jobs are wanted.

The next morning was fine, and the greens and browns were washed fresh after the heavy rain of the night. I would have liked to walk till evening, but such vague time-table as I had was thrown out by an appointment at Aberystwyth the following morning, and I knew that I would have to make use of a bus to reach my destination in time. I caught a bus and rode the last few miles into Machynlleth. Whether courtesy is an especial prerogative of the Crosville Bus Company, which operates over most of Wales, I do not know. But I noticed then and on other occasions that the busmen still fulfil many of the functions of the old-time carriers. The drivers and conductors on these country routes were infectiously cheerful souls. They picked up and put down without regard to the exactitude of the stops. They took messages for delivery and commissions for execution which were quite outside the letter of their duty. It did occur to me on my journeyings that I had not seen such friendliness and helpfulness shown in other parts of Britain, and that these bus-crews were made up of Welshmen.

I alighted in Machynlleth in mid-morning. The town is immortally remembered through the doings of Owain Glyndwr, whose house at Sycharth was not so very far away. Here, in the year 1402, he was crowned King of Wales, while the English still reeled and bled from his rapier thrusts.

I had descended from my bus in the centre of the place, where the roadway is as much a square as a street, and found myself opposite the Wynnstay Arms Hotel. I recalled that Borrow had spent a night here, and, entering, I asked whether I might leave my rucksack while I walked round the town. The manager was affable, and took my disreputable pack into his office.

Along the broad main street I came on a stone building with leaded windows which was of obvious antiquity. A notice stated that the building was used as a town institute, as reading-room, billiards hall, and café. It was named after Owain Glyndwr. The reading-room, which was detached from the main part, had been old Owain's Parliament House. I prowled about over the ground-floors of both buildings without meeting anyone, and was most impressed with the cleanliness: the crystal-clear windows; the scrubbed flagstones; and the polished woodwork. A faint reminder tapped at the door of my consciousness, but failed quite to cross the threshold from the subliminal.

In the café part, deserted at this time of year, was a counter on which I rapped. A young woman appeared, and at my request for information, asked me to wait, and retired. In a moment a very big, burly, dark man came from an inner room, and politely answered my questions.

I remarked to him that, if he was the caretaker, he was to be congratulated on the way he performed his duties.

"I was a Guardsman," he said, with divine simplicity.

I answered that I thought I had recognized a certain touch, and that now, of course, I realized that I had been reminded of the sterilized cleanliness of the Guards Depot at Caterham. Not, I added hastily, that the austerity was here too.

The large man became animated, and asked whether I had been in the Brigade. I told him that I was a Coldstreamer. He nipped round the counter with surprising speed, shook my hand, and declared that he was a Grenadier. I murmured a few words of consolation to establish between us proper relations as representatives of two regiments whose rivalry had afforded mutual pleasure and amusement for three centuries.

My new comrade gave a bellow of a quality which I had to admit was equal to that with which I had become familiar in my own regiment, and at once another man, equally tall, but thinner, doubled smartly out from an inner room.

"My name's Humphreys," said the first man. He indicated the newcomer. "My mate Evans," he introduced. On inquiry, Evans admitted to being a Grenadier also.

Humphreys asked me whether I would like to see over the place, and when I said that I had already looked round the ground floor he fetched a bunch of keys and led the way upstairs, with Evans as rearguard. The rooms up here were used mostly by the Council, and very fine they were. On a wall was a portrait of Owain Glyndwr himself which was probably a good likeness, for the face showed sympathy and intolerance, kindness and ferocity, dreaminess and resolution.

Humphreys adopted something of a weapon-training instructor's manner. Almost he said:

"Pay attention! What we're going on with first period is portraits. Next, it's history. Don't shuffle yer boots or I'll book yer."

In a subdued way I listened to what he had to tell me. There was an echo of Owain's experience at Beddgelert, when Humphreys mentioned that here too some one had tried to assassinate the old warrior. He believed the culprit had been detected and locked in a gaol still to be seen in another part of the town, but of his ultimate fate he was uncertain.

Borrow is more explicit. He says that the would-be murderer was Dafydd Gam, Crooked Davy, a chieftain from Breconshire who had a pro-English bias through friendship with John of Gaunt, and particularly through affection for John's son Henry Bolingbroke. Owain, says Borrow, confined Davydd Gam at Sycharth, from which durance he was released after Owain's downfall. But in the interval Owain had found time to burn down Davydd's home in Brecon, and to compose an englyn as he brooded over the smoking ruins:

Shouldst thou a little red man descry
  Asking about his dwelling fair,
Tell him it under the bank doth lie,
  And its brow the mark of the coal doth bear.

Later Davydd Gam followed Henry V to Agincourt, where he saved the life of the King at a dire moment in the battle. I wonder if he was friendly with that other Welshman in the bodyguard, Owen Tudor, the Rose of Anglesey.

When Humphreys had shown me all the overt treasures he unlocked a cupboard. I was startled to look into the eye of a fish, which, standing on its tail, and leaning negligently against the wall, was as tall as myself.

"Caught by Lord Vane Tempest in the River Boca Grande, South America, in 1900. Weight 117 pounds," said Humphreys in the tone of a serjeant enumerating the parts of the Bren gun. I expected him to bark out:

"Any questions!"

The fish and I regarded one another with distaste, but I was the first to move. Humphreys reverently relocked the door.

The two Grenadiers escorted me out on to the pavement. I thanked them very much for the trouble they had taken over a Coldstreamer, and suggested that next time I was in Machynlleth we might meet for some beer and regimental recrimination. To this the file agreed smartly, and we parted. I had not taken more than a few paces, however, before Evans overtook me. A Guardsman is ever an opportunist, and Evans remarked that, with beer, the time for it was the present. Since he and Humphreys had already arranged to be free in order to motor to Walsall they could well spare a few minutes.

Evans marched me briskly into an inn, and a moment later Humphreys joined us in walking-out order of clean silk shirt and well-pressed suit. Over the first pint I inquired why they had not joined the Welsh Guards.

"With me," said Humphreys, "it was like this. My dad was a shoemaker in Aberystwyth, but I didn't somehow take to it. Very tall and thin I was as a lad, and stooping terrible. Dad, he says I must find something to put weight on me and straighten me up. Well, I told him I fancied being a policeman, but he wouldn't have that. The Army was the proper place, he said, if I wanted for to be made a man of. I didn't mind the idea, and being so tall, like, I thought I'd try join the Welsh Guards. Dad said no. He said if I was going to broaden my shoulders I'd better broaden my mind while I was at it, and get away from my own people for a bit. I went and joined the Grenadiers."

Humphreys paused, and I had our glasses refilled, apprehensive of the outcome of this tale.

"I'd been told a bit about the Guards," went on Humphreys, "and I remembered in my mind that there'd be an old sweat in the rookies' barrack-room as we'd have to stand to attention to, and call 'Trained Soldier.' Well, I checked in at the Depot at Caterham, and when I came out of the office a rough-looking chap in denims was hanging about. He asked all about me, and what was my barrack-room, and I told him everything about my home, and Aberystwyth. In the end he took my old bag from me and said as how he'd show me the way to the barrack-room. There was some chaps being drilled on the square; being drilled something fierce they were. I asked what they were doing, and the chap with my bag said they were defaulters, and rookies like me, very likely. He said he knew one of them was on drills because he'd try to walk out of barracks inside the first five weeks of his training, when he wasn't allowed to put his nose out."

Humphreys drank emotionally.

"I laughed at that, and said I'd like to see anyone keep me in barracks for five weeks on end, or, if it come to that, wear scruffy old denims. The chap was very quiet, and said perhaps they wouldn't try it on with me, because he could see I was smarter than most. We got in the barrack-room, and there was no one in there yet, except for a sergeant. I knew he was a sergeant because he'd got three stripes like in the police. The chap who'd got my bag threw it on the floor, and looked at the sergeant.

"'What's that object you've brought in, Trained Soldier?' asks the Sergeant.

"Well, I knew I'd made a fool of myself not knowing the chap who'd took my bag was a Trained Soldier, because I'd been warned over and over to watch out for 'em.

"The Trained Soldier, he says very quiet:

"'It's a horrible bloody Taffy, Sergeant, but I can't say where he comes from on account of no one couldn't pronounce it, it being all spits and phlegm and such like. He isn't not going to walk out for five weeks, he isn't. He isn't going to wear scruffy denims, he isn't. He wants his red bloody tunic, he does.'

"The Sergeant he swells up till he nearly bust, and he lets out a shout at me:

"'You're a bloody Taffy!' he shouts. 'I don't like bloody Taffies! You and me ain't never going to be friends. But I'll teach you to be a soldier. By God how I won't teach you!'"

We all drank again at this, aghast at the horror of Humphreys' position.

"Well," he went on, after a heavy swallow, "it was a hard grind. They was all against me at first, and I might have tried to skip if it wasn't for fear of making myself look a fool at home. Anyway, in the end I won out; I made good friends, and when I turned out to be a champion quarter-miler everything got easier. But even when I was an old soldier I'd come up against it sometimes with N.C.O.'s who hated the Welsh. Not that they could say for why, if you was to ask them."

Evans had been silent through this, but now he took up the running.

"Very much the same it was with me," he said. "Caterham was a big change for a lad born and reared in Aberystwyth. My squad sergeant, like with Humphreys, was the first one to have a go at me.

"'What does a bloody Welshman like you want here?' he asks.

"'Excuse me, Sergeant,' I say, 'but we're all under one flag now Llywelyn's dead.'

"He was real angry at that.

"'Why didn't you join the Welsh Guards, not come here?' he yells.

"Well, I was angry myself by now, because I've got a very quick temper.

"'Because my father told me I'd find it easier here,' I answers.

"'On account of why'll you find it easier?' he asks.

"'My father said one Welsh Guardsman was equal to two of any other Guardsmen, and I'd find it easier to lick a Grenadier.'

"Well, that did it. A terrible time I had, man. One day the squad sergeant was at me again about being Welsh, and I was standing in front of him at attention. My temper was getting up; and when my temper's getting up there's a muscle twitches in my right cheek.

"'Take that grin off your face!' he shouts. 'You horrible Welshman, you.'

"'Excuse me, Sergeant,' I says, holding back not to hit him, me being a man for my fists, 'not grinning I am, but keeping my temper.'

"'You wait,' he says, 'I'll fix you proper.'

"He fixed me in a day or two, and I was confined to barracks, doing fatigues. I was carrying out swill from the cookhouse, not caring what happened any more, and slopping the muck all over. All I wanted was to get back home to Aberystwyth among my own people, and to have just one go at my sergeant first, because I knew there wasn't a man I couldn't handle in the Depot. As I was flipping the swill about, wondering whether I wouldn't go over the wall that minute, just as I was in my denims, I heard a bellow.

"'Come here, you!'

"Well, there was your Regimental Sergeant-Major Britain. You know Sergeant-Major Britain, and what his voice is like, and how he can look at you, though perhaps he hasn't looked at you like the way he looked at me that morning. This is it, I thought, I'm done for now. I doubled over and stood stiff in front of him.

"'You're Evans,' he says.

"'Sir!' I answers.

"'Making a bit of a mess of the job, aren't you, Evans?'

"I didn't say anything, because there wasn't anything to say, what with the swill all over the ground, and my denims stinking with it. The Sergeant-Major was gone very quiet.

"'Want a transfer, Evans?' he asks. 'Can't you take it, Evans?'

"'No, sir,' I says, 'I can stick it, sir.'

"'A boxer aren't you, Evans?'

"'Sir?' I answers.

"'When you're off this lot get along to the gym. and put the gloves on. Understand me, Evans?'

"I understood all right, and said 'Sir!' again.

"'I've got me eye on you, Evans,' the Sergeant-Major said, and told me to go away.

"After that I felt there was some one in the Depot who'd got an interest in me, apart from chasing me because I was Welsh, and I felt better in myself. I started boxing, and in no time I was fighting for the Regiment. I never looked back after that."

Long afterwards Evans lost a lung after a complicated tropical illness when with his regiment in Egypt, and his boxing days were ended.

My comradeship with these Welsh Grenadiers was firmly cemented when we discovered that one of their greatest friends had become my Regimental Sergeant-Major when I commanded an Airborne Unit in the last War.

A Sergeants' Mess Smoker atmosphere developed, to my horror, for I was anxious to move on to Aberystwyth. My resolution, however, was founded on shifting sand which successive pints of beer washed easily away. My friends had put aside all thought of journeying to Walsall, and, boxing me in one on either side, had no slightest intention of allowing the party to break up. The pangs of lunch-time hunger, stimulated by cooking-smells in some inn or other where we found ourselves at that time, waxed strong, then waned as the hour passed. We talked so busily of characters whom we had known in the Brigade that I forgot the time, and the road still before me.

The ex-Guardsmen assured me that there was an afternoon bus to Aberystwyth, and that I had better put aside thoughts of walking. Towards the bar closing-hour of three we were by chance at the Wynnstay Arms. When the hour struck I collected my rucksack from the manager's office, and, Evans having vanished, stayed on the pavement chatting with Humphreys. Evans reappeared from down the street, and we recalled another anecdote or two.

Finally, at about a quarter past the hour Evans told me he had a bus ready for me. It had been due out at three, but I need not hurry. Horrified, I hastened round the corner, and scrambled inside the vehicle followed by the winking conductor. The waiting passengers looked pleasantly philosophic, but I took a seat in some confusion. Evans and Humphreys cracked jokes with all and sundry, embarrassed me by telling the conductor to see I got out at the right point, and hammered enthusiastically at my window as the bus moved off.

After dinner at Aberystwyth that evening I walked along the sea front, and fell into conversation with an Englishman who had a business in the town. He was not happy. He had come from the Midlands six years before, and, though his business was doing well enough, was in process of making up his mind to return to his native parts. He detested the Welsh. Neither he nor his wife had, he said, made one Welsh friend during the six years of their life in the town. He did not trust the Welsh. He had found them mean and hypocritical.

This man was sincere, and was obviously in a miserable state of mind. I think it probable that the Welsh were not behaving towards him in a friendly way, or even that they were actively working against him. Yet I believe he might have evoked a different reaction to his presence, for the Welsh are one of the most responsive nations on earth; responsive to enmity; responsive to friendship. So responsive are they that they will swing to an extreme. Do a Welshman ill and he will contrive to repay with penal interest; do a Welshman a favour and he will return good tenfold. He will answer offhandedness with brusqueness, and discourtesy with downright rudeness; but the warm and courteous approach will be matched and overmatched.

The quality of the Welsh character is like that of the harp, of which the race is so fond. Touch the strings with a violent and untutored hand and there is discord; stroke them with gentle fingers and there is harmony.

Welsh character is unchanging. A trait which holds good to-day held good fourteen hundred years ago. For instance, in the year 597 Pope Gregory of Rome sent Augustine to Britain to enlist the help of the Celtic Church in an effort to convert the English to full Christianity. The Venerable Bede, an adherent of Rome, tells the story of the meeting and, being a true chronicler, lays the blame for failure at the right feet in spite of his prejudice against the Welsh.

The Celtic bishops were at a loss how to treat Augustine. They did not know whether to hear him with humility or to discuss the matter of his visit as equals. At last they decided that they would be guided by his own action at the first meeting. If he were to rise at their approach, giving courtesy, they would be ready to answer his requests submissively; if he stayed seated with a dictatorial assumption of arrogance they would have nothing to do with him.

Augustine remained in his seat and conducted the talks with haughty superiority. The Celtic bishops, firm in their decision, refused to help in the missionary work among the English, and later would not accept one or two changes of dogma urged by Rome. Yet had Augustine behaved with the courtesy which the Welsh had felt proper it is more than likely that he would have received from them all the help they could have given.

Apart from the clash of personalities, there were differences over the adoption of the Roman calculations for fixing Easter; the ordinance of baptism; and the firmness of the Celtic Bishops in refusing to help convert the English—a refusal based probably less on unwillingness to undertake the task than a dislike of working with Augustine. Later the Celtic Church refused to recognize the dictates of Canterbury, and of Augustine as Archbishop. The Church in Wales became free of Canterbury, the Holy Stranger, on Disestablishment thirteen hundred years later, which achievement was deserved by its pertinacity.

At the end of the abortive meeting, which was held, it is thought, at Aust on the Severn, the disgruntled Augustine made a prognostication which came true a few years later. He warned that, if the British refused to help in the conversion of the pagan English, a day would come when they would fall victim to their barbaric rage.

In the year 613 Æthelfrith of Northumbria, having driven a wedge between the Cymry of Wales and Strathclyde which finally separated them, appeared near Chester. The monks of Bangor Iscoed, on the Dee, joined the defending force of Selyf ap Cynan, King of Powys. The day went ill, and the monks were slaughtered to a man.

The representatives of this monastery at Bangor Iscoed had played a leading part in the negotiations with Augustine.

In any case, the Welsh possibly wished to leave the English to their paganism. As R. H. Hodgkin says of them in *The History of the Anglo-Saxons*: "It was a consolation to them to think that the invaders who had stolen their lands and slain their clergy were heading straight for hell-fire and an eternity of punishment."

There is another illustration of Welsh character four hundred years later. About the year 1040 Gruffydd ap Llywelyn, a prince of the line of Deheubarth, and descendant of Rhodri Mawr, was about to negotiate a treaty with England's Edward the Confessor. The two rulers were encamped with their attendants on opposite banks of the Severn, but neither was prepared to cross the river to the other's camp in case the move might be construed as an admission of inferiority. At last Edward became impatient of dignity, called for a boat, and his men began to row him across. At this gesture Gruffydd's warm Welsh heart burst the restraint of suspicion. He sprang down the river-bank, waded out into the water, plucked the English king from the boat, and carried him ashore on his own back.

As I talked to the angry English businessman by the beach at Aberystwyth, I wondered whether he, like so many of his countrymen, had brought with him arrogance and an assumption of superiority, as did Augustine. I do not believe that he made the first gesture of friendship, as had Edward, or he would have been rewarded by being met at least half-way.

Some Englishmen have put their unhappy experiences on record. During the Civil War Rupert of the Rhine was busy enlisting the aid of the Welsh, who were in the main sympathetically loyal to Charles I. The officers whom Rupert sent were high-handed and lacked courtesy. The Welsh responded in kind. Sir Thomas Dabridgecourt wrote to Rupert from near Chepstow:

> If your Highness shall be pleased to command me to the Turk, or Jew, or Gentile, I will go on my bare feet to serve you; but from the Welsh, good Lord, deliver me. And I shall beseech you to send me no more into this country, if you intend I shall do any service, without a strong party to compel them, not to entreat them. And then I will give them cause to put me in their Litany, as they have now given me cause to put them in mine.

This cry from the heart came in the year 1644. It is the same to-day. The Welsh may be lead through hell and high water. They will die before they will be driven. They may with justice be accused of being backward, suspicious, cussed, and tortuous. Yet if they had not these ingredients in their national character they would not have remained clearly defined as Welsh, emerging as Welshmen again and again from under the weight of successive waves of invasion. It is also probable that adversity and periodic subjugation has confirmed them in vices which they had found to be virtues when used as a defence.

CHAPTER FOURTEEN

Welsh National library—Ancient books—Bardic system—Welsh Plant Breeding Station—Vital upland regeneration—Controlled grass experiments—Cleaning seeds—Devil's Bridge—Visit to station's former hill farm—Johnes of Hafod—Borrow on sheep sickness—Reflections on drift to the towns

ON the morning after my arrival in Aberystwyth I walked out to the buildings of the Welsh Plant Breeding Station, close outside the town. I kept an appointment with the secretary, who passed me on to Llywelyn Phillips, who had formerly looked after the mountain farm worked under the Cahn Hill Improvement Scheme. Phillips was now at the Plant Breeding Station itself.

The Welsh National Library is near the Station, and, before we began to discuss matters agricultural, Phillips took me across to see it. The siting of the building on its hill, which looks across the chimneys of Aberystwyth to the waters of Cardigan Bay, and the impressively plain and massive design of it, proved that the Welsh can site and construct what is architecturally beautiful. The pity is that they so rarely try.

A very small librarian in black jacket and striped trousers guided us through the enormous rooms. His name was Ben Owen, and he had served with the Royal Air Force during the War. Ben Owen's interest reached back a few hundred years, and he quickly whisked us through the splendours of the great rooms to a narrow upstairs passage-way on either side of which fretted oak doors opened into little cells which were lined with shelves. Here dwelt ancient books, records, and documents which brooded on the past, like anchorites in their caves. Perhaps books, thought over and handled through the centuries, do retain some of the cerebral essence which has pondered over them. Ben Owen handled certain ones, his favourites, as if he loved the entity of the books, but was indifferent to their subject matter.

We came at last to a magnificent exhibition room whose door Ben unlocked. Many precious objects were here, but I was mainly thrilled by a few books, original volumes, of which I had read modern translations. There was the earliest written copy of *The Mabinogion,* Bishop Morgan's first Welsh Bible, the Laws of Hywel Dda, and the Black Book of Carmarthen. I was allowed to handle these; to feel the supple parchment pages; study the unfaded ink.

It was Bishop Morgan's Bible, translated into Welsh at the time of the Armada, which was responsible for rescuing the Welsh tongue from the anglicizing zeal of the Tudors. It was the peasantry who carried the torch of nationality at this time, and the Bible gave them a focal point on which to direct their uncertain resolution, and an assurance of the respectability of their wavering aim.

I had also read much of the laws of Hywel Dda; of how when he had made himself paramount in Wales he called an assembly of representatives from every part of the country, and in the year 942 set down in writing the ancient tribal customs of his race. These had been handed down through the generations, and jealously preserved by tradition, and now became the law in name which they had for so long been in fact. There is no surviving original copy, but at Aberystwyth the volume of the laws is ancient enough to have been touched by the fingers of Hywel's intention and authority. A model of humane jurisprudence are these laws, astoundingly fair in an age of inhumanity in other lands. It is in keeping with the consistency of the Welsh character that Hywel's original copy was written, not in Latin, but in his own language.

The Black Book of Carmarthen is the oldest extant Welsh manuscript, and holds a collection of poems which were put together towards the end of the twelfth century. It was only from this time onward that any considerable Welsh written literature began to develop. Before, tales and verses had been remembered orally. They were meant to be heard, not read. They were preserved intact by the bards, who had maintained the Druidical expertness of memory and recitation. There was a great amount of this romantic material stored in the professional minds of the bards, for the Welsh, like all pastoral and warlike people, had leisure for the enjoyment of such entertainment between spells of intense physical activity.

A fair number of these remembered themes were put down on paper when writing became more the practice, though Sir John Edward Lloyd says that some of the poetry had become conventional and lifeless, and probably did not survive its capture from brain to book. However, composition in Wales was ever a live art. There was no stultifying reliance on past glories, and hundreds of nimble minds were constantly offering, and are still offering, to transfuse fresh blood into the lifestream of Welsh literature.

Llywelyn Phillips dragged me away at last from the library, for he had planned a lengthy programme. We went back first to the home field of the Plant Breeding Station, and I began to learn at first hand from an expert the great importance of the work which was being done.

The work is of vital importance, and should be judged against a much wider backcloth. Britain to-day has largely exhausted the financial and material capital built up first by centuries of conquest, later by a hundred years of world leadership in the field of industry. Two total wars within the one tormented generation have laid violent claims to the treasure, and have cut off with their sabre strokes the flower of breeding. To-day our money is gone; our people are very tired.

The industrialist will say that we have with the ingenuity of our minds procreated machine-children to ease our work; to make goods for us which the world will buy, and, buying, refill our coffers. But the world is not buying. Other races now have machine-children of their own who brook no competition.

In Britain we have come to rely on our machines. In one century they have produced for us bartering counters in such profusion that we have, as a people, been able to make our threefold increase in numbers. The machines churn on. The goods pile up. The buyers one by one turn away. No longer can we exchange cotton-cloth for the cereals of the East, woollens for the wheat of North America, and tools for the meat of the Argentine. The food purveyors want cash from us now, not shiploads of manufactures. Worse still, the world market has little food to sell, even had we the money to pay for it. New lands have exhausted the original fertility of the soil, and are forced now to prepare for diminishing returns at greater cost. The standard of life in many peasant countries has been raised, and the surplus of food to be exported has shrunk. Britain is left with its swollen population, but without the means to sustain it by overseas purchases of food.

The industrialist says that we must build more and more factories; find more and more labour to feed the machines which, unthinking brutes of iron, are yet making us dance to the orchestra of cams and pulleys. This is the plunge of the Gadarene swine; the panic-stricken dash of the lemmings into the sea. We have become addicts of the machine, and nothing will satisfy us but bigger doses. But further mechanization is a drug, not a food or a buyer of food to fill the hungry gap.

If we have no cure in our gift, we have a palliative for our economic disease. We can look to our own land to close a part of the hungry gap. It is useless to look for a much increased contribution from the fat lowlands. The flat acres are incapable of much greater production. But very nearly one half of the surface of the British Isles is marginal and hill land—land undernourished, poorly drained, and, as a result, stocked far below its capacity. It is to the uplands we must lift our eyes for the meat we need. Here is the importance of the Plant Breeding Station at Aberystwyth. They have proved that the upland grass and the fodder which is grown in the hills can be increased vastly in quantity, and improved out of all knowledge in quality. Their experiments have reached the commercial stage. The guesswork is done with. This blue print drawn on the hills of Wales is a pattern which necessity has begun to force on the attention of England and Scotland.

The Welsh Plant Breeding Station was established in 1919 as a research department of the University College of Wales, at Aberystwyth. The first Director, who held that position for twenty-three years, was George Stapledon, who has now been knighted.

When we returned to the ground near the Station Llywelyn Phillips showed me first a row of fenced grass-plots, each about the size of a suburban front lawn. They had been managed in various ways. One was over-grazed; one was mown at haytime; one was under-grazed; and so on. In each case I could see just what effect different management produced. It was the last plot of all which most startled me. It had been untouched for twenty years. About a half of it was covered with dense bramble, seeded no doubt by birds; the grasses grew in rank and fibrous tufts separated by moss; and hawthorns and young ashes were well established. It was a frightening example of how untended land reverts to jungle.

Phillips leant on the fence and looked at the waste patch.

"It reminds me," he said, "of an old gardener I knew. His master was going away for a while, and set the old boy the job of clearing a neglected corner of the kitchen garden—a place something like this bit of wilderness. When the master came back from his trip, he was delighted with the old derelict corner. It was beautifully cleared, with the earth turned up and cleaned, and vegetable seedlings sprouting up in place of brambles and rushes. He congratulated the gardener.

"'It's a wonderful thing,' he said, 'what man and Providence can do together.'

"The old gardener wasn't too keen on sharing the credit. He said, 'Maybe you forget what this looked like when Providence was single-handed.'"

The phrase struck me forcefully, with my mind dwelling on the productivity of the uplands. Providence was certainly working single-handed up there.

Most of the ground round the main building of the Station was devoted to breeding pedigree grasses, which would continue to reproduce true to their strain. The quality of the various grasses, their suitability for certain climatic and soil conditions, the type of feed they would provide, and at what season, were intimately studied. By application of Mendel's law; by infinite patient seed-selection, fertilization, and cross-fertilization, steadfast types were bred which would thrive even under the severity of Welsh mountain conditions. These grasses were tried out with the help of many interested farmers, not only in Wales, but over the border and overseas. From time to time the seed of these pioneer grasses was brought back to the Station for 'growing-on' in order to check that the grass remained true.

Elsewhere varieties of oats, barley, and wheat were being bred which would crop well under hard conditions.

My impression was that, in their wisdom, the men of the

Station did not try to change Nature, but to assist her. That attitude is the prime ingredient of success in such work as theirs. The indigenous beasts and vegetation of an area anywhere in the wide world are the result of age-old trial and error by geography and climate. The native animals and growths should be helped to better themselves. They may not be supplanted without grave risk that the novelty of man's sponsoring is not accepted by Nature.

We moved about between the long rows of grass-plants, tens of thousands of them, each clump sprung from a known seed, each row pegged and labelled. Few humans have their ancestry so documented as those casual-seeming grasses at Aberystwyth.

We came to another field squared off into many sections by wire-netting fences. These were not of the original sward, as were those first squares, but had been ploughed and resown with different mixtures. Not only could the value of the mixtures be compared, but within each mixture different management was practised in its own private squares. Again some were grazed early, some late; some heavily, some lightly; some were mown, some not.

Now and then snips were cut from the many plots and taken to a room in the Station where the grasses of each snip were sorted into types and enumerated. Thus it could be discovered if one type in a mixture dominated others to their detriment; and whether early or late grazing or mowing worked against some strains or encouraged others, so altering the composition of the sward.

We walked on to a Station farm near by, where I saw seed being cleaned and bagged in the buildings. The men went to infinite care to ensure that not one—literally not one—alien seed remained in a sack of a given kind. One machine was of wonderful ingenuity. It was used to extract furry seeds from smooth. Iron filings were sprinkled in with the uncleaned material, which was agitated until specks of the filings adhered to the furred undesirables. The whole was then passed before a magnet which drew out the parasitic filings, and their hosts along with them. I watched this process until Llywelyn Phillips pulled me away.

Rats, he said, were dreaded in the storage sheds, and every precaution was taken to eliminate them in case they tore holes in the bags, and seeds became mixed.

We picked up a car at the farm to drive out beyond Devil's

Bridge to what had been until recently the hill-farm of the Station. Phillips himself had been resident there until lack of funds had caused the ground to be given up. I felt that this was a tragedy. Phillips agreed, but said that quite a few farmers were now using the Station's hill improvement methods, so that the staff were still able to experiment and to check the results of evolving methods.

We drove along a road which wound high above the valley of the Rheidol, climbing steadily across the typical rounded contours of this part of Wales. Presently Llywelyn Phillips stopped the car and nodded at the hillside. There were, he said, two farms up here which had been following the Station's methods for a long time. The farmers tackled a new part of the land each year—perhaps twenty or thirty acres—and were able to do this commercially. That was the vital lesson. It was possible for an upland farmer to tackle his land without any material help, other than the Government grants current from time to time, and to see a return within the year on his own share of the cost.

From where we sat in the car I saw the hillsides rolling in yellow-brown billows to a tumbled skyline. It was typical upland clothed in the colours of March, offering little but fibrous dead grasses to the thin population of sheep which lived upon it. But against this general winter colouring certain areas stood out in clear contrast; they were green, and sheep were thick upon the grass. There was no need for Phillips to say where the improved land was.

Lunch had been arranged at the Devil's Bridge Hotel. Very good it was, and pleasantly served by an elderly Swiss waiter who was quite at home in the wide-eaved, chalet-like hotel set in scenery which was, at that immediate spot, violently precipitous.

Borrow had stayed a night or two at the hotel, which he named "hospice." I had seen the falls and the old bridge before, and, time not allowing, did not propose to see the sights that day. Instead I recalled Borrow's awe and wonder at the scene of gorge and spuming water, and the magnificent array of adjectives which he lined up to match the wonders shown him. Also I remembered that he sat one night before the turf fire, and, having read a newspaper, fell to brooding on the Russian War.

We entered the car after lunch, and climbed eastward until we came to the land which formerly had been managed by Phillips for the Station. Here I saw again the contrast between the green patches, heavily grazed, and the typical dead mountain herbage, which supported few sheep.

We alighted and began to walk up the hillside, bent against a stiff breeze which whirled eddies of thin, wet mist. Phillips remembered the history of every hollow and slope, and told me how it had been first treated, and when, and what subsequent attention it had had. Basically the treatment had been the same all over the holding, and could be relied on to be effective over most ffridd type of hill pasture. The formula was to plough, perhaps to take one root or cereal crop, to lime heavily, and to resow to grass with an improved Station seed-mixture which contained wild white clover.

We knelt on the damp sward and picked among the grasses like prospectors searching for nuggets. The nuggets were there all right in the form of clover leaves which persisted in spite of lack of attention. Phillips said that lime, ground rather than burnt, was the key; that it conferred benefits more lasting than application of slag or phosphate alone.

I wondered whether ploughing was essential, and whether a thorough scarifying of the ground with a drastic harrow might not break up the mat of natural sward, aerate the soil, and rake out the mosses; and whether a liming and sowing on the torn ground would not be quite effective. Phillips did not scout this idea at all, but thought that such might prove a quick and cheap method of gaining marked improvement. In fact, he said that along the flat damp bottoms of the upland cwms something similar had been tried with success. The system was to burn off in winter the dead, paper-like leaves of the molinia grass, to plough a few furrows as surface drains, to dress heavily with lime and phosphate, and to broadcast new seed in late spring. The Station tried this experiment on one virtually useless patch, and established good grazing pasture which contained over 10 per cent. wild white clover. The reclaimed land kept cattle and horses in thriving condition.

Molinia will quickly die out if beasts can be tempted to graze its area hard. Unfortunately rushes will persist, but if they are mown a couple of times in the year they too will languish in the end.

A marsh experiment made on these trouble-free lines in 1940

showed the sort of improvement to be expected. The molinia, nardus, and weeds disappeared absolutely. Timothy grass supplanted them to a volume of 55 per cent., and wild white clover to 12 per cent. No trace of these had previously been in the sward.

These results are remarkable, and I have no doubt at all that they could be obtained over a very large area of hill-land. I met several of the Station men later, while staying in Aberystwyth. They were practical men, not theorists. They confirmed, each according to his view, that the mountain flocks and herds could be increased from three to five times, and maintain better condition at that.

There is more hope of stemming our economic landslide among the uplands than among the factories. We only build more and more machine-shops in the hope of selling automobiles to Detroit and bicycles to sophisticated savages. Our export attack is faltering against world sales resistance. The currency which we hope to exchange for food imports is drying up. In any case, there is less and less food on sale. It is really much simpler to produce more of the food here.

Llywelyn Phillips took me on to another place, where a hillside had been fenced into three equal areas. These were similar in soil and aspect, each rising to an altitude of 1300 feet. One patch had been left in its natural state, and was a particularly good bent-fescue pasture. The other two patches had been ploughed and resown in one case with ordinary commercial strains of a suitable mixture, in the other case with a similar mixture, but Station bred. The sheep put upon each of these three plots were of identical breeding.

Over a period of six years the unimproved pasture produced a total weight of lamb per acre of 298 pounds. The improved commercially sown area produced 747 pounds. The improved Station-sown area produced 840 pounds. In value the respective returns in the six years 1945 to 1951 were per acre £12 7*s.* 6*d.*, £36 3*s.*, and £42 3*s.*

The great difference between the improved plots and the unimproved was not entirely due to the heavier weight of individual lambs grown on the former, but also to a higher fertility rate among the ewes, a greater incidence of twin births, and lower mortality figures.

We drove back down the valley of the Ystwyth. At one point

we turned off from our road and took what seemed to be a private drive, which had been much cut up by heavy vehicles. Their purpose was apparent, for on the slopes lay the limbs of mighty trees whose trunks had been carried off.

Llywelyn Phillips now began to reveal another side of his character. The intensity of his instructional manner was relaxed. He ruffled up his thick black hair and turned into a knowledgable guide. We were, he told me, now driving through the graveyard of the woods of Hafod, whose old hardwood trees the Forestry Commission had cleared so that they could replant.

The Hafod Estate had been bought by Thomas Johnes towards the end of the eighteenth century. The original house was by Baldwin of Bath, though Nash designed the octagonal library and also had a hand in the lay-out of the grounds. Nash had conspired with Johnes to erect monuments on every bluff and in every coign of vantage. There was also a Garden of Eden, typically despoiled now by the hand of man, whose cold stone Eve could have expected little more from her male counterpart's clumsy ingenuity. Man has not changed much in character since the day of Adam.

The house was in ruins, although it had been rebuilt after a comprehensive fire in 1807. With it was destroyed unfortunately a great library which contained many unique Welsh manuscripts.

Johnes's most poignant monument stood on a knoll near the mansion to commemorate the very spot on which the female Johneses had stood in their night attire to view the holocaust.

Johnes has been described, rather dubiously, as a 'bibliomaniac,' and he even had his own printing press installed at Hafod, but, together with politics, literary work, and the erection of obelisks, he found time to introduce new farming methods on his estate, and to exhort his neighbours with a tract entitled *A Cardiganshire Landlord's Advice to his Tenants.*

But these new farming methods, Phillips told me, had run across the grain of nature, and had proved disastrous. He pointed out again the lesson learned at the Station: that nature may be helped, but not displaced.

As we drove slowly through the ruins of this restless man's overreaching an echo of a memory came back to me, and when I had the opportunity some time later I looked up my *Wild Wales.*

Sure enough, the indefatigable Borrow had fallen in hereabouts with a Durham man, who for thirty-five years had managed the lead-mines of a company known as Rheidol United. At that time the Duke of Newcastle lived in Johnes's old home of Hafod. As might be expected the Duke became acquainted with a fellow North-countryman in this foreign land, as the mining Captain told Borrow with pride. The Duke, said the miner, had brought wonderful improvements to the district. He had crossed the Welsh Black cattle with a Durham bull, and had also introduced North-country sheep to the hills.

The result of the cattle experiment is not given, but the miner admits that the sheep "caught the disease and the wool parted" so that they perished in the cold wet climate.

"But," said Borrow, never at a loss, "you should have told him about the salve made of bran, butter, and oil; you should have done that."

"Well, so I did, your honour; I told him about the salve, and the Duke listened to me, and the salve was made by these very hands; but when it was made, what do you think? The foolish Welsh wouldn't put it on, saying that it was against their laws and statties and religion to use it, and talked about Devil's salves and the Witch of Endor, and the sin against the Holy Ghost, and such-like nonsense. So to prevent a regular rebellion, the Duke gave up the salve and the poor sheep pined away and died, till at last there was not one left."

This non-co-operation by the local people may have been conservatism, but more likely it was from a disinclination to attempt to save a breed of sheep which would never thrive, and whose blood-strain might mix with and weaken the native. Yet to the English miner, to Borrow, and no doubt to the Duke the Welsh were intractable and ignorant.

In the nineteen-thirties a neighbour of mine in Wales, a shrewd North-countryman, had also introduced North-country sheep to his Welsh mountain near Capel Curig. They too had pined and perished, as all the local people had prophesied they would.

As Llywelyn Phillips would agree, it is one thing to improve the native strain, whether in stock, cereals, roots, grass, or trees. It is another matter, and one requiring much investigation before the doing, to uproot a strain and plant it in a strange place. The native strain is the result of a few tens of thousands of years of geological and climatic experiment. The freshly introduced strain is fortunate indeed if its own inherited characteristics fit it perfectly for life in a strange home.

As we drove down the valley of the Ystwyth we passed the old lead-workings. The Durham miner and his fellows of that period had left a legacy which was still remembered, for the spoil of the mines lay along the river-bank, their effluent still poisonous, so that fish no more lived in the water.

It was a very beautiful valley, sparely populated, with steep, wooded sides. Llywelyn Phillips was inspired to disclose himself personally as a poet, and to begin to quote from the works of other bards. His performance was brilliant. As a rock, or waterfall, or wood hanging on steep slope took his fancy he would quote aptly from some Welsh poem, interspersing the Welsh lines with a flowery English translation in the same metre. He had put aside the practical tone of the lecturer, which he had used to discuss the economics of agriculture, and now employed the rich, rolling, declamatory voice of the orator.

Yet, though there was beauty in the valley—beauty repeated without end throughout the rest of the Welsh hill-country—there was sadness. This vale and its fellows were so poor. Their possibilities had for so long been neglected, particularly since Wales had become an area for English industrial exploitation. The problem of the drift from the land, and especially from the remote upland, is general through Britain, but except for the Scottish Highlands an answer to it is most pressing in Wales.

The lot of the hill-farmer is a hard one. But a fraction of the holdings have piped water and modern sanitation, and a smaller fraction electricity. Most are at a distance from shops, railway stations, and such infrequently operated bus routes as there may be. It is the women who have started the drift. A young bride is no longer willing to set up housekeeping with the amenities of a century ago. She is not willing to trudge down a muddy hill-lane to stand in winter rain until a bus carries her to some small shopping town—a town which can probably not offer either café or cinema in which she can entertain herself when her purchases are made.

And on top of the money she spends for goods is the surcharge of the bus-fare, imposed because she is a countrywoman.

It is more costly and more troublesome even for her to listen to wireless programmes. Batteries cost more than mains units in a year. Also there is a tax on batteries, payable because the user has no mains into which to plug the set.

The young women find work in the larger towns, and naturally enough the young men follow.

The authorities always have a ready answer why it is not possible to take mains to out-of-the-way places; to run buses along thinly inhabited routes. The answer always is that the provision of such facilities would not pay. Yet how much more expensive is the burden of land which is becoming derelict; how much greater is the strain on industry, which is trying to make and sell abroad more and more goods to exchange for the food which deserted home acres no longer produce; how much more costly will be the result of the loss of balance between factory and field.

The price of bringing amenities to the remote countryside is part of the price of food, and food is the essential of national survival.

It is fortunate that the Welsh people do not readily leave the land, on which they have lived since fifteen hundred years before William of Normandy conquered England. Their love of their land, physically and spiritually, has kept them wedded to it when economics are trying to force a divorce. But necessity, not the death of affection, is beginning to break up the association.

That day, I had seen a little of what could be done to increase several-fold the produce from these wild hillsides. Yet all plans fail when the human element begins to falter.

Llywelyn Phillips, between bouts of versifying, agreed with my depressing observations, and we reached Aberystwyth in a sad frame of mind.

CHAPTER FIFTEEN

National Eisteddfod—History—The Gorsedd—The Bronze age and Welsh lustreware—Old Iolo—Eisteddfod ceremonial and symbolism—Costs and difficulties—A hill farm on Plynlimon—A wonderful hat—Practical grass improvement—Sir George Stapledon—Hardy cattle—lambs and infra-red—Wool Marketing Board—Rural Industries Bureau—Country amenities curtailed—Evils of afforestation

THE National Eisteddfod was to be held at Aberystwyth later in the year. The Eisteddfod moves from place to place, alternating between North and South, and confined by no means to the larger towns. This share-out of the honour of holding the festival is on a par with the circulations of the Archbishopric. A favourite Welsh expression is 'fair play.'

The Eisteddfod has its roots in the Druid practices. After the religious influence of this old priesthood was gone the bardic system survived, and the privileges and duties of the bards were exactly prescribed. A bard was as much a part of a great house as would be a secretary to-day. In the time of Hywel Dda, who died in 950, the Pencerdd, or chief bard, had his own special chair at Court. It may be that these chairs were won in contests, but more likely they were simply reserved seats in the halls of the great. From this old privilege springs the modern ceremony of chairing the bardic winners, with the difference that instead merely of having the right to sit in it, the bard now takes his chair home with him.

There is little written history of the early Eisteddfodau, for it has never been the Welsh way to inscribe records, though now and again a gathering is documented: at Carmarthen in 1450; Caerwys in 1523, and again in 1568. It is certain, however, that if National Eisteddfodau were not regularly held owing to difficulties of communication, then local ones were arranged, just as they are to-day.

With the anglicizing of the Welsh nobles through the Tudor influence abuse crept into Bardic circles. Without much doubt many of the strolling poets and players were little better than buskers performing for their suppers. Queen Elizabeth I arrested the decay of a great tradition of ability, because, perhaps, her own Welsh blood curdled at bad versifying. She appointed a board of twenty able men of Gwynedd to examine aspirants to bardic honour, to issue certificates of merit to such as deserved them, and to prevent those who did not know an englyn from a sonnet from plaguing the highly critical ears of their patrons.

In the eighteenth century bardic merit declined from the standard which Elizabeth had set. The great houses no longer supported poets, and once again the craft fell into disrepute. Fortunately, an energetic and inventive man from Corwen named Thomas Jones began to take an interest in Eisteddfodau. He arranged one at Corwen in 1789. This was no slapdash affair of imbibing and improvising. The meeting had been announced a year in advance, and the subjects set, so that competitors came prepared. It was a success, perhaps not altogether because it was held at the Owain Glyndwr Hotel, and was the father of the present-day events, with their meticulous organization.

The famous Twm o'r Nant, whose history Borrow gives in detail, was a competitor, but, though much fancied by some of the judges, he did not gain the principal prize.

Thirty years later pageantry began to colour the Eisteddfod. The Gorsedd, a kind of Chapel of Bards, had been formed as, in effect, a rival institution, but was now blended with the Eisteddfod. I am not sure to what extent the robing and ritual of the Gorsedd are spurious. So little is known of Druid practice, though indeed inferences can be made, that the very exactitude of the ceremonial puts a doubt in one's mind. Nevertheless, a little colour sells many tickets.

The Llangollen Eisteddfod of 1858 was notable for the dress and antics of some of the organizers. One of them wore an egg pendant from a necklace; another a tarboosh of fox-skin. Nevertheless, cheap railway excursions had been arranged, and the charade was a great financial success. After all, the English visitors were not to be disappointed if they came in expectation of viewing something odd and barbaric in comical Wales. There is a parallel to this Welsh wish to do what pleases the mentality of their visitors; the famous Llanfairpwllgwyngyll in Anglesey is a name created solely for display on the railway platform and on local picture postcards to delight the summer tourist trade. The joke never fails to convulse the Midlands visitors, who, by comparison, feel themselves to be linguistically concise.

However, following this 1858 Llangollen Eisteddfod a council was set up, which twenty-two years later became the National Eisteddfod Association. This controls the annual function to this day.

The Association used to work in conjunction with the Gorsedd of Bards and the local committee of the town currently preparing for the Eisteddfod. No doubt a great deal of efficiency was dropped between the three stools, and after 1937 a single Council was formed to do the executive work of the Association and the Gorsedd. It is this Council which weighs up the claims of towns, and decides which shall be honoured by a visitation; and which lays down the conditions of competition.

Out of its funds the Council helps the Local Committee if necessary, and also undertakes the publication of prize compositions which might otherwise be lost to Welsh literature.

The Gorsedd has not been robbed of all its influence. It is the Gorsedd which attributes to God the symbol known as Y Nod Cyfrin, the Mystic Mark, which is written as /|\. The sign depicts the three rays of Love, Justice, and Truth. When God spoke His name He said /|\, and at the breath of His voice matter and life were born.

At the centre of the Gorsedd Circle is the stone called the Maen Llog, the stone in front of the Portal lies due east of the Maen Llog. The northern Portal stone faces the rising sun of the longest day, and the southern faces the rising sun of the shortest day. Lines drawn from the Maen Llog to the three Portal stones form, Y Nod Cyfrin: /|\

While I was still at Aberystwyth Llywelyn Phillips, the exponent of hill-farming technique, called in at my hotel to invite me round to his house. I bowed imperceptibly to the deities shaped like lustre jugs in the hall, as I always do in a Welshman's home. It is possible that this lustreware, whose possession is universal in Wales from bothy to manor house, is the oldest household ornament in general use in Britain, in symbolism if not intrinsically. Two and a half thousand years ago, when iron began to replace bronze in these islands, the British housewife grumbled:

"Dull-looking old stuff it is, and rub as much as you like, but you won't get a shine on it. Look at grandmother's bronze bowls. There's lovely now, isn't it?"

But, just the same, bronze slowly died out of practical use. However, an astute potter discovered that the sheen of coppery metal could be reproduced on clay if the vessel were dipped in hæmatite, the iron oxide, then polished. Thus was born the ancestor of lustreware to brighten the Iron Age house. Its descendant still brightens the Welsh home.

Lustreware is a faint reminder of the beautiful Celtic art which flowered at its finest in the La Tène period, and which is now said to mark a milestone in man's upward progress. Jacquetta Hawkes, in the book *Prehistoric Britain*, says that Celtic chiefs took pride in their collection of magnificently worked bronze and gold drinking-vessels, for these nobles were much addicted to Macedonian wines. She quotes a saying that La Tène art may largely have owed its existence to Celtic thirst.

I settled down in Phillips's sitting-room to talk with his wife and him.

I knew that my host had won a prize for verse at the National Eisteddfod, and asked his opinion of the Gorsedd. He would not commit himself, but went so far as to say that Iolo Morganwg had had something to do with the revival of pageantry. Phillips kept referring to the bard as old Iolo, and used the tone of a man who expects a neighbour to drop in at any moment.

Old Iolo made his mark at the end of the eighteenth century. Iolo to-day would be known as a proper card. He took his bardic title from his county of Glamorgan, of whose credit he was very jealous. So jealous was he that he told the Gwyneddigion, the Society of the men of North Wales, that Glamorgan had produced innumerable poets of greater quality than those of Gwynedd. To prove this he wrote a great deal of first-rate verse in the names of various of the deceased Glamorgan minor poets, and arranged for it to be discovered in their former haunts. He was a distant parallel of Van Meegeren, and his little deception was not exposed until long after his death, when close study revealed anachronisms in his etymology.

Phillips, very drily, considered it possible, therefore, that old Iolo's imaginative flair might have improved to some extent on the Druid ritual. Be that as it may, Iolo, whose everyday name was Edward Williams, and who was a stonemason by trade, showed great talents. Among his hobby-horses was a passion for fraternity and equality, which hobby-horses he exercised sympathetically round the guillotines of revolutionary Paris. So as not to bore his public by consistency he wrote an *Invocation to Peace* in 1799, which is always published in the yearly Gorsedd programme.

But though quite a number of Welsh Eisteddfod followers watch the Gorsedd ritual tongue in cheek, it has to-day been brought to a well-drilled display. So retentive is Welsh race-memory that old Iolo may not have been so very inaccurate when he rehearsed his bardic *corps de ballet*.

It is an inspiring scene when the Gorsedd Session is opened, the members in green or blue or white robes according to their rank in the order. The Archdruid partly withdraws the Grand Sword from its scabbard and cries three times, "Is it peace?" Three times the assembled bards reply, "Peace."

Then a matron of the district offers the Hirlas Horn to the Archdruid in symbolism of welcoming libations, and a maid proffers the Aberthged, or Corn Sheaf. These acts are indeed echoes from the depths of mythology.

One other piece of the Regalia is significant: the Half Sword. This weapon is split down the length of its blade, and the missing half lies with the bards of Brittany, who in Druid days followed the lead of the priests of Mona. The halves are only joined at a Joint Gorsedd of the Welsh and Breton bards, and the whole sword becomes a reminder of King Arthur's brand, Excalibur.

Somewhere back along this road of memory which traverses the Celtic past King Arthur must have ridden. If the thought of his chivalry can spur pale inspiration to-day old Iolo must be forgiven much.

I went one day to see Dafydd Morris Jones, the secretary of the

Local Committee, who was very busy organizing for the visit of the Eisteddfod to the town during the first week of August. His offices were reached through a narrow alley, off which one ascended steep stairs which exhorted three times to mind the head. Dafydd Morris Jones had been at work for two years co-ordinating the various local committees, reconciling their decisions with those of the National Council. He was a young, keen-featured, dynamic man who had taken on the job straight from college. He would leave it when he had cleared up the aftermath of the meeting, but no doubt his experience gained in organization would stand him in very good stead when he came to take up a permanent career. There is no continuing paid Secretary of the National Council. This is probably a fault, for without one there can be no continuity of progressive organization through the years. As a result each temporary local secretary must learn the ins and outs from scratch, not benefiting from what was learned by previous secretaries in their brief tenure of office.

Dafydd Morris Jones told me that there are so few buildings scattered about Wales which are large enough to hold the Eisteddfod crowds that the Council has bought a vast wooden pavilion. This is moved yearly to the next town whose turn it is, and thus minor places are equipped to cope with the six-day crowds which may total one hundred and thirty thousand people. To demolish, transport, and re-erect the pavilion costs to-day about £13,000.

I have a feeling that the executive machinery of the National Eisteddfod is top-heavy; that there is dead wood there which trips those who have much to do with the meeting's practical well-being. This accumulation of lumber is often found in ancient institutions. It is to be hoped that the Welsh people will not allow so much lumber to pile up that there is no room for the furnishing of new ideas. A tradition, like a language, must be receptive, or it dies. The tradition of a great regiment, though founded on prowess with pikes, can only continue if it has progressed to muzzle-loaders, and thence to automatic weapons. Similarly, the Eisteddfod tradition might be strengthened if it grafted more modernity on to the firm base of its established custom.

I left Dafydd Morris Jones to his problems, thankful that they were his, not mine, and made my way down the stairs. Unfortunately I forgot the third Mind-your-head, and reached the street with as bad a headache as the Secretary's.

At the Plant Breeding Station I had heard much theory and seen some practice of hill regeneration. During my own farming days in the North I had heard from time to time of the doings of an ebullient character who ran stock on Plynlimon, one Captain Bennett Evans, of Manod. The Captain had begun his then unconventional experiments in conjunction with George Stapledon, who was the foundation genius of the Station. I now arranged to go to see whether commercial practice could follow theory.

It was a pleasant morning when Captain Bennett Evans's son picked me up in a Land Rover at Pont Erwyd, a tiny village a few miles from Manod. He was a young man aged about twenty, quiet and capable. As we drove along he pointed out the Forestry plantations where trees grew on tractor country, on ffridd ground, above which reared the hill sheep-walks, virtually worthless now that their lower lying complement was taken.

Captain Bennett Evans himself was awaiting us by the roadside, a lone figure in that high vale, walled by bulky, sprawling ridges. When I alighted to shake hands I found him to be a small man to tame so great a mountain as Plynlimon, but he had the sort of eyes which Moses must have had: the eyes of a man who looks for a promised land and inspires other men to forget their doubts; indomitable eyes burning with enthusiasm, and, as I later found, flaming with interest at the mention of any subject for discussion under the sun. The Captain carried a funny old stick; was followed by two terriers; wore tweeds, boots, and a remarkable hat. This was the sort of hat anyone could buy, a simple trilby, but, instead of denting it horizontally in what an Army instructor would call the 'proper manner,' he had allowed the crown to work up to a point, with one vertical indentation for each of the four points of the compass. The Royal Canadian Mounted Police attempt the same effect.

We went first to the house for a cup of coffee. The house was as unusual as the Captain's hat. The Captain explained that he had put the building together during the lean years of sheep-farming, and that they had all grown so attached to it that they had done little to alter it, though now he proposed to build another wing.

The building consisted of two railway carriages set at an obtuse angle to one another, and joined by a central nucleus of brick. Entrance was gained by an inclined slatted ramp copied from the approach to a sheep-dip bath, which allows the dirt to fall through from the cloven hoof.

The sitting-room was the central bit and surprisingly pleasant. It was comfortable, lived-in, oak-furnished, garnished with pewter tankards, and presided over by two large lustreware dogs. A daughter, convalescing from hospital, lay knitting in a bed by the fireplace, where stood an electric heater which glowed with the warmth generated by a cold river without, through the medium of turbine and dynamo.

This upland stock-farming is a fascinating business. The daughter, the son, the Captain, and Mrs Bennett Evans were all steeped in the lore of the hills, and infectiously enthusiastic. The older pair must have been enthusiastic for a good many decades, and the flame burned the brighter with age. So brightly did it burn that it was not long before I was in the Land Rover again, pitching up an old track which wound up a valley towards a played-out lead-mine under the final hump of Plynlimon.

This accessiblity is an advantage which the hill-farms of Gwynedd do not share with Mid-Wales. It was even possible to shepherd on pony-back at Manod.

We alighted at the end of the track, and began pawing the sward. The Captain's formula was much the same as Llywelyn Phillips's; the plough, lime or slag, a first crop of oats for silage, then a long ley with wild white clover among the seed-mixture. Big areas had been so treated, and one or two surprisingly steep slopes had been worked with a Ferguson tractor. So far the method was conventional. Now, however, Bennett Evans pointed out another type of reclamation. Cattle had done the work for him here. He had run them there in winter, when their hooves had been able to cut into the moist ground, breaking the age-old surface-mat of decayed vegetation, and aerating the peaty soil beneath it. We pawed the grass again. Sure enough, there was wild white clover and one or two decent grasses, seeded from droppings, for the cattle had had access to an improved strip near by. This example illustrated how stock will spread the benefits of reclamation.

We climbed higher to a grassy spur above the 1500-foot contour. Here was a wired enclosure so placed that beasts could descend off the crest for shelter to either side. Within was a herd of pedigree Welsh Black cattle, with suckling calves and a bull. These cattle were a permanent acclimatized herd, managed just like a mountain sheep flock. When a beast was sold it was replaced by a calf bred within the herd. The cattle never saw the inside of a building, yet their condition in a wild climate, and at a high altitude, was better than that of many a lowland lot who wintered indoors at night.

"You must harden your heart when you start this game," said the Captain. "You lie in bed sometimes and listen to the weather roaring and drenching outside, and you think of the cattle up here, and you lose your nerve. But they thrive on it if you make them stick it. Once you relent you're done for. Out they must stay in snow and ice and rain and wind. We get no losses except for very rare accidents—a tumble into a hole, maybe."

Alongside the paddock, and indeed the reason for its location, was an area under reclamation. The crop of oats had been grown at that altitude, cut for silage, and pitted just outside the wire fence. In other words, the cattle had been brought to their winter fodder: a system most economical of labour.

We descended to the track, rode a while in the Land Rover, and came to the sheep-pens. Here the Captain's restless, inquisitive enthusiasm was evident, for he had streamlined his pens. I had never thought to see such modernity in Wales' oldest industry, which is a stronghold of tradition and conservatism. The length of the hill-lands the pens are the same: dry-stone walled, with rickety gates which have to be opened against the press of sheep; little holes left under walls, blocked by slate slabs when not wanted for sorting; a dip-bath into which each animal must be lifted and thrown at great cumulative effort to the thrower.

The Captain's pens were different. From the main enclosure the sheep, urged by a little effortless 'shooing,' tripped along a passage just wide enough for single-file. In section, the passage was 'V' shaped, so that any horned animals could take their heads with them, held at natural level in the upper width of the 'V.' In the sides of the passage, opposite one another, were two openings into side-pens. A gate was so hung that when swung it blocked the passage and obscured one or other of the two openings, as the operator desired. The sheep were thus sorted to this pen or that with no more work than the swing of the little gate. The other gates were hung from tall frames of two uprights and a cross-piece. They slid up in grooves, like guillotines, but with their weight eased by counterpoises. This way of opening must have been a great time-saver, for in ordinary pens the gates work in the traditional horizontal manner, and, traditionally, there are always a couple of hundred sheep leaning against them.

The show piece of the pens, however, was the dip-bath. Sheep, not being fools, dislike dip. They struggle against immersion as fiercely as would a pagan against baptism. Captain Bennett Evans, therefore, had done his best to outwit his sheep. The approach to the noisome bath was by concealed ways out of whose confines the animals could not see. At the last moment there was an incline, beyond whose blind crest lay a steep slide, well greased with old tractor-sump oil, which shot the victim straight into the bath. The principle was that of the old-time comic film, where the gang of ruffians emerges member by member through a trap-door, and is eliminated individually by a hero with an iron-bar and a good ball eye.

I remarked with delight on the beauty of the conception, but young Bennett Evans, with one eye on his father, confessed that in the second year the method had not given such satisfaction as in the first. The Captain agreed, glumly.

"You've been a sheep-farmer," he said. "You know sheep are far from being fools. They were caught first time, but the next year they remembered all about it. It's a job to get them to the top of the slippery slide now."

During the morning we were drenched by a couple of heavy downpours, drying off each time in the stiff breeze which is more effective than heat. The Captain was not a young man, but recked as little of the rain as did his son. He had walked the slopes of Plynlimon for so long that he was as impervious as they were to weather. He had begun to farm before the First German War. On its outbreak he and his shepherd decided that one of them must go, and after weighing the pros and cons of which peg to which hole Bennett Evans left his mountain in the care of the shepherd.

When both contestants had slaked their blood-lust, and peace blossomed briefly, he returned to Plynlimon to find that his shepherd had played his own part well. The flock had increased and there was money in the bank. From year to year thereafter Bennett Evans had increased the scope of his farming. He impressed me as a man who was not, as are so many Welshmen, ironbound by tradition, but who, while drawing strength from these old roots, yet adapted present growth to present times. From his conversation it was clear that he was considerate of any and every new idea which bore upon upland farming. Here he showed me a strip of hill, the first which he had ploughed to resow with better grasses; here was the area where he and the now Sir George Stapledon had experimented with pasture improvement; here was a slope which had been fertilized by air-freighter; here was a slope which, in a favourable wind, he proposed to spread with burnt lime by means of a giant fan drawn on a sled.

Of all his restless experimenting I was most interested in that which he showed me in a shearing-shed as we neared the house for lunch. He was here trying to find the answer to the great upland problem of wintering the season's lambs. While the hill sheep-flock is bred for hardihood to withstand the climate, its ewe lambs, and such wether lambs as are to be kept, must be given the flying start of a first winter away in some softer district. This wintering is expensive. In the late nineteen-thirties it cost up to ten shillings per head. In the early nineteen-fifties it cost twenty-five shillings per head. This is a big bill to meet when three or four hundred lambs are sent away, as they often are from the bigger hill-farms.

What is more, wintering at any price has become difficult to find. The great expansion of the milk industry, often taking in farms which are quite unsuitable, has much reduced the number of low-land farmers who accept mountain lambs for wintering.

Bennett Evans had put his shearing-shed to winter use by keeping in it a hundred wether lambs in pens of half-a-dozen or so. The lambs were turned out by day into a small paddock through which ran a stream, where, besides the water, there was an exiguous bite of grass. In the shed the lambs were fed a pound and a half of hay apiece daily. There had been no losses. I saw the wether lambs out in their paddock. They were a fine colour, alert and contented.

Possibly they were lighter in weight than those which had wintered outdoors in the lowlands, but I am not sure they had not grown bigger frames. At any rate, there was little doubt that, after a summer on the mountain, they would be at least as forward as the other yearlings.

There was only one question in my mind, and the Captain, too, had asked it of himself. We wondered if, in any way, the stamina of the stock to resist the harsh weather of their future outdoor mountain winters would be reduced. Only time could answer.

The coming winter the Captain proposed to continue his experiment, this time with ewe-lambs. When turned out in the spring these would be marked, and they and their progeny would be watched for several generations. For a fractional deterioration in a generation of ewes builds up within a few years to a cumulative decline in the standard of a flock.

After my several hours with Bennett Evans I was not prepared to accept his wintering experiment in all its apparent simplicity. I had noticed a curious kind of lamp above the pens in the shearing-shed. The Captain told me that these were infra-red, and that he considered they had given great benefit to his indoor wether lambs. The little river which spun the turbine by the house was thus being laden with responsibility.

The Captain had given thought to the floors of the pens. These were formed of slats, bevelled away on the underside, so that droppings fell easily through. He was now considering whether to dry and package the droppings with suitable artificial additives for sale as fertilizer.

We returned for lunch, which was preceded by some pleasant dry sherry. Two more visitors had arrived without warning in the meantime, and there was news of a third on the way.

"It never rains but it pours," remarked Mrs Bennett Evans, but she did not mean it unkindly.

So often it is the same in remote places. Weeks may pass without sight of a strange face, then for one reason and another a dozen people will appear within a few hours. Perhaps the action of one telepathically brings the intention of the others to the point.

After lunch the Captain and I talked about wool over our coffee. He was recently appointed a member of the Wales Region of the

British Wool Marketing Board: named in Wales the *Bwrdd Marchnata Gwlan Prydain.* I argued that this title was misleading: that Wales was synonymous with Britain; that there could not be a Wales region of Prydain; but that there were English, Scottish, and Northern Irish regions of Prydain. We agreed heartily on this; then Bennett Evans explained briefly how the marketing system worked.

The idea was to smooth the wild fluctuations of wool prices, and to ensure good grading and storage. The Board bought from the producers at a declared annual price. It then sold by auction to the users. If it made, as so far it had, a profit, then some of the surplus was paid over to the producers as an addition to the original cheques, and the balance was held over against a drop in price levels, so that in a poor year the producers might receive more than the auction price.

Most farmers with whom I had talked had approved of the operations of the Board. An exception, perhaps, was the co-operative group of Merioneth farmers who had put their money into the mill at Dinas Mawddwy. I now realized more clearly what they had desired. No doubt they had wished their co-operative to be licensed as an 'A' merchant. An 'A' merchant was one of the former big men of free marketing days, who, because of his experienced grading staff and good storage facilities, was licensed by the Board to continue to perform those functions on its behalf. For this work the 'A' merchant currently received twopence-halfpenny per pound handled.

I expect the Board argued that the Dinas Mawddwy co-operative did not possess the qualifications. Just the same, I felt that a rigid system might be relaxed to embrace such small concerns which, with encouragement in their many difficulties, could do much to provide a reservoir of work in parts where emigration to the overloaded industrial areas was becoming the practice of the young.

Before I made my farewells the Captain and I took a stroll along the bottom lands. I saw his hydro-electric set, motivated by a short leat of substantial capacity whose considerable water did the work on a drop of only seventeen feet. Across the river which was his boundary rose the lumpy group of hills whose highest point was Bryn Garw. The Forestry Commission had planted extensively up to the tree-line, leaving the mountain-top bald, difficult of access for shepherding, and unbalanced without its ffridd. The Captain deplored the planting policy. For every acre planted at least another was rendered useless. It seemed to me that the Commission's activities in Mid-Wales, and as I later saw in South Wales, were more detrimental to hill-farming than they were in Eryri. There, at any rate, the precipitous nature of the ground ensured that a proportion of non-tractor country was put to use. Most probably this was better employed under trees than sheep. After all, afforestation and stock-rearing are two methods of land utilization. They should be complementary to one another, not inimical. There are in every upland region areas where trees are likely to be more profitable to the nation than stock, and areas where the reverse applies. The only excuse for trees on country where the tractor can improve the sward is that they should form shelter belts. These the Commission are loth to plant for internal economic reasons of their own. It is important that Forestry activities are integrated with agriculture before more meat-producing land is lost. When planted with trees the land is virtually lost to stock for all time.

Wherever trees are planted, on suitable land or otherwise, there is the problem of vermin who breed in the sanctuary of the plantations. This is a heavy liability to impose on neighbouring farmers. It is not the loss of a few fowls which is the probability, but the slaughter by foxes of perhaps 10 per cent. of a lamb crop. But life presents a balance sheet. We must accept a debit for every credit. The object, however, should be to keep the debits low. It is bad national management to debit agriculture with loss of land better used for stock—which is an avoidable debit—as well as losses by vermin, which must be accepted if we want home-grown trees.

Captain Bennett Evans had planted shelter belts up on Plynlimon to mark the birth of each of his children. He was thus able to remember the age of his offspring, or possibly it was the other way round.

I left the high, lonely valley in an exhilarated frame of mind. The Captain's enthusiasm, his restless, eager search for new ideas, and his fearless trial of the many he found was an inspiration. He and the few like him are the yeast which would leaven the dough of that Welsh conservatism which, admirable in its virtues, yet carries the germ of stagnation.

Before I went on south from Aberystwyth, I doubled back on my tracks to Machynlleth. On my earlier visit, due to my capture by the two Welsh Grenadier Guardsmen, I had been forced to forego a visit I had wished to make there and to supplant it with several other visits of a less solid, in fact liquid, character. My return now was to see the Rural Industries Bureau, whose help had been praised by Mr Jones Flannel Mill.

The man I saw was Mr Morison, an Edinburgh Scot, who was expert in both the technique of weaving and in designing. He received me in a large room in a dilapidated mansion known as the Plas, which also housed other institutes, societies, bureaux, and committees. His room was filled with looms, designs, and patterns.

Mr Morison told me something of his work. In the main, he visited mills and advised on plant, production problems, and designs. I said that Mr Jones Flannel Mill had favourably mentioned the Bureau, and was told that my forthright acquaintance of Llangollen had been sitting in my very chair a couple of days before, discussing designs for furnishing fabric. Mr Morison had also advised the co-operative Dinas Mawddwy venture.

Another function of the Bureau was to arrange courses for operatives, with expenses paid in many cases by the education authorities, and sometimes for willing mill-owners themselves. These usually took place in Scotland. I know some of the small Scottish mills, and undoubtedly their tweeds are more pleasing to the modern eye than are the Welsh. Here again was that stumbling block of ultra-conservatism over which progress trips in Wales. In the woollen industry, at any rate, comparable mills in Scotland were keeping pace with changed demands. Until recently Welsh mills still wove for great-grandfather. There is now, largely under Scottish tutelage, a marked turn for the better.

I expressed this view to Mr Morison, with the reservation that some of the Welsh quilted designs had always been delightful, and with a further admonition—though off the subject—that Highland farmers might learn much from the shepherds of the Welsh hills.

The Bureau did not directly do much about marketing. Most of the little mills sold locally to visitors or residents: only one or two used agents in London. Yet I have always felt that there would be a market for short lengths of female suiting woven to the special order of the great dress-houses. The Welsh mills cannot compete with Yorkshire in mass-production, but they could certainly compete in a small specialist trade. And I know that some Welsh mills would be prepared to weave short lengths to an exclusive design.

This presupposes that they would know how. Mr Morison said that he had found many mills ignorant of the versatility of their machines; that some had needed to be shown how to alter from the diagonal weave of a twill to the zigzag of a herring-bone. He said that the change was simple.

We parted after rather a harrowing incident. A knock at the door presaged the entrance of a Flag Day lady. I was, fortunately, screened by a loom, but Mr Morison was caught in the open. He paid up without hesitation. Scots always do. Thrifty they may be; mean never.

The Rural Industries Bureau is a robust organization, and not to be identified with the type of Arts and Crafts shop which is burlesqued by humorists. Its purpose is to assist blacksmiths, agricultural engineers, wheelwrights, carpenters, boat-builders, thatchers, basket-makers, potters, brick-makers, saddlers, and any other country workmen who can put up a case for help. It has funds granted from the Treasury—in other words, from all of us, since all of us pour money into the Exchequer. With these funds it maintains advisory technicians and makes loans to individual craftsmen for the purchase of equipment. It provides the advice on costing, planning, sometimes marketing, and on every aspect of country industry for which a large urban industrial concern would maintain special departments. Its activities may help to stem the drift from the countryside, which is making the many great wens of the cities larger and uglier and less economic as communities than ever they were before.

When I left Mr Morison I had an hour or so to spare before a bus would carry me back to Aberystwyth. After some thought I called at Owain Glyndwr's old Parliament House to greet Mr Humphreys, the Welsh Grenadier. He was supervising lunches in the café, and, duty being duty, had little time to chat, but when I was leaving did threaten that he might have a few moments to spare later, and might be able to bring Evans along. If so, where would I be? I suggested the Wynnstay.

I had sandwiches and a glass of beer at the Wynnstay, eating and drinking with one eye on the door, and renewing from time to time a resolution not to miss my bus, whatever intervened.

There was another man in the bar; an Englishman. His talk was largely of the sale of railway sleepers. Presently I asked him if he was connected with the dismantling of the branch line from Cemmaes Road to Dinas Mawddwy. He said that he was, in fact, in charge of the work on behalf of a North-country firm whose tender for the demolition had been accepted by British Railways.

He told me that the line had, in any event, been uneconomic, and that the *coup de grâce* had been delivered by a landslide at Mallwyd and a flood on the River Dovey near Cemmaes which had moved the span of the rail-bridge. To rebuild the bridge and clear the slide was not financial sense. In any case, only two trains weekly had run to Dinas.

I suppose he was right. Yet this curtailing of country amenities in order to afford yet more amenities for the townsman has started a vicious circle. The countryman tends to follow the amenities to the towns. When he goes, still more rural services become uneconomic. As a result they are cut further, and as a result of the cuts more countryfolk drift away. Lack of frequent public transport services is a major factor to spur the flight from the countryside. The townsman, unfortunately, holds the heavier vote, cares little for the balance of economy, and faintly despises those straw-in-the-hair rustics who man agriculture, our greatest industry, and its many ancillaries. He would be horrified if country transport services were scheduled which did not directly pay their way. The indirect return to the community does not interest him. Yet an unbalanced national economy must in the end topple, propped though it may be by makeshifts.

I did not mention these sad reflections to the uprooter of the Cemmaes to Dinas Mawddwy railway, for he was, I gathered, a

Sheffield man with no nonsense about him. Instead, I asked what he was doing with the scrap. Much of the steel, he said, had been sold provisionally at a pre-determined price before his firm knew that their tender to British Railways was accepted. This was a pity, for when they began the demolition the price of steel scrap had vastly increased, but they had to honour the lower selling-price which had been agreed earlier with their customers.

The wooden sleepers went to all sorts of people. Mostly they were sold by the ton, which was made up with sixteen of them. The better ones went to box-manufacturers, who cut them up as required. The poorer found a ready local market with farmers for gate-posts and bridging. The cost of an individual sleeper varied from four to ten shillings according to condition.

I asked if the labour was brought from Sheffield. My acquaintance said not. His gang of a dozen or so was provided through the Machynlleth Labour Exchange. They had proved very good chaps except for two of them. One of these was always idle, the other usually so. But this latter man was very strong, and sometimes was in the mood to work. On these days he did as much as every one else combined. However, if he dared, said the Sheffield foreman, he would sack the lazy couple. But if he did he realized that he would lose all the rest.

"Clannish!" he remarked. "Clannish! I've never seen nothing like it. The gang's happy to carry the two no-good ones so long as they all stay together."

My bus was by now due, and I went out, casting an apprehensive eye up the street for Humphreys and Evans. All, however, was quiet, and I enjoyed a sober and peaceful journey back to Aberystwyth.

That evening in the lounge of my hotel I met by chance an old acquaintance of mine from pre-War days, an agricultural botanist from the University College of North Wales, at Bangor. We talked a little of farming, and I gave my impressions of the Plant Breeding Station and of Bennett Evans's work. From here the talked moved to afforestation, and I deplored, rather vehemently, not the planting of trees, but the areas in which they were planted. My friend did not disagree, but seemed unwilling to express any violent opinion. He turned to a man sitting in the next arm-chair and made an introduction between us. I learned that the stranger was Lord Robinson, Chairman of the Forestry Commission. It was an excellent opportunity to learn more of the Commission's policy, but, perhaps fortunately, Llywelyn Phillips came in to take me out in the town.

CHAPTER SIXTEEN

Agricultural economy—Lampeter—St David's College—Nonconformity and the Church—Financial struggles—English indifference—Welsh intelligence—Status of St David's—A productive farm—Labour shortage—Reclaimed moorland

I LEFT Aberystwyth next morning, for I had arranged to visit St David's College, Lampeter, later in the day. Before going from the town, however, I called on the Livestock Research Officer, Richard Phillips. His namesake, Llywelyn, had asked on my behalf for some figures of Welsh agricultural production.

Richard Phillips was recovering from a mild gastric affliction. He received me by his study fire, and his wife and daughter joined us for coffee. Afterwards he handed me two cards on both sides of each of which were neatly tabulated figures.

"That's what you want," he said.

I thanked him, but he brushed the words aside.

"I love figures," he remarked. "It's a pleasure to me to handle them."

With a touch of polite curiosity he inquired why I had sought the facts of Welsh agricultural production. I told him that I was soon to stay a night with Gwynfor Evans, the President of the Welsh National Party, and that, before I met him, I wished to find out how far I might honestly agree with him. At this Richard Phillips began to go through his figures with me, and I soon saw that the many Nationalists who had talked to me had not overstated their case in this direction at least. Indeed, before my present visit to Wales, my wife and I had worked out that the country would be self-supporting for unrationed food if it were not compulsorily exporting to feed the teeming millions of England.

Richard Phillips had based his figures on the current ration scale applied to all Great Britain. The first side of the first postcard dealt with milk. Wales produced 179 million gallons annually. It provided out of this total for its own individual ration of three-quarters of a pint daily for its population of two and a half millions. This absorbed eighty-two million gallons. The balance of ninety-seven million gallons went over the border.

Were this export milk to be retained within Wales, the country could produce for itself—as one suggestion—ten pounds of cheese per head, and eleven pounds of butter per head each year. The present butter ration was at the annual rate of nine and three-quarter pounds.

It seemed to me to be clear enough that Wales, if free of the Westminster economy, could be self-supporting in dairy products, unrationed.

The figures for meat production were interesting, but not so clear-cut. In various areas the Welsh figures were joined in with those of a region which straddled the border, and were difficult to disentangle from those of the English output. However, Phillips had played for safety, and had enumerated only those beasts which had been killed in Welsh slaughter-houses.

On this basis, to meet a meat-ration assumed to total ninety-seven pounds per head per year, the United Kingdom produced fifty-two pounds; imported forty-five. Wales produced sixty-two pounds; imported thirty-five.

Now, these figures were not so favourable to Wales as they might be. Firstly, the greater Welsh production had boosted the United Kingdom figure, a percentage of which should be discounted. Secondly, a proportion of Welsh fat stock was killed in English abattoirs, and Phillips's figures could not show credit for them. Thirdly, and far the most important, was the tremendous annual export of store beasts, particularly lambs, to England. Of this last category Richard Phillips was prepared to say that, with its inclusion in the general figures, it could be proven that Wales was self-supporting for meat if left to itself, and that it could maintain entirely from its own resources a higher ration than the present one. It was possible, even, that rationing could be dispensed with without recourse to any importation of meat.

I thanked Phillips for the vast amount of work which he had done to provide these few simple figures, and was about to go when he asked me if I was free that evening. I said that I was free, but would be at Lampeter. Whereupon he offered to pick me up from there in his car and take me to see a small dairy farm which he and some of his colleagues had assisted the tenant to plan. We arranged to meet at the Black Lion Hotel, and I took my leave.

On arrival at the Black Lion I found myself in the midst of a wedding party. The guests, male and female, were partly concealed by individual button-holes and sprays, respective to sex, of white carnations backed by a fistful of fern. So large were these embellishments that a mixed darts four in the bar reminded me of primitive native hunters hurling spears from behind a bush. All, however, were cheerful. I joined in the merriment until lunch-time and might have lingered longer but that I remembered I was to meet the Principal of St David's College at three o'clock, and was nervous of making an entrance into his house heralded by the fumes of ale.

I arrived in the College with a few minutes to spare. There were two main buildings, separated by wide, well-kept lawns. It was now vacation time and I could discover no one in the grounds to direct me. At the side of the larger building, however, I discovered a door marked 'Principal.' I rang the bell; rang again; and yet again. Presently I tested the latch, found the door to be unbarred, and entered the hall. The first sight which greeted me was, on my right-hand side, a very long row of clerical hats on hooks, and nestling among them one huge straw cartwheel hat, gaily coloured, and of obvious feminine ownership. I prowled about unremarked by any, coughed a time or two, and tried to stamp with my rubber-soled shoes. At last, defeated, I retreated past the hats into the open air, and began a cautious circumnavigation of the building. An arch in the main frontage led me into a pleasant quadrangle, cloistered at the far end. Here I found notice-boards, with directives signed by the astral Principal.

By this time, a feeling of unreality possessed me, and when I saw a door marked 'Principal' I refused for a moment to fall into the trap, for I knew perfectly well that that door belonged round the side, and was, in any case, a snare. A second glance revealed wording beneath 'Principal.' I moved closer and read nervously.

"Don't ring," it said. "Enter and close the door. Pass through and close next door. Knock on study."

I looked back through the striped shadows of the cloisters, quite prepared to see the White Rabbit scuttling towards me with anxious glances at his watch. He was evidently very late indeed, and there was nothing for it but to go on alone. This I did, meticulously obeying instructions. Within the second door I found myself in a hall. On my left hand side was a very long row of clerical hats on hooks, and nestling among them one huge straw cartwheel hat, gaily coloured, and of obvious feminine ownership.

This is monstrous, I thought indignantly. A few minutes ago the hats were on my right-hand side.

I was confusedly working out how objects were positioned when seen through a looking glass, and was sympathizing with the difficulties which Alice must have experienced, when I noticed opposite me across the hall the door through which I had made my first entrance from the side of the building. I was still a little uncertain whether I had been baffled by geography or bedevilment, and rapped quickly on the interior door which I took to be the study. I entered, at a voice, and was relieved to be greeted by the Principal. The Rev. H. K. Archdall was not very clerical in appearance. He was, I knew, a much-travelled Irish-Australian. Had he worn a secular collar he might have been taken for anything from a rancher to a politician.

I sat down opposite his desk, and found myself surrounded by learning in the form of books which lined all the wall-space from floor to ceiling, and which a later covert inspection proved to bear mostly upon philosophy and theology. When I had begun to visit people at the start of my tour I had for the first few times been a little nervous of how to explain myself; how to tell what information I wished to extract. Often I had not known what I wanted, though, like a prospector, I may have felt that some precious metal or other was there to be found. With a little experience I developed a technique of letting the talk wander wherever it might be edged by statement or question, and almost always a trend manifested itself after what had first seemed aimlessness.

On this occasion, not a trend, but a positive stampede took place immediately when I referred to St David's as a theological college. It was not, I was told firmly, any such thing. It was an independent college which taught the classical languages, mathematics, Hebrew, and modern subjects such as chemistry, botany, and zoology. It was entitled to grant the degrees of Bachelor of Arts and Bachelor of Divinity. Though four-fifths of its students later entered Holy Orders, the College, just the same, gave what might be termed secular instruction in the Arts. Those students who dedicated themselves to the Church took a post-graduate course in the Theological Hall—the lesser of the two main buildings which I had seen.

Our conversation flowed more easily after time had begun to heal the wound caused by my false description of the College. Little by little I began to realize how remarkable had been the survival of St David's. For a hundred and fifty years the hand of most men had been against it. Yet it lived. In fact now it was by no means turning the bruised Christian cheek, and I detected in its recent militant history the fourteen years of vigorous leadership of the Irish-Australian Principal.

The College was founded in 1822 by Dr Thomas Burgess, Bishop of St David's, a broad-minded man for those days, who felt that culture of a general nature was not incompatible with religion. To-day, I suppose, many people feel that religion is not compatible with culture. George IV granted the College its first royal charter in 1829, and three further charters were granted before the end of the century.

Apart from the original poverty of the foundation, not much helped by a disinterested Church of England, the Holy Stranger of Canterbury, and doubtless harried by Welsh Nonconformity, a problem arose when about the year 1852 there was a movement to obtain university status for St David's. This movement certainly stirred up sects and cliques. Within a few years came a counter-suggestion that a University of Wales should be formed, and that possibly St David's might be a constituent College. At that time there was strong popular objection to the inclusion of theology as part of a Welsh university education. Perhaps the objectors were wise, for in those days of narrower thought the dogma of religion was ever a cause for quarrels, as for centuries it had been a cause for wars. St David's, however, held to Dr Burgess's tenets, refused to drop theology, and thus remained outside the University of Wales.

The University College of Aberystwyth was the first of the four colleges of the University of Wales to be founded. This was in 1872. It is significant of Anglo-Welsh relations that the new foundation received no State help. The £400 per annum of which St David's had been in receipt for fifty years—not a generous sum—was withdrawn at that time. The Cathedrals Act of 1840 had empowered the Ecclesiastical Commissioners to endow St David's, but no move was made by them to assist the lonely College which was fighting the battle of the Church of England in a Nonconformist Wales. This indifference was, no doubt, because the institution was Welsh.

I asked the Principal why Nonconformity had gained such a quick and strong initial hold upon Wales. His opinion was that the French Revolution, which had profoundly affected Welsh thought, had prepared the ground. Old Iolo Morganwg had done his bit here. It must be remembered that when the Welsh people put their Henry Tudor upon the throne they had thought their days of oppression were done. They put up with enactments from the Tudors which, from other rulers, would have roused them to bloody rebellion. Their squirearchy was deliberately anglicized by this ruling house, and the common people were left to find their own salvation without their brilliant traditional leaders. There must have been resentment against the great families, now largely absentees.

This resentment came to include the Church, whose ministers were often products of English universities, and were also hand in glove with the squires, when these were to be found at home. In other words, there was a reaction against a squire-church authority which had ceased to speak for its own country. The discontent was stirred by the new ideas of brotherhood which permeated across the water from revolutionary France. The ideas were probably cleansed of their bloodstains by the time they reached Wales. They came in the ideal form, not in their practical shape of animal blood-lust. They must have seemed attractive to a leaderless people who ruminated on their history of successful defiance to great pressure, and who felt that the mighty of their race were now fallen to the enticements of the enemy.

The heralds of Nonconformity found minds fertile to germinate the seed of their instruction. "Away with our traitor leaders and their Church sycophants," the people cried. They accepted Nonconformity as a weapon to break spiritual bondage, and speedily found the new tool to be a new master. Their traditional gaiety left the Celts. They plagued themselves with the terrors of the new dogmas. They wore repentance like a hair-shirt to exorcise devils by which, perhaps, they had never been possessed. They lay shivering in the shadows, and shrank from the sunlight in which Jesus had expounded his philosophy.

I believe that the bitter interpretation which a large section of the Welsh have put on Nonconformity is out of character with the ebullient nature of the race and that the mixture has gone sour. There are many signs in Wales of a more open approach to religion. Within this century I think we shall see the chapels changing to centres of happiness from being, sometimes, prisons of repression. Yet their ministers are a fine body of sincere men who devote their lives to the furthering of their convictions, and take a pittance of money with which, somehow, they feed and clothe themselves and their families. This poverty in itself tends to breed a bitterness and narrowness which cramps the wide objective outlook.

I have spoken in Wales with many people who are tired of bigotry. I have heard of a bishop who has stated that he could fill the livings of his diocese with ministers who would leave Nonconformity. I do not know if this is true, or, if true, desirable. But I am certain that the trend is towards broadmindedness and enlightenment, and that goal certainly is desirable.

Whatever the future may be of Nonconformity, there is no doubt that Wales owes to the Methodist revival in the last half of the eighteenth century its release from a mental apathy which had persisted since the Edwardian Conquest.

The Principal of St David's confirmed the accuracy of the impressions I had gained throughout Wales. He said that, while the College had at times not had co-operation—to say the least of it—from Councils and from the University of Wales, a change had set in. Several benefactors of the College were now Nonconformists. Indeed, before I left, he showed me a magnificent set of oak-tables and forms which had been presented by a Nonconformist for use in the dining-hall.

We talked a little of the Welsh character. The Principal remarked on the brilliant intellect of many of his students who had come from the poorest of homes. He was almost prepared to say that there were no intellectually stupid Welshmen. It was, we agreed, in the application of their intellect that often the Welsh failed. There is no doubt that the Welshman does not like to face unpleasant facts. Ignore them, he hopes, and they will vanish. This is the attitude of a subject with delirium tremens. In defence of it, I feel, however, that English eyes, or Irish-Australian ones for that matter, see values differently. Many a train of events which would exercise an Englishman's mind to the utmost would rouse no interest in a Welshman. He must not be chided, therefore, if he remains unmoved by some problem which would, in England, be a burning one. However, there are plenty of problems which do come within his range of evaluation, and too often he refuses to recognize them. Here, once more, is the Eastern touch.

Abroad, in his travels in Australia, New Zealand, and the Americas, the Principal had found Welshmen mostly in prominent positions. Perhaps this was because in an alien country they were forced to stand on their own feet in practical matters. They could not rest on the ready sympathy of their own race, nor let the present do its worst while shielding themselves with thoughts of the historic past. Their lively intelligence was forced to switch its focus from the abstract to the concrete.

The Principal walked me round his College, which was pleasantly laid out, and well designed and equipped in spite of the many handicaps under which it had suffered. As we strolled he told me rather guardedly of a new development. Nearly a year previously the College had brought an action in the Chancery Division of the High Court of Justice against the Ministry of Education. The object of the action was to gain a declaration that the College was a University, and was as such entitled to certain benefits for students. I obtained later a verbatim transcript of Mr Justice Vaisey's judgment. It was the first such which I had read unabridged, and, apart from my interest in it because of St David's, I found it fascinating in itself. The judicial mind points its expression with a sword of clarity which slices through every knot of complexity and circumlocution left tangled by lesser brains.

The whole affair seems to have been conducted most amicably. Even when this is not so, however, I understand that the opposing advocates are frequently inimical in court only, and, a case ended, doff their wigs and dine together.

When the parties met to hear judgment delivered Mr Justice Vaisey first complimented both sides upon the manner in which each had treated the other: evidently an "After you, Claud" affair. Then he enumerated the grounds upon which a tutorial establishment might claim university status. These were that it should be incorporated by the highest authority—that was, he said, the sovereign power which succeeded in this country papal authority; it must be open to students from the world over; there must be a plurality of masters; one at least of the higher faculties must be taught, by which he meant, he said, theology, law or philosophy, or medicine; that students must reside in or near the institution; that the institution must have power to grant degrees.

Mr Justice Vaisey then decided that St David's College possessed all these desiderata in full, except the last, wherein its power to confer degrees was limited to Bachelor of Arts and Bachelor of Divinity.

The learned judge then asked himself the question whether the man in the street really regarded St David's, with its one hundred and seventy students and faculty of a dozen or so, as a university. He was bound to say that he did not think so. On this he stated that he was unable to make the declaration of university status asked by St David's, the plaintiffs.

The Principal, however, seemed well satisfied with the result of his action, though the College had not won, for its status was now clarified. I guessed that Ministerial authority had been stirred to action by the searchlight of publicity, and that benefits to the College were soon to accrue. The action was probably a masterly tactical move camouflaged as strategy, and I daresay the idea emanated from the shrewd and pugnacious Principal.

I wished the Rev. H. K. Archdall good-bye and good fortune in his administrative battle, and walked back to the Black Lion, where Richard Phillips was waiting for me.

It was a beautiful evening, the country glowing with the peculiar luminosity of late sunshine. Phillips drove at a leisurely pace, discoursing on this and that. I told him how interested I had been in his figures of Welsh livestock production, and suggested that with a proper programme of assistance and advice they could be improved to a point where the country, if self-governed, could not only dispense with rationing, but export a surplus to England. Phillips agreed, and said that the farm we were about to see would show me how readily possible this was.

Now, just as national economic advisers ignore all factors but the industrial, so, I find, do many agricultural advisers—themselves ignored by the first sort—ignore or take little note of upland farming. Therefore when I said that Wales, especially, should look to its hill and marginal lands for the greatest percentage gain in any scheme of regeneration Phillips would not fully agree. He said that the farm we were about to see—a dairy farm—was the sort on which to concentrate. He added that he had no doubt one could grow wheat on top of Snowdon after using gold-dust for fertilizer. We argued happily until, having passed through the village of Llandyssul, we took to the lanes, and arrived at last in a farmyard.

I had been told something of what to expect. The farmer, Mr Evans, was a tenant. His house and buildings had been poor, and the land mid-way between marginal and good. Phillips and two or three of his colleagues had offered to advise on planning for milk production. They planned crop rotations and advised on seeds. In return the farmer costed his operations meticulously. The result was that the farm produced annually twenty thousand gallons of milk from sixty-eight acres, on a minimum purchase of foodstuffs from outside.

Mr Evans was a small, quiet young man, with a keen face and a reddish tinge to his hair. He was in the roughest clothes, as befitted a working farmer at close on milking-time. As we walked round the fields the pattern became clearer. Evans treated his land largely as a grass factory. He was able to give the soil plenty of muck, and to supplement it with artificial fertilizers. As a result it carried nearly a cow per acre, and produced the bulk of the winter fodder in the form of silage.

Evans attached great importance to controlled grazing, and practised the strip method with the help of electric fencing.

I began to think of the primitive farm-buildings we had seen in the yard. They had been improved as much as was possible, and were scrupulously clean, but their lay-out was not helpful to large-scale milk production. I thought also of the labour of hauling silage daily from the pits in winter, and of the tremendous work of intensive field cultivation. I asked how many men Mr Evans employed.

He employed one man and one boy. The boy would not long be with him because he had come to do his National Service on the land rather than in the Forces. Nor was the lad interested in farming so much as mechanics. This complaint is a usual one, for the rising generation look upon both stock and land only as an excuse to drive machinery. The refinements of husbandry bore the present young.

Evans said that, if he could find one more reliable adult worker, he could still further increase production: he was prepared to pay very good wages. He said too that he did not ask his people to work week-end overtime, because few labourers were prepared to do so. As a result he and his wife had become slaves to their stock.

I was interested to listen to Evans and Phillips talking of the individual fields through which we walked. They discussed the history of each, the future management, the production figures in terms of crop or grazing with the exactitude of engineers chatting about a set of precision machines. Evans and his advisers had, without doubt, built a grass and silage factory whose turnover was a matter for scientific calculation. There was something rather cold about the thought, but I suppose the norm of production must to-day be turned loose on the land.

Mr Evans was urgently wanted at the milking, and after we took our leave of him Phillips suggested a detour on the return journey. As we drove, casting appraising eyes at the countryside, he said that what Evans had done others could do. He thought that too many Welsh farmers were too conservative.

He began to describe some researches he had been making over a long period into stock mortality, fertility, and weights of fat stock when slaughtered. The most favourable figures, working from west to east, came from the low ground of Pembroke, in the South, and the Lleyn Peninsula, in the North. Further inland there was a trend towards higher mortality and lower weights, with big local fluctuations, until the breadth of England was traversed. In the eastern counties the figures were good again. Phillips had sought the reason for this consistent regional condition. He had tried to find a common factor whose variation matched the changing stock statistics. He examined soil, rainfall, altitude, latitude, and other factors. In the end only one fitted into the puzzle. Sunshine figures could be superimposed on the stock figures, and proportionately matched with them, largely overriding other considerations.

I suppose man, from the earliest days, has not blindly worshipped the sun without the prompting of sound instinct. Phillips was satisfied that the warmth of the mother, or, as some astronomers claim, the foster-mother, of our planetary system was a prime agent to promote fertility, disease resistance, and bodily growth.

We had by now come to a moorland region. Phillips gave an exclamation, stopped the car, and we stood on a viewpoint which disclosed mile upon mile of rolling country. My companion was quite excited.

"Well!" he exclaimed. "It's a long time since I've been this way. There's a great change."

As far as we could see was good grassland which was just then supporting large numbers of ewes and lambs, obviously in thriving condition. The W.A.E.C. Phillips told me, had taken over these moors during the War, had ploughed through the gorse and heather, and finally sown to grass.

I pointed out in some triumph that this illustrated my earlier argument; that the production of few lowland farms could be increased five-fold, but that that of most upland farms could be so. Phillips, still tut-tutting and peering here and there into the gentle hollows, and over the soft-rising ridges, did not directly answer, but muttered again and again, "Remarkable! Splendid!"

Here and there we saw land which showed signs of reversion to the wilderness. Phillips said that newly won pasture should be ploughed and reseeded after the first four or five years, but that the necessity for this would become less frequent as time went on.

For the rest of our drive back to Lampeter, where Richard Phillips said good-bye, I brooded on the rich upland heritage of Wales and other parts of Britain, which lay like a hoard of buried talents, waiting men with the vision to dig them out and put them to use.

CHAPTER SEVENTEEN

Llangadog—Welsh National Party—Tomato-growing—Carreg Cennen and the Last Llywelyn—Llandilo, an architectural achievement—Black Mountains and coloured cottages—Limestone and Rebecca riots—Going 'over the hill'—The fairies of Llyn y Fan—An Eisteddfod y Plant—Teetotalism—The case for Home Rule—The words of the old man of Pencader

GWYNFOR Evans, the President of the Welsh National Party, lived a little way outside Llangadog. He had arranged to meet me in the town, for his farm lay, he had said, up a complex series of byroads in which I would lose myself.

I was most interested to find out what kind of man my host would be. I wondered whether he were crank, fanatic, politician, or something more. He was continuing the course pointed out by the later part of the great tradition of the House of Cunedda. The aim of the House, consistently, had been the independence of Welsh race and territory, until the Tudors' deliberate policy of Welsh-English unification.

I wondered whether the giant sword of the ancient Princes were not too heavy a weapon for the National Party to wield easily. I had reasons for so wondering, and hoped that the President would not take offence when I put them to him.

My first surprise was Gwynfor Evans's age. I suppose my rucksack had marked me out, for he drew his car alongside me and verified my name. I entered the car. When I looked at him I judged him to be in the early thirties; a tall, rather fair man. As we drove along I studied him more closely. He had a determined chin and mouth, and the eyes of a man who sees his goal clearly, but sees too the difficulties of the way. He was, I thought, of the quality which makes a martyr, and which, perhaps, prefers personal abnegation so that others may gain the reward which it purchases. Perhaps

I was reading too much in a fleeting glance, for our conversation was about tomatoes.

Gwynfor Evans grew tomatoes on a large scale. We stopped a moment by his glasshouses, nearly two acres of them, and he took me on a quick tour. Although it was but Easter, the plants in the most forward house were forming the third truss of fruits. I thought of our few plants at home, whose seed my wife had germinated in the airing cupboard, and was rendered silent as I thought of the soil sterilization, the pinching-out, the tying-up, and, indeed, the picking, which there would be on such a scale as I now saw.

Evans was no longer planting out his seedlings in boxes, but in compressed blocks of loam and peat, pot-shaped, which he made with one of the types of compressing tools now on the market. He claimed that the earth-blocks took less space than the boxes, and that there was no further transplanting with them since they were put straight into the beds without disturbing the plants growing in them.

There were no labour problems. It was a clean occupation, much sought after. Four or five men were employed the year round, and at picking time half a dozen women came temporarily to help.

I remarked on the size of the latest and largest heating boiler, and learned that it burnt over a ton of anthracite a day.

"Welsh anthracite," Evans pointed out, "mined just over the mountain there. I buy it from the English Coal Board."

We reached the house in time for lunch. Mrs Evan's mother was staying for the week-end; I found that there were six Evans children, ranged from nine years to a few months; and learned that the maid had fallen downstairs quite recently and broken her arm. Mrs Evans, however, seemed unperturbed at the addition of another hungry mouth. The children ate in a lair of their own, although every now and then a pair of eyes peered round the door to examine the foreigner. The young ones and I could not say much to one another, for they spoke no English, and I had largely forgotten my little Welsh during the War and the years after.

Gwynfor Evans had the day free both from his farm and his political activities—unless, indeed, I was one of the latter—and after lunch we began a leisurely drive round quite an area of Carmarthenshire.

We went first to the castle of Carreg Cennen. This was a natural choice for my guide, for it was a Welsh castle, built by the great Rhys family, which persisted through the centuries until Rhys ap Thomas marched to Bosworth with Henry Tudor. At one time, after the expulsion of the Normans from the greater part of Wales, the castle was a bastion against those of the invaders who retained their foothold along the easily penetrable coastal strip to the south. It sang its swan song to the tune of bowstrings in the day of Llywelyn ap Gruffydd—Llywelyn the Last—when his men took and held it as the high-water mark of his great endeavour.

We saw the castle first from a distance. It crowned a conical hill which rose from the floor of a broad vale. It sat squat and grim, and implacable on its eminence; I thought its position the most impressive in all Wales, the country of castles. Invader after invader had built, like Ozymandias, the monuments to his power, the footholds from which he never dreamed but that he would retain it. But the invaders were gone, and the Welsh people remained.

Here was the castle of the Welsh themselves, and unlike the others, the race which had built it lived about it, and spoke their language, and carried on their customs.

We left the car in a farmyard and climbed on foot a steep grass slope until we stood beneath the walls, which sprang from the rock below the turf on which we stepped. There was no pandering to the eye of beauty, no thought to the amenities of peace, about this castle. In the result it was handsome above all others, with the functional grandeur of a building dedicated to the one purpose. I was surprised to see how small were the stones of which the great curtain-walls were built. They were not, like those of Caernarvon Castle, for instance, huge dressed blocks, but small stones, such as a farmer might use in a boundary wall. Yet they had withstood, and they withstood still.

We went inside the confines, and to do so passed along a gallery, guarded by a low parapet, which led to the right-handed curved stairway through the thickness of the walls into the central court. The gallery was poised on the lip of a sheer and spectacular drop which fell to the valley bottom many hundreds of feet below. So steep was the drop that from this side the castle was unassailable, and the walls were but lightly pierced with arrowslits. Not even a Wolfe could have persuaded his men to scale those heights.

The atmosphere of great events lay so heavily within the walls that I think a sleeping man would have dreamed the past. Awake, and in daylight, my mind still was turned back just seven centuries to the occupation by the men of Llywelyn ap Gruffydd. A great prince was Llywelyn the Last; a prince who deserves an illuminated page in Welsh history, yet one who has been accorded too little honour. He died obscurely; his grave is lost; he is unsung. Yet he united Wales and its mutually suspicious princelings more completely than did his grandfather, Llywelyn the Great. He wrung from the reluctant English throne a complete and full recognition for himself and his heirs of the title "Prince of Wales." Yet the only title which was to sustain him to the end was that traditional inspiration "Lord of Snowdon."

At the Treaty of Montgomery, where Henry III of England was forced to accept Llywelyn's independence, the Welsh Prince was even conceded border-lands reft from Wales by the Norman free-booters of William I. The next decade was as glorious and as brief as an Indian summer, though there were rumblings of thunder towards the end of it, when Edward I came to the throne of England.

Llywelyn would pay no fealty to Edward, as did Alexander of Scotland. He did not attend his coronation. Perhaps in this intransigence he fell short of the statesmanship of his grandfather, Llywelyn the Great. As a result the tide turned and set against him. His brother David, ever jealous of him, was a friend of Edward. The border barons were urged against him—though they needed no more than a nod of approval to take up arms. The decade so brilliantly begun, ended with the Treaty of Aberconway, and Llywelyn ap Gruffydd was stripped of all his power except the Princedom of Gwynedd, where had always burned the small unquenchable flame whose intensity had ever and again set all Wales ablaze in revolt against subjugation. Yet even Gwynedd was now, by Treaty, without the rich lands beyond the Conway, and Llywelyn the Last took his troubles to the old, unchanging mountains of Eryri.

I wondered, as I prowled about the ruins of the castle of Carreg Cennen, whether Llywelyn had thought to re-establish his power there when he made his last desperate bid, springing, from the fastnesses of Eryri. Even brother David was now in sympathy with him, and Wales was at his back, internal dissensions subordinated to the hatred of English officialdom, which was oppressing the Welsh people to a degree which Edward did not realize.

Gwynedd was hard pressed, though not to be overrun by any sudden assault, and Llywelyn slipped south to enthuse the men of Mid-Wales and to distract the English from the northern mountain keep. On December 11, 1282, he died by a lance-thrust on the banks of the River Irfon, near Builth. His slayer, Stephen Frankton, knew not the man he had killed; the occasion was but a skirmish. Thus was the great cause lost which might yet have gained much had its leader lived.

Celtic prophecy often fulfils itself in a terrible way. It had been said that Llywelyn would be crowned in London. The English severed his head from his body, took it to their capital, and crowned it ironically with ivy-leaves. A few months later Llywelyn's vacillating brother David was executed horribly at Shrewsbury.

Gwenllian, the daughter and only child of Llywelyn and Eleanor his wife, daughter of Simon de Montfort, was taken away and immured for life with the nuns of Sempringham. Thus, cynically, was the recognition of the rights of Llywelyn's heirs, given at the the Treaty of Montgomery, mocked.

Henry Treece writes of the betrayal of a pact. He tells of:

> The gentle lord who walked without a sword,
>   Believing tales of peace among the hills,
> Trusting the word, the signatory name,
>   Forgetting the black seasons of a race.

Yet history has a way of demanding payment. The English throne had not finished with the Llywelyns. Edward forgot that their blood lived on in the Mortimers, through the marriage of Llywelyn the Great's daughter, Gwladys the Dark, with Ralph. Over a century later Owain Glyndwr remembered, but failed to make a Mortimer Prince of Wales. But in 1486 Henry Tudor took Elizabeth Beaufort as Queen. She was a direct descendant of Ralph and Gwladys.

Gwynfor Evans too was brooding. I said something of my thoughts about the last Llywelyn.

"It was a tragedy the way he died, and the time he died," he said. He might have been speaking of a friend who had lost his life in a recent war, so fresh in his mind was the memory of the man who was killed six and a half centuries ago; a friend of promise, who might have achieved much.

It is thus that the Welsh remember what has gone before. There is no past; there is only the root of to-day.

Gwynfor and I explored farther. We went deep beneath the castle down a passage-way eaten out of the rock on which it was built. A little light filtered through holes cut through the face of the great precipice. Down here, in the heart of the hill, was the water-well. Down here too were dungeons to strike a chill in the heart.

We left Carreg Cennen, and Gwynfor Evans drove on, making a circular tour. We went through the village of Llandilo, which I thought most interesting. It had been burned down towards the end of the eighteenth century, and was then largely rebuilt. The architecture was plain, and as satisfying to the eye as the Georgian style of England. It proved to me that until the Welsh became bad copyists of the Victorians, they were capable of working out their own architectural salvation.

Gwynfor Evans had recently been elected to the County Council —an achievement for a man of extreme political views—and he stopped here and there to thank his supporters for their help. One such place was a smithy. It was the tidiest I had ever seen, well painted, and garnished about with trees and shrubs in tubs. The smith was a great man for music and singing, as was his wife, and a large shed, no longer used for anvil and bellows, had been converted to a choir-room. Here met the people of the scattered farms to practise for their competitions. In his own village of Llangadog, Gwynfor told me, the chief artistic club was run by the cobbler, who sponsored a literary circle.

We continued on our way, and passed a house which had, I understood, belonged to the Rhys ap Thomas who had gone to greet Henry Tudor at Milford Haven. I thought the place looked rather modern, and, remarking so, was told that it had been rebuilt. I felt that my conductor disapproved of the modern construction on the foundation of Rhys's edifice.

My eyes had long been set upon the outlines of the Black

Mountains, to the east of us, and presently Gwynfor Evans turned towards them. He suggested that we should drive over their crest, and pointed out that in the south the contours of the hills were such that roads passed over the mountains and not, as in the north of Wales, between their rugged peaks.

I began to be impressed by the neatness of the countryside in Carmarthenshire. The cottages were beautifully kept; their walls colour-washed in blues, pinks, and creams; their gardens brilliant in rivalry. In dour Gwynedd there was no such pandering to the softness of life. The nature of the country was hard as the rock whose contorted shape formed it; the dwellings functional to the point of grimness; the spirit of the people tempered by labour, climate, and warfare. Yet it was Gwynedd I loved.

We had a mild argument about the respective virtues of North and South. Gwynfor Evans had to admit that the strength of the nationalist movement lay among those untamed Northern mountains, but he maintained, and rightly, that the intellectual force now lay to the southward of Eryri. The people of the South sharpened their wits in the world of industry and commerce, yet, Gwynfor insisted, they were not losing their identity.

The men of Gwynedd might still, to-day, follow a leader bearing a sword. The men of the South saw no glory in a forlorn hope, but would fall in behind the man whose weapon was subtlety.

There is a profound difference between Gwynedd and the rest of Wales. The change becomes marked in the region of Aberystwyth, the line running south-east towards the border by Builth. The farther south the greater is the gulf. To the north live the dark Iberian people, lightly mixed with Celt; hard people; fatalistic people; terrible enemies ruled by the head; warm friends, to such as they admit to friendship, ruled by the heart; quiet yet turbulent people unlike any others in the world, difficult to explain, and resentful of explanation.

The men of the Mid and South are bigger, blonder, more Celtic; perhaps more superficial. Although the men of Cardigan are said to be so shrewd in business that no Jew has set up shop in the county. At any rate, very few have.

As Gwynfor and I argued in a lazy sort of way the road mounted in curves and zigzags up the swelling slopes of the Black Mountains.

I was assured that in certain conditions of light the mountains did look black, though to-day, lying relaxed in sunshine, the short turf which clothed their limestone bones was very green. Man was burrowing here and there for the limestone, which was of special value in Wales to counteract the acid of the peaty soil.

In this small country were all the ingredients of prosperity. There were this and other limestone formations to counter-balance the peat; there were rich cereal lands in Anglesey, Lleyn, and Pembroke to complement the hill-grazings; there were minerals in the rocks; there were coalfields both north and south; there were safe harbours along the coasts and good fishing-grounds in the bordering sea. Yet Wales remained a poor country in spite of the wealth which was being wrested from the growth of her soil and from the strata which underlay it.

Here was an echo of the Roman cry: "Væ victis!" Woe, indeed, to the conquered. Yet Wales did not consider herself conquered. She spoke her tongue and followed still her way of life. In remaining the same she took too little note of new exploitations by foreign hands. Thus poor she remained while the wealth which she disregarded was transported to another land.

These limestone workings of the Black Mountains had been the indirect cause of the Rebecca riots of 1843. The small farmers would come with their horses and carts from the farthermost parts of Carmarthenshire, and from neighbouring counties too, to collect the one load of lime to which money and labour limited them. So many were the toll-gates through which they must pass that the addition of the many tolls often totalled more than the value of the lime. The Welsh have never taken kindly to this form of foreign oppression. To show that the old spirit was still bred in them, bands of men, behind a hefty leader in woman's clothes, struck here and there throughout the county, destroying the turnpikes. They kept close counsel, for it was a long while before authority was restored. Many of the turnpikes never were so.

The crest of our road crossed a divide which was not only a watershed, but a line of demarcation between two ways of life. We had at our backs the rolling pastoral landscape; in front of us the fringe of the South Wales coalfield. Yet, so Gwynfor Evans said, there was a close affiliation between the mines and the farms which had lost their sons to the pits. Looking back, Gwynfor pointed out a scattered community of holdings in the old Welsh pattern which did not take the form of a village. In the last century, he said, the pastor there had given a letter to each departing member of his flock to make introduction to the pastors of the mining villages to which they were going. In the space of forty years the pastor wrote a thousand letters for people who went over the hill. But the exiles kept in touch with home, and visited, and maintained their roots.

The population of that parish was now less than four hundred.

The coal valleys were predominantly Welsh, Gwynfor said, in spite of a big influx of English, particularly Somerset men. If the language was weak in the coalfields the Welsh customs were strong.

The Welshman without roots becomes as rudderless as a man without a belief. On my way through Wales there was scarcely a village where some one had not pointed out to me a cottage from which had sprung a man of note. Gwynfor agreed that such a manifestation was generally true, but said that over the last century or two there were areas which had not given the country many men of merit. Those were areas where there had been much dilution with foreign blood. He instanced Radnor and parts of Brecon. Here, he maintained, the people had become severed from their roots, and had wilted intellectually.

From where we stood we could see far to the west the outlines of the Mynydd Prescelly, from where the sarsen stones were taken to form the inner ring of Stonehenge. The Welsh claim a hand in this feat. As H. L. R. Edwards says:

> Pembroke to Stonehenge. With bleeding nails
> Lugging the holy sandstone through the scrub
> My countrymen, chanting.

But it must have been the Iberian strain of the Welsh who did the work, long before the Celts fused with them. Perhaps these stones were not hewn specially for Stonehenge, but were already erected in Pembroke. It is unlikely that this prodigious task of transportation would have been undertaken for the sake of just any old stones. They were certainly special stones, long steeped in the virtues of the essence of ancestors, and well fitted for a place in the new temple on Salisbury Plain.

Close by where Gwynfor and I had paused was Llyn y Fan Fach, which some say is the most beautiful lake in Wales. Gwynfor told me that recently some one in London had, as he put it, stuck a pin in a map and decided to use the area round the Llyn as a military training ground. Intense national opposition had scotched the scheme.

At Llyn y Fan Fach is the root of an extraordinary race-memory which flowered in historic times, when there lived at Myddfai, in Carmarthenshire, a widely respected family of herbalists and physicians. This family was said to derive from the marriage of a farmer with a fairy of Llyn y Fan.

One day, when the farmer was tending his sheep in the Black Mountains, he saw the fairy, like Aphrodite, rise out of the water. He fell in love with her beauty, but his advances at first were repelled. The fairy taunted him, naming him "Cras dy fara," meaning that he ate hard-baked bread. The farmer was a resourceful fellow, and, after returning home, went again to the lake, and wooed the lady with bread which had been soaked, whereupon she named him "Llaith dy fara," or man of the soggy bread. Nothing daunted, he finally tried her with bread lightly baked, and she allowed him to pay his addresses.

Her father said that he would give consent to a marriage if the farmer were able to pick his bride out from among her sisters, who were of identical appearance to her. The clever lover managed this feat, and the marriage took place. But there was a condition that he must never touch his new wife with iron.

The fairy brought with her a dowry of fine cattle, and the couple were very happy, though she forbade her husband to plough up the grass near the house. They reared a large family of children.

But one unfortunate day, when he was trying to halter a half-broken horse, the farmer accidentally touched his wife with an iron part of a bridle. Immediately she vanished, and her husband was left alone and desolate to brood over his lost love on the shores of remote Llyn y Fan where first he had seen her rise in her loveliness.

A famous authority on folk-lore, the late Sir John Rhys, Principal of Jesus College, Oxford, gives a list of interesting deductions from a summary of the many versions of the tale, of which W. J. Gruffydd writes in his book *South Wales and the Marches*. He deduces from the various accounts that the very ancient people were sallow, small, and lived in underground or lake dwellings; that they disliked the newfangled use of iron; that their homes were poor; that they viewed ploughing with suspicion; that they could only count to the extent of the numbers of their fingers; that they knew little of baking and less of the schooling of horses.

This may seem a great deal to surmise from a fairy story, however clearly it has persisted. Yet the more one probes folk-lore the more its incidents marry with the probabilities which archæologists and the like are only now beginning to relate to history.

A seed of fact lies at the root of almost every legend, however flamboyant is its growth.

Gwynfor Evans and I drove back to his house for tea, and afterwards he took me to an Eisteddfod in Llangadog. The meeting was held in a large marquee, for the Church authorities, I gathered, had forbidden the use of the Y.M.C.A. hall on Good Friday for so profane a purpose as the playing of music, singing of songs, and recitation of verse. I wondered whether Jesus would have issued a different directive.

On this particular evening it was an Eisteddfod y Plant—a children's competition. There must have been five hundred people in the tent: mothers grooming their young; fathers making last-minute admonitions; self-possessed young people grouped in the grass aisles in readiness to perform.

We heard recitations, duets, trios, choirs, and piano soloists. After each section of the contest one of the several adjudicators would give a detailed verdict, taking each competing child in turn, giving praise, blame, or encouragement, and announcing finally the winner. One soloist girl of thirteen years posed a problem, for she had elected to play Schumann's *Arabesque*. This seemed to me ambitious, for she was required to render the piece from memory. This she succeeded in doing without fault, and, what was more, put a virtuosity into her playing which surprised even the adjudicator, who sat behind her stool holding the music-sheet to check her notes.

The difficulty was that a boy of sixteen played his piece even better, which would have seemed impossible. The young lady was given second place because, apparently, her piece was one in which much was left to the interpretative imagination of the pianist, and the adjudicator had a feeling that he had heard one or two passages better expressed at the Albert Hall, in London.

We had sat a long time on our hard chairs, and I was a little tired too with the strain of trying to understand the gist of the Welsh pronouncements from the stage. I had relapsed into a semi-coma when I was startled into wakefulness by a short speech from the stage. The words might have flowed past my ears unheeded if I had not caught the English title of a previous book of mine. People were peering about at their neighbours, and began to clap in the rather threatening way which the French sometimes employ before they pelt an entertainer.

I started to look about me too, in the hope that I had misheard, but Gwynfor Evans gave me a nudge with his elbow, and said that I was wanted up there.

The Welsh are difficult people to follow on a platform. They are blessed with a complete lack of self-consciousness. I went up, made a kind of bow to the chief adjudicator, and shook hands. We had a little talk, and I hoped that that would be the end of it, but as I made to go away the adjudicator directed me to say a few words out loud to the audience.

This request, somehow, I managed to fulfil. It occurred to me to mention that the Welsh Eisteddfod was a unique survival in British life, and from there the path led easily to one or two other apposite remarks. Indeed, inspired by the atmosphere of peroration in which I had for so long sat, I might have run on for quite a time, except that I saw the children next for duty becoming restive.

When I returned to my chair Gwynfor seemed quite pleased.

"I'd no idea they'd get you up there," he whispered, "but it went very well, impromptu."

I looked at him with sharp recollection. I remembered that soon after our arrival he had written a note and had it passed to the stage. It was obvious that he had been responsible for the publicity. It was not so much that which I minded, as that I had innocently lent him my pen with which to write his note.

We left soon afterwards, and Gwynfor took me for a stroll through the lamp-lit streets of Llangadog. I was very ready for a glass of ale, but it was at the back of my mind that my host was teetotal. And so he was, for, sensing my feeling as we passed one cosy inn after another, he suggested that I refresh myself while he awaited me. This I did not feel able to do, and asked from what reason sprang his antipathy to strong drink; not, I pointed out, that beer deserved that title these days.

As usually was the temperance reply to such a question, it was because evil followed in the train of alcohol. There had once, I was told, been eighteen inns to serve the thirsty inhabitants of Llangadog village. Their numbers had been stimulated by the customers of the limestone quarries which we had seen earlier that day. The visitors had often put up for the night at Llangadog before they went on next morning to the Black Mountains.

We did not have an argument, for Gwynfor Evans was one of those eminently reasonable men who would not belabour others with personal prejudices. He half agreed with me that there was no preoccupation which could not, by excess, be turned to vice, whether it was love of woman, keenness on sport, or a liking for a glass of ale. Even excessive overt worship of God might become religious mania.

Later that night at Gwynfor's home we were left to ourselves, with the rest of the house abed. We sat in a large room which had once, I guessed, been the farm kitchen, for the bacon-hooks were still in the beams of the ceiling, and the dog-grate burned within a deep recess where once must have been a cooking-range. Midnight is an intimate hour, and I found it easy to say what I felt.

I felt that two factors worked against the establishment of a truly national National Party: geography and suspicion.

Geography had constructed Wales in pockets which, even to-day, were almost watertight. For instance, to travel by rail the eighty miles from Conway to Aberystwyth required six hours and at least two changes. There was no through motor-road from north to south. National committees and councils, such as those of the Eisteddfod and the University of Wales, met usually in Shrewsbury, which was a more convenient venue from all parts of Wales than was any town within the country.

Geography too interfered with national broadcasting from Cardiff, for Northern listeners could not receive their own home programme. Television viewing would prove to be even more restricted when the new transmitter was set up outside Cardiff.

This barrier of topography within the country had always been a barrier to the mutual exchange of Welsh ideas. It continued to be a barrier even in this modern day.

But suspicion was the greatest enemy which the National Party must face. Suspicion comes readily to the Welshman. Because of the watertight pockets of countryside in which he had dwelt so long he is wary of those who live across the mountain, for, often developing in different directions, neighbouring districts have not seen eye to eye. Overriding this internal distrust was the general suspicion in which the people over the border were held, a suspicion which successive races—Jutes, Angles, Romans, and Normans—had done their worst to justify. Any Welsh political party which hoped to obtain general backing must therefore disarm the mistrust which the native people have been taught by history to use as a protective shield against threats both within the country and outside it.

Gwynfor Evans did not disagree with me. He realized, of course, how the poor communications within the country militated against a cohesive line of action. The warlike past had pointed the handicap time and again. But he did insist that the Party was well aware of the difficulty, and that they had striven to have it removed. The trouble was, he said, that, joined as it was to the English economy, Westminster was concerned only to have good access into Wales from the border. The Welsh demand for a central north to south road had been kept in a pigeon-hole without proper examination.

An excuse to refuse the construction was given by the Labour Government in 1946. They said, according to Hansard:

"Such a road would have to traverse mountainous country at a height of over eight hundred feet, and would be both difficult and expensive to construct."

Gwynfor and I thought that any Continental engineer would make no great fuss about such a work even if a nought were added to the altitude figure.

On the other hand, Gwynfor was not sorry that the mountains would bar universal television until in the end numerous transmitters were set up. He feared television's impact on Welsh life, as he deplored the effect of the impact which films and radio had already made. This attitude, I thought, was defeatist. These inventions, whether retrograde or progressive, had come to stay. The Party could not, like a collective Canute, stay the tide. They could, however, like Maelgwn seated on his chair of goose-quills, float with it. They could do their utmost to see that a sufficient proportion of Welsh radio programmes tied with the traditional past, and that when television became commonplace the Welsh way of life was adequately depicted.

As to Welsh distrust of the new idea, my host had less to say. But he did know that many of his countrymen showed little interest in the aim of the Party of which he was the President, whether their reason was antipathy or indifference.

I took the risk of telling him what I had learned in many a conversation with many people in different parts and of different occupations. The Welsh, I believed, were afraid, not of nationalism, but of the National Party. One man of the North, an old friend, had been frank enough to say that, while he was, for the sake of his upbringing, prepared to be dictated to by the Nonconformist conscience on one day in seven, he was not prepared to listen to its dictation all week. Then there was the strong pacifist flavour of the Party. Gwynfor Evans himself was a sincere pacifist, as, I believe, every thinking person must be in theory. But a person who thinks deeply realizes that the way to godliness is long, and that pacifism is not practical until the human race nears the end of the road.

From a financial viewpoint, it is easier to reduce taxation if there are no military obligations to fulfil. Yet the Party does not wish to take Wales out of the Commonwealth, to which the Welsh people themselves have lent the title 'British.' If a self-governed Wales remained within the Commonwealth it could not gain financial easement by refusing to pay for its share of arms and fighting men unless it lost honour. That, I had reason to believe, the Welsh people were not prepared to barter for temporary financial gain.

Gwynfor told me that, as was well known, his own convictions were pacifist, but that a Welsh Government would reflect the will of the Welsh people, whatever that might be. Again, this theory was sound. But in practice does a Government always reflect the will of the people? Often it becomes an old man of the sea riding the nation's back in perverse directions. The people of the country, I thought, knew of this danger, and feared it.

On another cause for mistrust we were in full agreement. Welsh local politics have a bad name among the electorate. I had been told time and again over a period of many years that the members of councils and committees were all too often self-seeking to an unusual degree. Recently people had instanced to me this unfortunate trait in minor politics, and had said how much the more scope there would be for its exercise in a Welsh Parliament.

Others had asked who was to govern the country if Home Rule was won. Few Welsh members of the Westminster Parliament had been men of stature. Of recent years they had ever been willing to let the cause of their country go by default. In the judgment of their own country, while some may have been reasonably good Parliamentarians, most had been poor Welshmen. The people felt that they would not find the leadership they wanted from among the ranks of those who had served in Westminster.

After all, political work to-day is no longer a sinecure, but a full-time occupation. Welsh men or women who wish to make politics a career must strive in the larger sphere of the London Parliament. There they are caught up in affairs nine-tenths of which are no concern of Wales directly. Their racial identity is lost, and their national feeling stultified.

The Welsh are a race who may be moved temporarily in either of two ways: by an appeal to the reason of the head; by a call to the inspiration of the heart. But neither method alone will hold their attention for long. To grip them permanently they must be shown the cold blue-print of a plan, and at the same time their enthusiasm must be fired by colourful leadership. They wish the simultaneous appeal to heart and head.

The National Party have the blue-print, but I doubt if one Welshman in fifty has glanced at it. For this ignorance the Party is not directly to be blamed, for men who could inspire the commonalty to read it are not made, but born; and that at rare intervals.

The blue-print plans a decentralization within the country so that families may own their farms or businesses. This is a good conception for the dignity of the human animal, and particularly for the Welshman, in whom runs so strong a vein of individual independence. It plans also for the application of co-operative principles in large ventures, and for the grouping for certain purposes of smaller ones. Thus the plan hopes to provide incentive.

There would be credit for agriculture to aid the immense marginal regeneration scheme, which is long overdue, and which would in the most conservative estimate double the output of the hill-lands.

There is a plan to electrify the country by means of both hydro and coal power-stations. The tourist industry would not be harmed by the hydro-schemes, for these need not be set up in areas where they would be detrimental to the scenery. Wales has a greater proportional surplus of coal than any nation in the world, and could well afford to drive the turbines of its power-stations by steam if the use of mountain water was not expedient.

The aim of the Welsh National Party is good, but I personally fear that the sights are out of alignment. I fear a driving-force which is as much anti-English as pro-Welsh, and which brands every move from Westminster as Imperialism. What is wrong with Imperialism? The strong will always overlay the weak, though often enough they do not crush the smaller nations, but breathe new life into them. This is not to say that Wales should not govern herself if she can find men of wide, liberal views to lead her. After all, if the Gold Coast is fit I daresay Wales is capable too. But I see a narrowness of outlook and a bitterness of mind reflected in the pronouncements of the Party. Intense patriotism is there, as is sincerity, but a policy conceived in hatred, born in intolerance, and suckled with the sour milk of disapproval will grow into a bitter princeling to rule a laughter-loving land.

I told Gwynfor these personal views, and he was not offended.

As we sat by the last lazy flickering of the fire we spoke dreamily of the country an independent Wales might become. She could feed herself, and, when her land was improved, even export meat and milk in exchange for such few crops as she could not grow. She had slate and stone for her houses. She had wool to clothe her people. She had lime, iron, lead, zinc, copper, and even a trace of gold. She had water-power. She had a great tourist industry. Above all, she had coal.

Coal would be the key to prosperity in an independent Wales. Its export sale would liberally provide the money for land improvement, houses, schools, and all the desiderata of modern government. For each living soul the known Welsh coal reserves are eight times greater than those of England and Scotland combined. Her miners produce at the rate of ten tons yearly for every man, woman, and child in Wales. The comparable English and Scottish figure is four tons. It is a fact too that the South Wales coalfield produces the more costly grades, including anthracite, the most valuable of all. There is here a golden source of revenue were Wales to retain the credit won by its mineral wealth.

The question is not so much "Can Wales do without England?" but "Can England, in the present state of her economy, do without Wales?" England is in no condition to drive a path contrary to world temper. Overseas it is a country which has been respected, but rarely loved. Weakened and impoverished, it would be wiser now for it to seek co-operation rather than to try to command an obedience which it can no longer enforce. English economy is poised to-day on so sharp a razor's edge that the withdrawal of Welsh contributions to the common exchequer might tip the balance on to the side of ruin.

I told Gwynfor of an incident which had happened to me in Devon not many weeks before. I was talking at a party to a retired English Major of the Regular Army, and remarked idly that my family and I were shortly going to Wales for a few months. The Major looked at me sympathetically. He said that he had never been in the country, but that he frequently heard the language broadcast from Cardiff. What damned impertinence it was, he thought, to take up useful air-space with their stupid tongue.

The average Englishman is often his country's worst ambassador. He usually has taken the stand that it is improper for a nation to speak its own language in his hearing or continue its native customs within his view.

Gwynfor went to a cupboard and withdrew from it a roll of parchment. He explained that the lettering, in Welsh, was a facsimile of an inscription which the National Party was about to set up at Pencader, not far away. The words had been spoken by an old man in that village to England's Henry II. Henry had asked what the peasant thought of his army, and whether it could subdue the rebellious people of Wales.

In free translation the old man of Pencader had answered:

"This nation may indeed be oppressed, and, to a great degree, weakened and destroyed by your powers, O King, and by others who may come after you. It will suffer now and many times again under the weight of its deserts. But never shall the race be destroyed completely by the wrath of man, unless one day the wrath of God be joined to it.

"At the day of Judgment, so I believe, O King, no other race, and no other language save ours, shall answer for this Welsh corner of the earth."

Gwynfor put away his scroll, and we trooped off thoughtfully to bed.

CHAPTER EIGHTEEN

I fall into a religious schism—Brecon—Congregational College—My energetic host—Magnificent farm-houses—Potent cider—Dafydd Gam and Owain Glyndwr again—The ladies and 'Sospan Fach'

I SAID good-bye to the numerous Evans family next morning, and Gwynfor, on his way to a meeting at Aberystwyth, dropped me off in the village of Llangadog. We were shaking hands at parting when I was accosted by a parson. I remembered him as the army padre who had been at the Airborne Forces Depot when I became Commandant after the end of the War, and I recalled that he had once told me that he was taking up a living at Llangadog.

My wits could not have been working well at that hour of the morning, because, after we had chatted busily about old times, I noticed that my recent host and the parson were not communicating. Absurdly, I made the introduction, unmindful of the fact that the two must be well acquainted. There was an icy politeness in their mutual acknowledgments, and brief admissions that they did, of course, already know one another. I realized that the two must be in opposing camps, since their convictions on religion and war were so different, and that there must have been a very recent brush over last night's Eisteddfod and the use of the Y.M.C.A. hall.

I was quite glad to jump on a Brecon-bound bus to escape the coldness in the air.

This was an example of the intolerance which religion has brought to Welsh life, and which does not confine itself to ritual and dogma within the places of worship, but permeates many secular activities, isolating soul from soul. Man sets himself up to practise a discrimination which Jesus was at pains to avoid.

The day was Easter Saturday, and Brecon was very crowded.

I had been asked to spend the holiday week-end with an old friend of army days at a village outside the town, but before I moved on I wanted to call at the Congregational College. My rucksack had grown extraordinarily heavy owing to the repeated gifts of pamphlets from people I had visited, and, having bought goodwill with custom, I left it at a hotel. In a guide-book I had once read the terse statement about Brecon:

"Cathedral was Priory Church of St John. Mrs Siddons, the actress, was born in a public house in High Street."

But whether my pack was resting where once the feet of the Siddons had tripped, no one was able to tell me.

I found the Congregational College at some little distance from the town, and discovered the same vacation difficulties as at St David's, Lampeter, of finding the man I wanted. I was looking for the Vice-Principal, Dr Pennar Davies, and only provoked a response after the belated discovery of a side-door from within which I heard children's voices. It turned out to be the Doctor himself who opened to me, and asked me into his study. He was a big, fair man, looking more practical than the usual practitioner of religion.

I hoped to learn more about the trend of Nonconformity in Wales, and after some general talk about the country asked whether my impression was correct that there was a loosening of its ties. But the Doctor was an adroit fencer, and showed a subtle guard with a bland ease. I did gather from him that Nonconformity, in common with the Church in Wales, was affected by the general touch of indifference towards organized religion, but he avoided saying whether or not Nonconformity was suffering more than its share of that indifference.

We sparred cheerfully with each other until the Doctor's charming wife brought refreshments of tea and cake, after which I took my leave baffled by evasive discourse.

I walked back to where I had left my rucksack, guarded perhaps by the shade of Mrs Siddons. A slight tiredness told me that I was ready for an Easter break, and I prepared to enjoy it. Indeed, from past experience of my host, I feared that I might enjoy the week-end too much. I remembered Andy, my host-to-be, as the early-morning bane of a large mess. Breakfast is a grim meal in an army barracks. The hour is early; the waiters sullenly sleepy-eyed; the officers often making silent renunciation of late parties; the events of the day looming urgently, brooking no delay, demanding a spruce appearance and mentality which will stand the test of many disillusioned eyes. Yet at this forbidding meal, in spite of, or perhaps because of, a serious head-wound, Andy had always appeared in the guise of the cheerful cricket, his moustache a-bristle with vitamins, his face ruddy with health and carbolic soap, his greeting jovial and persistent against the defensive mechanisms of his fellows.

In the end we forbade him to speak at breakfast.

As, at last, I passed through the village at the far side of which Andy now lived, I found the street ripped up to a degree which required a long diversion for wheeled traffic. Although the purpose of the excavations was evidently to lay service mains of one sort or another, I was half-prepared to credit the eruption to Andy's ebullience.

I found him tearing at a waste patch in the corner of the garden of a brand-new house which, I later learned, he had but recently thrown up. His superabundant energy had, since our last meeting, snatched him a wife, a calm young lady who allowed the tide to flow past her, and also a son. Except for the moustache, the babe was very like his father, and equally cheerful.

Andy was now a Group Secretary for the National Farmers' Union, and in tweed cap and hacking jacket was as rural as he had once been military. I scarcely had time to drop my rucksack and wave at wife and baby, before I was touring the county in my host's car. He was on intimate terms with his farmers, whom he felt I should meet.

These Brecon farm-houses were unlike any I had ever seen in Wales. They were large as mansions, with spacious beamed rooms, huge fireplaces, and often with staircases of real splendour. At the very first we visited no one was about. Andy stumped through the door into the great kitchen, which was deserted, then through the chain of big rooms which was the ground floor. I followed more slowly, admiring the magnificent furniture, collectors' pieces put to the daily work for which they were intended. The oak of Brecon is different from that of the North. It is not the black bog-oak, but a dark golden wood glowing with light from within, and, in all cases that I saw, gleaming with a mirror-finish of surface polishing which must have been inherited from several generations of female arms.

Still no one appeared at this first place of call despite Andy's shouts and stamps. Whereupon he withdrew me from contemplation of an ancient dresser, laden with pewter and willow-pattern plates, and whisked me through the farmyard to an open shed in which stood two huge cider-barrels, with a capacity I should judge of seventy-two gallons apiece. Andy told me that the far one was empty and directed me to take the much thumbed glass from the top of the other, and fill it. This I did.

"It'll blow the top of your head off," Andy remarked.

Metaphorically, he was right. I handed him the glass, speechlessly.

"It's the one drink I can't touch," he said in smug refusal. "Bad for my head. You have another."

I did so, and clambered back into the car in a state of near-paralysis. I was well used to Devon cider, but it had no more fitted me to encounter this Brecon brand than an aptitude on a donkey fits a man to undertake the Grand National Course.

I did not find Brecon to be a typically Welsh county. It was delightful in soft scenery and pleasant architecture. The people reflected the comfortable spaciousness of their surroundings, but, in many cases, I felt that this very comfort was theirs at the cost of the underlying core of hardness of body and spirit which becomes more steely the farther one travels towards the North. Some plants flourish among rock, relishing rough weather, but fade to a shadow of their glory if translated to the ease of the herbaceous border. So I feel does the Welsh character become blunted without the whetstone of hardship.

One of Andy's friends was an auctioneer. He took me to visit him during the morning of Easter Sunday. Such fine furniture as I had already seen in the district was nondescript when compared with the pieces in the house of the auctioneer. Again, much of their appeal was because they were in full use. Many a man might have treated them as museum objects. When I had admired and breathed envy, I asked Andy's friend whether property was selling well in those parts. He gave me a few values from which to form an opinion, then remarked:

"By the way, Dafydd Gam's house comes up for auction next week."

I was, by now, fully reconditioned after my absence from the country to the co-existent past and present of the Welsh, and found no difficulty in slipping back five hundred and fifty years.

"Surely it was burned down," I said. "Old Owain Glyndwr set fire to it."

"Oh! Not that house," explained the auctioneer. "I mean the one he built when he came back from France with England's King Henry V."

Andy did not neglect evening entertainment either. On one night we repaired to an inn on the side of the River Usk. It was a convivial place. I talked to some of Andy's farmer friends who bewailed the lack of useful agricultural labour. Our discussion was interrupted by an invasion of women with, in their midst, one solitary male charabanc-driver. He looked as nervous as a captive among the females of a Bedouin tribe, and accepted a glass of stout from his dismounted passengers with an air of mingled suspicion and resignation.

The ladies, for the most part, took gin. None were young, few handsome, but all radiated good cheer. When their second drink came up, the ringleader, a plump matron in purple, waved a slow arm. Her companions formed a half-circle in front of her, and, at a signal, broke into the song *Sospan Fach*. The singing in a Welsh inn is always good; never a rowdy bawling. But this performance was extra special. If the singers were more homely than enticing, the quality of voice belonged with the angels.

There were riotous encores. The ladies obliged with *Bless this House*, and one listener wept freely. Finally, two of the old dears entranced Andy and me by rendering *My Brother Silvest* with more vigour than we had heard it receive from any battalion of fighting men. While the audience cried for more the ladies vanished as suddenly as they had come, their driver, distinguished by his peaked hat, swept away with them like a non-swimmer in a flood.

Some one in the bar told us that we had just heard the finest women's choir in all Swansea, who were on their return from a concert up-country.

It was satisfactory to reflect that we had all had a private performance.

On Bank Holiday Monday I said good-bye to Andy and his cheerful family, and took train for Cardiff. My rucksack bulged with pamphlets on Eisteddfodau, Hill Lamb Production, Self-government for Wales, the Rural Woollen Industry, and Is Monmouthshire in Wales?

I thought the information contained therein too weighty for a hiker.

CHAPTER NINETEEN

Cardiff, a raw new city—Glamorgan and the rest of Wales—B.B.C.—Provincial newspaper—Rhondda—The grey ghosts—Hywel and Blodwen—Tonypandy—Toll of the mines—Politics—Monmouthshire—Its allegiance—The mountain wall—The spiritual barrier between Welsh and English—Desire for independence—Old age of Y Draig Goch

CARDIFF was a busy city on that evening of Easter Monday. The sidewalks were blocked by cinema queues, and the public houses filled to the doors with a boisterous, friendly crowd. I realized suddenly that here in Cardiff and its county of Glamorganshire there now played and worked, loved and died, a half of the population of Wales. I wondered whether a man who, as I did, sought an up-to-date impression of the country should therefore spend a half of his time in Cardiff and Swansea and the coal valleys which fanned northward like the fingers of a hand.

To do so, however, would be to gain a distorted impression. Industry superimposes a pattern of life which varies but little from country to country, and which is not necessarily indigenous. The law of the machine is international. The real heart of Wales beats yet in the hills and cwms, and the men who have gone over the mountain, exchanging green grass for black diamonds, still have their roots in the pastures they remember from boyhood, and about whose freshness they sing when they are old men in the black shadows of the tips. It may not be very long since they left the pastures, for the dust of the hard anthracite grinds away time and often brings old age directly to meet youth.

There are ancient cities of the world which reflect a nation's history. A writer must give full place to Rome, London, or Paris when he tells of the countries whose story has for so long been interwoven with the life of their capital towns. But the newly expanded modern towns of South Wales have no place in Welsh history. They scarcely have a civic history of their own yet.

Cardiff to-day is a raw, gangling youth of a place. Nearly a quarter of a million people live there. A century and a half ago it was a babe among towns, with 1870 persons. At that time Merthyr Tydfil was the most considerable town in Wales with less than 8000 dwellers. This mushroom growth of the South seaports and the strips of dense population along the coal-measures has been too recent for the areas to do more than form a pattern of life for themselves. They have not swayed the greater, ultra-conservative extent of the rest of Wales. They cannot be read as a pattern of the whole country, but only as one more example of the exploitation of British industrial resources made in the catchpenny Victorian Age. This age made Britain rich, but now the other side of the balance sheet was being presented: the side where was debited ill-health; human and material waste as a result of lack of thought for the future; and, in Wales, the cost of uprooting a large section of the people rather than transplanting them with care.

As I thought these things in crowded Cardiff I felt that I would present a more accurate picture if I were to give Glamorganshire no more prominence than any other Welsh county. For though its coal and its industrial capacity are of great importance, and would be a tremendous factor were Wales to be self-governing, Welsh character has become so set in the mould of history that it will be long before it is easily altered by the pressure of industry.

When Bank Holiday was over, and the workers had gone back to their masters, the machines, I rang up the British Broadcasting Corporation, where worked the brother of a history lecturer whom I had met at Aberystwyth. I had not before met Hywel Davies, but he asked me to call on him at noon for one o'clock lunch. I found that the Cardiff studios of the B.B.C. were a conversion of dwelling-houses, and, whether convenient or not, had a more friendly and homely air than the morally therapeutic building in London.

Hywel Davies turned out to be quite young, big, burly, dark, wearing a moustache and a cheerful expression. When I came to know him better, I learned that he was a connexion of his namesake, Hywel Dda.

We lunched down in the canteen with the Director. I broached some of the problems which worried the National Party: the proportion of Welsh to English programmes; the need for more plays and talks in the Welsh vein, whatever the language; the fear that the proposed new television station would make a destructive impact on Welsh tradition. The answer was that the Cardiff station reached a large non-Welsh speaking public both within and without the country, and that it was necessary to serve up entertainment more in English than Welsh. There seemed to be difficulty too in encouraging enough good Welsh material.

One retort which the broadcasters made to the National Party was that the Party must accept the fact that radio was now a part of the home, and that, if they wished its voice to reflect the Welsh way of life, they must help to produce the suitable broadcasting material which was so difficult to find. It was of no use to pretend that radio did not exist, or, if its existence was admitted, that its effect must be retrograde.

The National Party has long sought to obtain for the country a Welsh Broadcasting Corporation. There would be both profit and danger in this. The profit is obvious for a race which is intensely jealous of its separate entity, the danger less obvious. The danger would be that the transmitter might be used as an instrument of propaganda. The result of the use of radio for political purposes can be seen in many Western countries. Those minds which are not drugged become embittered.

The Welsh Members of Parliament have not, as seems usually to be their way, done much to further Wales' claim for its own Corporation.

Lunching in the canteen that day was a journalist of the *Western Mail* group to whom I was introduced. Like so many progressive Welshmen I had met, it was my impression that he was as alive to his country's proper claim to self-government as was any member of the National Party, but, like the others of his calibre, was by no means certain that the best form of government would result from present political material. Hywel Davies became due to oversee his share of the ether, and, when he left us, the journalist and I walked through the city, arguing which taxes could be repealed were Wales free to sell its agricultural and mineral products

P

for its own benefit, and were it not placed statistically with England.

We came at last outside the offices of the *Western Mail*, and my new acquaintance asked me in to see the presses at work producing fodder for the minds of the people. The collection and dissemination of news gives impressive examples of man's ingenuity. Unfortunately, the product is a drug. It is not enough to take in news with the breakfast meal. The stimulant is required again at midday and at intervals from about 3.30 in the afternoon until late-night-final. To satisfy the addiction of the public the men who serve the printing presses work to a relentless time-margin, and keep up their strength by feeding on their own nerves. Wynford Jones, my new acquaintance, took me down to see the type-setting machines; the formes which set the reverse impression of the news-page; the rolling machines to which the formes were taken, covered with a 'flong' of papier mâché, and put through a mangling process which forced the type impression into the flong, now called a matrix.

We followed a matrix down to the basement, where I saw it within an ante-plate machine which flooded its surface with molten alloy, and delivered a curved metal printing-plate on which the recessed lettering of the matrix was transposed in relief. From this plate the paper was printed. There were seven printing-machines, each of which could deliver sixty thousand copies an hour.

As we watched I saw a machine flipping out its complete newspapers on to an elevator which took the batches aloft and delivered them to the open doors of the news-vans.

The process of news production is complex, the stages timed to the second, its success dependent on team-work. Printers are queer cusses. When Wynford Jones had first taken me into the type-setting room he was explaining to me the intricate machinery. An elderly man, not unlike a bishop in appearance except that his apron was oily, watched us dispassionately for a while. Presently he brushed past, and, as he went, thrust a pamphlet into my hand.

"Read all about it!" he said, wrinkling his nose at Wynford Jones. "It's got it right in here."

The pamphlet described the news-routine from first to last, and was simply entitled *How It's Done*.

I could not but think the printer's gesture more deflationary than kind, but Wynford Jones seemed resigned to it.

I went one day to Tonypandy, in the Rhondda Valley, to see a friend of Griffiths y Dydd. This vale I find not so depressing as the coal valleys to the east—as, for instance, the bleak upland of Dowlais Top, towards the head of the River Taff, where the barren pyramids of the tips stand as monuments to buried souls. I saw Dowlais Top once on a wet Sunday, with the mist lying not thick enough to hide the scars of the moors, and I have never forgotten it.

Yet the Welsh have a great capacity for making a home, and neither do they forget it, even if the home be set up in the industrial belt, whose atmosphere is alien to the pastoral history of their people.

Idris Davies gives a glimpse of the Welsh nostalgia:

Where are you going to, Hywell and Blodwen,
  With your eyes as sad as your shoes?
We are going to learn a nimble language
  By the waters of the Ouse.

We are tramping through Gloucester and through Leicester,
  We hope we shall not drop
And we talk as we go of the Merthyr streets
  And a house at Dowlais Top.

We have triads and englyns from pagan Dyfed
  To brace us in a fight,
And three or four hundred Methodist hymns
  To sing on a starless night.

We shall grumble and laugh and trudge together
  Till we reach the stark North Sea,
And talk till we die of Pantycelyn
  And the eighteenth century.

We shall try to forget the Sunday squabbles,
  And the foreign magistrate,
And the stupid head of the preacher's wife,
  And the broken iron gate.

So here we say farewell and wish you
  Less trouble and less pain,
And we trust you to breed a happier people
  Ere our blood flows back again.

This poem may be slight, yet it is so much in character. The Welshman thinks of his past; the foreign imposition on his country; the religious quarrels which he now accepts as inevitable, but not necessarily deadly; and, if he must go away, at the back of his mind is always the thought of return by him or his descendants.

"Land of my Fathers" is no trite phrase, but holds a significance for the Welshman close to worship.

Rupert Brooke's *Grantchester* and Gray's *Elegy* are superficial in their nostalgia. The English seem to recall only the sensory memories. Brooke again speaks to his countrymen in *The Great Lover*. His loves are objects of sight and smell and touch.

The Welshman remembers more the abstracts of home atmosphere, sadness, gaiety or magnificence.

The Vale of Rhondda illustrates the descent of man. It opens with clean farming country, fresh pasture, stock quietly grazing; the only sign of what lies higher up the valley given by the river, whose banks are rimed with dirt, whose waters are black under scuds of grey scum. Below Pontypridd is the factory area of Treforest; well enough laid out, with spacious modern, clean works set well apart, and rows of little houses where the people live and die who tend the machines.

Higher up, the tips become more frequent; the embankments of road and railway are covered with the litter of a generation or two. The drear stone houses, dark-windowed, are strung in a monotone of long rows as if a giant child had laid them down with no eye to the shelter of ridge or hollow, but only with a wild impatience to dump them so that his mannikins might be thrust inside.

One cannot walk very far through any of the bleak village streets before seeing the grey ghost of silicosis. The incidence of the disease in the hard-coal areas of South Wales is one hundred times greater than in the soft-coalfields of England. A few years ago a committee of the Medical Research Council found that in one colliery just under one-half of the underground workers showed an abnormal lung condition. The Welsh anthracite miner is a man hunted by a persistent enemy, and with every year of work the odds on his survival shorten. This same committee showed that three-quarters of the miners at the colliery they investigated were normal after ten years' work, but that after twenty years only a quarter were normal.

The grey ghosts are unmistakable. They have a clear pallor of the skin through which the bones show. They walk very slowly, pausing often. There is no hurry for them, because the end of their road is near.

Tonypandy is not unlike most other Welsh mining-towns. It is not so much ugly as featureless. It is a child forced to a premature birth so that it may more quickly become a wage-earner. It is strung together, added to, altered, and adapted not for the benefit of its human dwellers, but to meet the changing whim of the pits.

Neither here nor in most of the coal-towns has there been thought given to the bodies of the people who are housed like draft-oxen close to the places where they must toil. The evil expediency begun a century ago by the men who first saw the possibilities of modern industry has left ineradicable scars.

Yet, however their bodies are treated, the Welsh miners are still rooted over the mountain, and from their dark warrens they project their minds across the walls of the hillsides and refresh that part of them which industry cannot chain. They have their dreams like the collier's lad spreading his wings in the sunlight, but destined for the pit-cage, of whom Vernon Watkins writes:

> And when I went to the County School
>   I worked in a shaft of light.
> In the wood of the desk I cut my name:
>   Dai for Dynamite.

I walked through the steep streets of Tonypandy, crossed a garbage-filled stream which Nature had meant for a clear mountain torrent, and came to the printing-works where I hoped to see the friend of Griffiths Y Dydd. I was lucky, for Bob Jones was there dressed in a dustcoat, tending a machine. He was an alert man of middle height, dark, with quick eyes. It seemed that he had been expecting me, for Wales is an intimate country, and he had from time to time heard that I was moving towards the South.

We talked at first of Wales in general. The Welsh of the

industrial parts are passionately interested in the greater, thinly populated area of their country. They may never have seen the cwms and mountains where the shepherds live, and more than likely they never will see them, but the knowledge that the old way of life persists seems to bring to them in mine and factory a glow to lighten darkness, and a key to unlock the closed door.

Bob Jones had been born in Glamorgan. Almost alone among his school classmates he had turned from the broad-trodden track to the pits, continued to educate himself, and taken to printing. Except for three or four of them, those school friends of his were dead.

"Old at thirty was a man in the mines," Bob said. "I used to meet my old school-fellows sometimes, and one after another I'd see the lung-disease had got them. They'd come home from the pits played out. You'd see them walking up a bit of a hill, or up the stairs in the house. They'd take it slow, not wanting anyone to notice, like a man on a mountain stops to look at the view, or tie a bootlace, when he's pretending he's not tired. Hard it was to get the compensation. The doctors would say it was T.B., and the man had had it before ever he began in the pits."

Bob looked at me to see how strong my stomach was before he went on.

"The women would stand by the bed of a dying man. Often with his last breath he'd cough up not blood, but a hard black plug that was a bit of his brittle lung, and that was the proof he'd died of silicosis."

The scourge had ravaged the anthracite areas with especial venom, but now, Bob said, there was a notable change for the better. So well were the conditions being controlled which bred the disease that miners were again allowing their sons to be recruited for the pits.

Except towards the heads of the valleys little Welsh is spoken, and less read, in the coalfield. Yet the soft Southern Welsh accent is strong, and the poetry and warmth of the Celt are as evident as in the rest of Wales. There is, however, a much stronger political awareness, and allegiance is given so strongly to the Labour movement that for practical purposes the mining South is exclusively Red, shaded from left-wing socialism to Communism.

As some one had said to me:

"You could put up a lobster for candidate down here, and they'd vote him in if he'd been boiled long enough."

This leaning is strong beyond the point of bigotry, bred from hardship and bitterness. When I later talked to the principal of a concern, a man in a good way of business, employing others, he, too, was a socialist. He only thought himself worth a pound or two a week more than his top employees. I said that I felt a man was worth as much as he could earn; that in general no man received more than his worth now that the days of nepotism were nearly passed. But my acquaintance would not have it so, insisting that all men were as equal as made no matter.

I wondered how this great body of opinion, bolstered by half the voting-power of Wales, which was concentrated in this one small corner, would swing the policy of self-government should the country achieve it. It is possible that, under its influence, Wales might try a social experiment in equality worked out from its own pattern, not that of Russia. The trends of Welsh history and the development of Welsh character had always been towards liberality of thought in the humanitarian sense. The present economic policy of the National Party already favours co-operatives joined with individual endeavour.

Yet I have little faith in the success of any political experiment which equates human values. Men are not equal one to another, and most of them are individual enough to wish not to be. Wales, however, is well equipped by tradition and by the high intellectual standard of her people to build a near-classless social structure on the Scandinavian pattern.

The Welsh miner is at once to be pitied and to be envied. He is to be pitied because his native romanticism must struggle to survive in an environment not suited to a poetic and imaginative people. He is to be envied because his romanticism *has* survived in spite of a drab environment. Here, at least, are the hackneyed lines true that "Stone walls do not a prison make, nor iron bars a cage." The mind of the Welsh miner is not yet subordinated to corporeal confinement, but wings high into the clouds to join them in their play about the mountain-tops.

When I returned to Cardiff my time in Wales was drawing to a close. I had, however, some business to see to at Newport in Monmouthshire. Always I had been plagued to know in which country the county lay, England or Wales. I am still not clear about it, so that when I entered Monmouthshire I was unsure if Wales was now left behind me.

The National Party make out a very good claim that Monmouthshire is rightfully Welsh. Geographically, of course, it lies within the rim of the great South Wales coal-basin, and its coastal plain is one with that of Glamorgan. But boundaries do not always follow the topographical divisions, more is the pity. The arbitrary divisions of modern Europe are each individually root causes of future war. Korea is a warning in the East.

Indeed, one of the few arbitrary boundaries with a settled and amicable future is that between the United States and Canada.

The days of war between Wales and England are long over, but now that there is so strong a Welsh resurgence towards the goal of Home Rule, Monmouthshire may one day be the subject of wrangling and embitterment. It is this possibility of future Welsh self-government which gives practical importance to the status of the county.

History sides with the National Party, and that early Englishman Offa underlined the appropriate page. He built his dyke to exclude Monmouthshire from his territories, and to let it lie on the British side. Up to the time of William the Norman it was a part of the South Wales kingdom of Morgannwg—from which the name Glamorgan is derived. It was in the area of Morgannwg known as Gwent.

Gwent fought stoutly against the Normans, but, once the Wye was crossed, the end was quick, and the invaders built their garrison towns at Newport, Abergavenny, and Chepstow. Outside these towns the Welsh way of life continued, just as through the rest of Wales a thousand years before it had continued outside the military posts of the Roman occupiers.

In bardic tradition and national feeling the area now called Monmouthshire was Welsh up to the Act of Union, in 1536. The county was formed at that time from the lands of the former Lords Marchers, together with Denbigh, Montgomery, Radnor, and Brecon. In the appropriate sections of the Act the new county was treated in all ways except one as were the other four new shires of the Marches. The one difference was that Monmouthshire was included in an English assize circuit with Hereford and Gloucester. The National Party point out, rightly, I am sure, that this inclusion was administrative only. To confound those who would argue, they state that at the same time Cheshire was joined to a Welsh circuit. They wonder if Wales should lay claim to that county on the same grounds as England's claim to Monmouth.

I am not sure if England does claim Monmouthshire. Through the years since the Act of Union there are innumerable English references to it as a Welsh county, and there is no doubt that its language and customs were as Welsh as those of any border county up to the middle of the last century. The strength of the language has faded to-day, as might be expected in an area so accessible to England.

Yet Monmouthshire is administered by Wales for Education and Health and for most agricultural matters. It is joined to Wales in the Welsh Church Act and the Tithe Act, and in the Charter of the University of Wales.

But in the county there is a strong anti-Welsh force at work. This realizes that Westminster cannot sit indefinitely on its non-committal fence, and it wishes to have the county firmly attached to England before there is further devolution of governing responsibility to Wales. The active anti-Welsh force is not numerically strong, but is entrenched in official positions.

God forbid that the plebiscite should come to Britain on such a question, but if one were taken I do not believe that Monmouthshire would join a self-governing Wales unless that Government had some years of successful administration behind it. It is possible that if Wales received the monetary credit for her rich resources she would rapidly become a more prosperous and less-taxed country than England. Then, perhaps, Monmouth would knock on the door and ask to be let in. Unfortunately the rest of England might do the same, and that would spoil the party.

George Bernard Shaw posed a similar problem in *The Apple Cart.*

Monmouth has lain close to England for too long readily to turn her eyes elsewhere. Drs D. J. and Noelle Davies have written a pamphlet showing the traditional ties of Monmouth with Wales.

At the end, they quote: "Look unto the rock whence ye were hewn." I think Monmouthshire has by now forgotten the direction of the rock. My companion in Newport was an estate agent, an Englishman, whose family had worked in the county for a long while. He did not realize that there was a question of suzerainty. When a cause is unrecognized as such, then it is but the ashes of a cold fire.

On my personal business in the county the estate agent took me to the top of a low hill to see a view of a district pertaining to our private dealings. Behind, over my right shoulder, was the moat of the Bristol Channel; in front was open, rolling country; but to the left, and stretching northward into a haze, was the mountain rampart of Wales. The agent must have thought me dense and uncommunicative. My mind was not on his discussions, but dwelt beyond that austere wall of hills over which the British had lived through the tens of centuries, and lived still.

The wall was a barrier to understanding, as well as to physical mingling. It was a mental barrier of the same nature as a ha-ha ditch and wall, formed to be invisible from the English side, but an obstacle from the Welsh. For the English do not realize that, to the Welsh, a barrier exists between the two races. Until they do realize it their treatment of the Welsh may continue often to be gauche and unacceptable.

It is their long race-memory which reminds the Welsh of ancient suspicions even after most of them have forgotten the causes. The causes are rooted fifteen hundred years ago, when the Angles swarmed into what is now England on the heels of the departing Roman legions. It is a pity that the newcomers were members of Teuton tribes which had remained beyond the farthest fringe of the Roman Empire, and had never known the Roman system of government, their laws, nor the Christianity they had embraced. They came as aliens, and as aliens in thought, to the Romanized Britons of England, and they annihilated the British in England as far as it is possible for one race to annihilate another. In England there was within a short time no trace left of religion, custom, laws, or language. There are to-day in England but a handful of place-names which are not Teuton or Danish.

It is not likely that many Britons fled from England to their brothers in the Western hills. Forest, swamp, river-crossings, wild beasts, and warlocks would have rendered such a journey almost impossible for families burdened with their household goods. They stayed where they were, and hoped and prayed; and community by community they died.

The extrovert modern Englishman, with the practical Danish and Norman blood mixed with the Teuton in his veins, does not see the mental ha-ha between himself and the Britons who survive yet in those Western hills. Or if he does see, he is impatient. But, right or wrong, the Welsh see the barrier, and it cannot, in their eyes, be removed by ignoring it. Yet implicitly the English do recognize the barrier. They still call the only surviving Britons 'Welshmen,' a word of Teutonic origin which means 'foreigners.'

As late as 1682 an English traveller expressed the hope and belief that "the British lingua may be quite extinct, and may be English'd out of Wales, as Latin was barbarously Goth'd out of Italy."

His analogy was unflattering to his countrymen, and his belief was mistaken for such time ahead as he could foresee. Yet, at last, there are signs that modernity is doing what the English failed to do. Native Wales survived many battles any of which might have ended in her death, but to-day she is losing the last battle against a modernity cast largely in the English-speaking mould: commerce, radio, television, films, theatre, newspapers, and books. The Welsh, in all their struggles from Anglo-Norman days until Bosworth Field, were consistently outnumbered by about fifteen to one, yet the most their conquerors could ever impose was physical subjugation; they failed always to destroy or absorb. The spirit of the country sustained the wounded flesh. Wales still dare not lose her racial identity, for, more than most nations, she would disintegrate without the unifying love of land and breed.

As Gwilym Lloyd had said at Dolgelley, a Welshman without his roots at home was lost.

Perhaps that is why so many Welsh to-day are fiercely possessive of what is left to them. History has often taken the wrong turn for the Welsh. It was the son of their own first Tudor king who so nearly destroyed Welsh Wales four hundred years ago by the instrument of his Act of Union.

The people remember it still. Emrys Humphreys speaks for them:

Spirits grow tired of waiting—
  Four hundred years upon a rock
Of disappearing Hope—
  Freedom will you not come back?
Our souls are hungry!

But many Welsh realize that the practical English are not to be much moved by the nostalgic heartburning of a small romantic nation. These Welsh point to the words in the preamble of the Act of Union which describe their land as the "dominion, principality, and country of Wales." They say that Wales is the oldest and the only British-speaking dominion in the British Commonwealth. They ask why it may not rule itself, and by so doing retain the spiritual possessions which remain to it.

Henry Treece has written a poem about the Red Dragon, who has survived for so very long against all the guile of many hunters.

Ho, Draig Goch! They tell me you are dead;
  They say they heard you weeping in the hills
For all your children gone to London Town.
  They say your tears set Tawe in a flood.

I'm older now, but still I like to think
  Of your great glass-green eyes fixed on the Fferm,
Guarding the children, keeping them from harm.

Don't die, old Dragon, wait a few years more,
  I shall come back, and bring you boys to love.

The Welsh do not want to preserve the Red Dragon in a shrine of memory. They wish him to pass his old age among the youth of a living country.

ACKNOWLEDGMENTS

I have found the following books to be particularly informative:

BORROW, GEORGE: *Wild Wales.*
CAMPBELL, B., SCOTT, R., AND NORTH, F. J.: *Snowdonia.*
CARR, H. R. C., AND LISTER, G. A.: *The Mountains of Snowdonia.*
EDWARDS, OWEN: *A Short History of Wales.*
EVANS, WILLIAM: *The Meini Hirion and Sarns of Anglesey.*
FLEURE, H. J.: *A Natural History of Man in Britain.*
HAWKES, CHRISTOPHER AND JACQUETTA: *Prehistoric Britain.*
LLOYD, D. MYRDDIN (Ed.): *The Historical Basis of Welsh Nationalism.*
LLOYD, SIR JOHN EDWARD: *A History of Wales.*
RHYS, JOHN, AND BRYNMOR-JONES, DAVID: *The Welsh People.*
ROWLANDS, HENRY: *Mona Antiqua Restaurata.*
VALE, EDMUND: *The World of Wales.*
WILLIAMS, A. H.: *An Introduction to the History of Wales.*
WILLIAMS, W. S. GWYNN: *Welsh National Music and Dance.*
The Mabinogion.

T. F.

The British Line to Henry VIII

Edeyrn (Eternus)

Padarn Beisrudd (Paternus of the Red Robe)

Tegid (Tacitus)

CUNEDDA WLEDIG (Duke of Britain)
(Probably defended Hadrian's Wall against Picts and Scots. Drove Irish from N. Wales about A.D. 410.)

Einion Yrth (eighth son)

Cadwallon Lawhir (Longhand)

MAELGWN HIR (The Tall) (*d.* 547

Rhun Hir

Belyn

Jacob

Cadfan (Was ruling in 613.)

Cadwallon (*d.* 634)

CADWALLADR (The Blessed) (*d.* 664)

Idwal Yrth

Rhodri Molwynog (*d.* 754)

Cynan Tindaethwy (*d.* 817)

Esyllt (heir) = Merfyn Frych (The Freckled) (*d.* 844)

RHODRI MAWR (The Great) = ANGHARAD (last of the line founded by Ceredig, Duke of Britain, son of Cunedda Wledig)

Anarawd (*d.* 916)

Cadel (*d.* 909)

HYWEL DDA (The Good) (*d.* 950)

Some of the British rulers before Rhodri Mawr are shadowy figures whose lives rest on tradition. It should be borne in mind, however, that Welsh law, for various purposes, required a Welshman to know his ancestry to the respective degrees of fourth, seventh, and ninth. A litigant concerned with proving the seventh degree would need to quote all the descendants, male and female, of his sixty-four great-great-great-grandparents. The highly developed bardic system helped laymen with such feats of memory. There is no doubt that the self-interest of a horde of relatives is a surer guarantee of authenticity of descent than is the scrap of paper purporting to be a family tree.

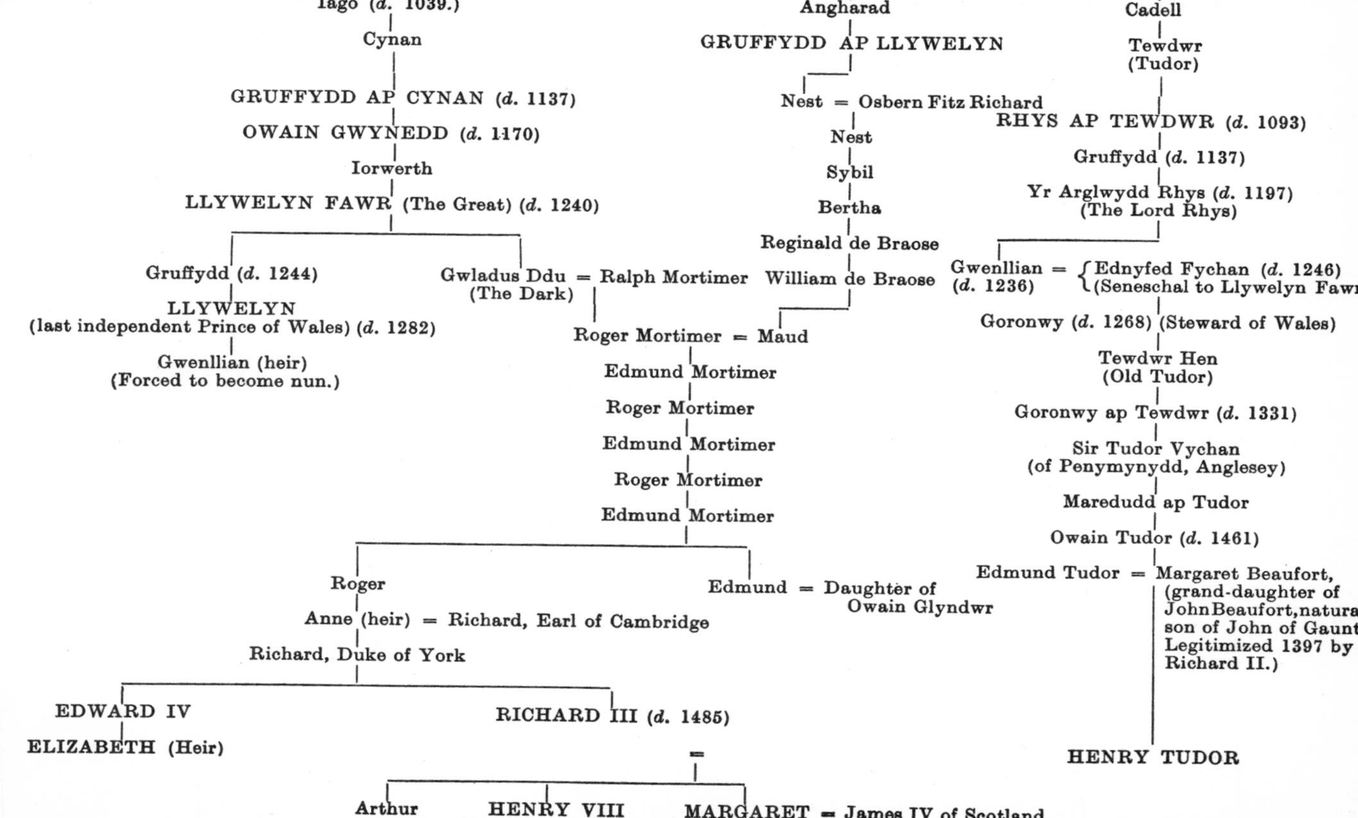
Iago (d. 1039.)
Cynan
GRUFFYDD AP CYNAN (d. 1137)
OWAIN GWYNEDD (d. 1170)
Iorwerth
LLYWELYN FAWR (The Great) (d. 1240)
Gruffydd (d. 1244)
LLYWELYN
(last independent Prince of Wales) (d. 1282)
Gwenllian (heir)
(Forced to become nun.)
Gwladus Ddu = Ralph Mortimer
(The Dark)
Angharad
GRUFFYDD AP LLYWELYN
Nest = Osbern Fitz Richard
Nest
Sybil
Bertha
Reginald de Braose
William de Braose
Roger Mortimer = Maud
Edmund Mortimer
Roger Mortimer
Edmund Mortimer
Roger Mortimer
Edmund Mortimer
Roger
Anne (heir) = Richard, Earl of Cambridge
Richard, Duke of York
EDWARD IV
ELIZABETH (Heir)
RICHARD III (d. 1485)
Edmund = Daughter of
Owain Glyndwr
Cadell
Tewdwr
(Tudor)
RHYS AP TEWDWR (d. 1093)
Gruffydd (d. 1137)
Yr Arglwydd Rhys (d. 1197)
(The Lord Rhys)
Gwenllian
(d. 1236)
= Ednyfed Fychan (d. 1246)
(Seneschal to Llywelyn Fawr)
Goronwy (d. 1268) (Steward of Wales)
Tewdwr Hen
(Old Tudor)
Goronwy ap Tewdwr (d. 1331)
Sir Tudor Vychan
(of Penymynydd, Anglesey)
Maredudd ap Tudor
Owain Tudor (d. 1461)
Edmund Tudor = Margaret Beaufort,
(grand-daughter of
John Beaufort, natural
son of John of Gaunt.
Legitimized 1397 by
Richard II.)
HENRY TUDOR
=
Arthur
HENRY VIII
MARGARET = James IV of Scotland

Important Events
in the History of the English Race up to the Reign of its First British Ruler

410. Last Romans leave Britain.

Invasions of Heathen Teutons (Angles, Saxons, Jutes) continue. Cerdic, Saxon Alderman, settles in Hampshire. (*d.* 534.)

587. Augustine, emissary of Pope Gregory I, lands in Kent to convert Anglo-Saxons, thus ensuring their allegiance to Rome, and not to the Celtic Church.

655. British defeat at Winwaed Field isolates Britons of Wales.

789. Heathen Danish invasions begin.

802. Egbert, King of Wessex, is first king to be styled 'King of the English.'

900. In this century the word 'England' is first used to denote area conquered by Anglo-Saxons.

1013. Swegen Forkbeard, King of Denmark, becomes first Danish King of England.

1066. Duke William of Normandy lands in England, kills Harold II at Hastings. First Norman King of England.

1282. Edward I conquers Wales. Llywelyn the Last killed. Edward's son first English Prince of Wales.

1485. Henry Tudor returns to Wales. Kills Richard III at Bosworth Field. First British King of England. His heirs have ruled Britain ever since, except during the Commonwealth, 1649–60.

Note. Morgan Williams of Glamorgan followed the Tudor fortunes to London. He married a sister of Thomas Cromwell. Their son Richard assumed his mother's name, and his descendants, Oliver and Richard Cromwell, ruled as Lords Protector during the Commonwealth.